W9-ANM-521

"As a Marine I had to admire the courage and discipline of the North Vietnamese and the Vietcong but no more than I did my own men," said Capt. Myron C. Harrington, commanding officer of Delta Company of the 1st Battalion, 5th Marines, which had fought in the Citadel. "We were both in a face-to-face, eyeball-to-eyeball confrontation. Sometimes they were only 20 or 30 yards from us, and once we killed a sniper only 10 yards away. I don't think that the North Vietnamese and Vietcong were about to give up even if we'd surrounded Hue and tried to starve them out. We had to go in and get them out. There was no other way, except to dig them out."

Books published by The Ballantine Publishing Group
are available at quantity discounts on bulk purchases
for premium, educational, fund-raising, and special
sales use. For details, please call 1-800-733-3000.

THE SIEGE
AT HUE

George W. Smith

BALLANTINE BOOKS • NEW YORK

Sale of this book without a front cover may be unauthorized. If this book is coverless, it may have been reported to the publisher as "unsold or destroyed" and neither the author nor the publisher may have received payment for it.

A Ballantine Book
Published by The Ballantine Publishing Group
Copyright © 1999 by George W. Smith

All rights reserved under International and Pan-American Copyright Conventions. Published in the United States by The Ballantine Publishing Group, a division of Random House, Inc., New York, and simultaneously in Canada by Random House of Canada Limited, Toronto.

Ballantine and colophon are registered trademarks of Random House, Inc.

www.randomhouse.com/BB/

Library of Congress Catalog Card Number: 00-190739

ISBN 0-8041-1946-5

This edition published by arrangement with Lynne Reinner Publishers, Inc.

Manufactured in the United States of America

First Edition: July 2000

10 9 8 7 6 5 4 3 2 1

CONTENTS

PREFACE

The smell attacked my senses like a blast of hot air from an oven. It was a sour, pungent odor that reminded me of decaying garbage. The first whiff was the worst. Once I started breathing through my mouth it wasn't so bad.

Old women, aided by their children, carefully scooped away handfuls of sand from an individual grave in a football-sized field just outside the walled city of Hue. The diggers, a tattered crew of dirty ragamuffins, wore bandanas over their faces to keep from gagging on the smell.

Slowly, as the sand was removed, part of a body came into view. Then another and another. The bodies of men, women, and even children were uncovered, some after weeks of repose in their sandy graves. Some had bullet wounds, others had their arms bound from behind by rope or wire. Many had their mouths open, silent screams frozen on their faces.

The bodies were wet, as if they had been drenched in water before being interred. It appeared that many had been buried alive.

The old women knelt beside each pit and, in slow rocking motions, lifted their faces and blackened teeth to the sky and filled the air with long, mournful cries. Their faces were distorted in agony, and the moaning, interrupted only by sobbing and rhythmic breathing, continued for half an hour or more.

Ten feet away, another group unearthed another body to more wailing. Another and another. Soon, the smell and mournful baying rolled across the barren landscape. The sound reminded me of a pack of wolves howling at a new moon.

Each body was gently dragged to a piece of level ground. The families gathered around and the weeping intensified. Those dead who were bound with wire or rope had their shackles gently removed, and their arms were positioned across their chests. Wooden flatbed wagons appeared, and the bodies were loaded aboard for the trip to a family burial plot. The holes in the ground were left unfilled.

It was warm and sunny that unforgettable morning in March of 1968, the first pleasant weather in Hue in almost two months. How ironic that something so heinous had been discovered on such a lovely day.

My jeep driver and I stayed behind, watching the families plodding slowly back toward the city with their human cargo. We stared into the vacant holes without a word passing between us. After the previous month's carnage during the Battle of Hue, both of us were numbed by the sights and smells of death.

The Battle of Hue, which raged from 31 January to 25 February of 1968, was the largest single engagement of the Vietnam War, claiming a total of 5,713 lives (142 U.S. Marines, 74 U.S. Army, 384 Army of the Republic of Vietnam, and 5,113 enemy). In the weeks and months following the battle, between 2,800 and 3,000 more bodies, many of them civilians, were discovered in shallow graves around the city, most of them victims of cold-blooded murder by North Vietnamese and Vietcong troops and their sympathizers.

The world paid little attention to these atrocities in Hue. Unlike the My Lai massacre by U.S. troops, which occurred at about the same time but was covered up for 20 months, the ghastly events at Hue became mere footnotes in a highly unpopular war.

Historians agree, however, that Hue was the scene of the most vicious street fighting since Seoul in the Korean War. With South Vietnamese and U.S. units surprised by superior forces and hovering on the brink of annihilation for so many days, the struggle at Hue reminded some of the older U.S. veterans of World War II's Battle of the Bulge.

Few doubt that the Tet offensive of 1968, and the Battle of Hue in particular, was the turning point in U.S. involvement in the Vietnam War. Even though the North Vietnamese and the Vietcong sustained huge losses and failed to accomplish their primary purpose—to rally the South Vietnamese to their side—they had shown an amazing willingness to endure the U.S. forces' awesome firepower beyond anyone's expectations and often to the bitter end.

Other experts believe that the North Vietnamese took full control of the war after the Tet offensive. They had to because the Vietcong were virtually wiped out. The Tet offensive of 1968 and the long siege at Hue caused the United States to reexamine its policy in Vietnam and then slowly reverse its involvement.

To those of us on the ground in Hue there was little thought given to any long-term consequences. We took it one day at a time, just praying to survive.

Although I personally witnessed many of the events in this book and have relied heavily on my own notes, records, and interviews, my memory was refreshed by rereading the many after-action reports filed by the various participating units, some of which I wrote myself. Also of great help were the dozens of newspaper clippings and magazine articles on the battle that I perused at my local library. I found the two main books on the battle, Keith Nolan's *Battle for Hue* and Eric Hammel's *Fire in the Streets*, to be very accurate and well done, especially when documenting the contributions of the U.S. Marine Corps. Last, I want to thank the dozens of people I interviewed and reinterviewed in recent years, particularly Brig. Gen. Ngo Quang Truong and Capt. Tran Ngoc Hue and all the U.S. advisers with the ARVN 1st Division and the Vietnamese Airborne—the "Red Hats"—for their cooperation and kindness. Without their help and encouragement this book would have added little to the knowledge we already had on the Battle of Hue.

G.W.S.

CHRONOLOGY

Allies

Jan. 31, 1968, 0340, NVA rocket attack on all sections of Hue. Enemy troops overrun all of city except the ARVN 1st Division headquarters in the northern corner of the Citadel and the MACV compound in the southern section of Hue. At 0800, National Liberation Front flag raised over Citadel; 1420, two U.S. Marine companies from Phu Bai, 11 kilometers south of Hue, arrive at MACV compound.

Feb. 1, ARVN relief forces arrive at 1st Division headquarters in Citadel from the north; another U.S. Marine company arrives at MACV compound.

Feb. 2, a fourth U.S. Marine company arrives at MACV compound.

Feb. 3, U.S. Marines set up regimental headquarters at MACV compound; U.S. Army commits battalion from 1st Air Cav northwest of city.

Feb. 4, An Cuu Bridge on Route 1, 3 kilometers south of city, blown up.

Feb. 5, a second air cavalry battalion committed northwest of city.

Feb. 6, U.S. Marines take Thua Thien provincial headquarters and prison complex.

Feb. 7, 0500, enemy sappers blow up main bridge across Perfume River; General Westmoreland flies to Da Nang to assess situation.

Feb. 11, two U.S. Marine companies and five tanks arrive in Citadel.

Feb. 12, rest of U.S. Marine battalion and two Vietnamese marine battalions arrive in Citadel; three Vietnamese airborne battalions depart for Saigon.

Feb. 13, initial U.S. Marine attack stymied at line of departure; Gen. Creighton W. Abrams establishes MACV forward headquarters command post at Phu Bai.

Feb. 14–15, huge bombardment of supporting fire directed against enemy strongpoints in Citadel.

Feb. 16, ARVN 1st Division commander, Brig. Gen. Ngo Quang Truong, flies to Phu Bai to brief Vice President Nguyen Cao Ky; a company from U.S. 101st Airborne committed northwest of city; a third Vietnamese marine battalion arrives in Citadel.

Feb. 19, a third air cavalry battalion committed northwest of city.

Feb. 21, U.S. Army forces overrun enemy regimental headquarters at La Chu northwest of city; U.S. Marine replacement company arrives in Citadel.

Feb. 22, two Vietnamese ranger battalions arrive in Citadel.

Feb. 24, 0500, ARVN troops raise South Vietnamese flag over Citadel; 1515, Vietnamese Black Panthers sweep through Citadel's Imperial Palace area.

Feb. 25, Citadel officially declared secure; President Nguyen Van Thieu arrives in Citadel to congratulate defenders.

Enemy

(From captured document, entitled "Twenty-Five Days and Nights of Continuous Fighting for the Wonderful Victory")

Jan. 31, 1968, 1233, attack and control the city. Assault eight advances; strike and kill one hundred enemy; destroy four M113s and many aircraft.

Feb. 1, attack Tay Loc airfield, destroy 40 aircraft and beat back all counterattacks; kill many enemy.

Feb. 3, continue to beat back counterattacks and destroy and kill hundreds of enemy and completely control the city.

Feb. 4–6, destroy nine supply boats (4th, two boats; 5th, two boats; 6th, five boats) all loaded with U.S. troops and weapons.

Feb. 7, destroy one battalion and one company of enemy at Chanh Tay Gate (northwest wall) and Theu Quan culvert (center of west wall).

Feb. 8–10, beat back many phases of enemy assaults and destroy many enemy.

Feb. 11, kill 40 enemy at Chanh Tay Gate; destroy one boat and capture many prisoners, one a captain of the puppet troops.

Feb. 12–13, beat back counterattacks and seize the locations.

Feb. 14, beat back 10 assaults at Dong Ba Gate (center of northeast wall) and at Thuong Tu Gate (southeast corner) and Chanh Tay Gate and Cuang De Street (western corner); kill four hundred enemy, down one aircraft, destroy two APCs; one cell of VC fight the enemy the entire day and destroy 50 enemy and seize the locations, destroy one more boat.

Feb. 17, beat down five phases of assaults, kill hundreds of enemy; capture eight.

Feb. 18, beat back five counterattacks, kill 190; destroy two APCs; bring down two airplanes; destroy six boats (supply boats containing 40,000 liters of gasoline).

Feb. 19, beat back three phases of counterattacks; kill two hundred enemy; destroy one boat.

Feb. 20–21, engage with enemy forces in Bon Tri, Bon Pha (to the northwest); kill more than two hundred Americans, shoot down three combat boats loading enemy troops and weapons.

Feb. 22, beat back seven phases of counterattacks, kill hundreds of enemy in Citadel; kill one hundred Americans (including 30 Korean troops "Pac Chung Hy"), destroy two trucks, two boats, kill 80 more Americans in La Chu.

Feb. 23, counterattack and kill 50 enemy, destroy one assault boat, two other boats, kill 23 Americans in Thuong Tu Gate, Dong Ba Gate; capture 25 rifles; during 3 days (21–23) kill four hundred Americans at An Hoa (outside northeast corner); shoot and burn one helicopter.

In February 1966, at a strategy meeting in Honolulu, President Lyndon Johnson asked his commander in Vietnam, Gen. William Westmoreland, what his next step might be if he were the enemy commander.

"Capture Hue," General Westmoreland answered without hesitation, explaining that the city was the symbol of a unified Vietnam. "Taking it would have a profound psychological impact on the Vietnamese in both the North and the South, and in the process the North Vietnamese might seize the two northern provinces as bargaining points in any negotiations."

Two years later—almost to the day—the enemy overwhelmed Hue and held much of it for nearly a month. The only combat troops to resist the initial assault were a depleted South Vietnamese company. The nearest U.S. troops were seven miles away.

CHAPTER ONE

Next Stop, Vietnam

The road to Vietnam began for me in Panama in mid-July of 1967, where I was sent to attend a two-week jungle warfare course.

I was 27 and a U.S. Army captain with over 3 years of active-duty service, and I had just completed a 17-month stint in a mechanized infantry battalion in West Germany. Most of the officers in my unit were West Pointers, and a few had already served in Vietnam as advisors. Some of the enlisted men had earned their combat infantryman badges in World War II and Korea. One officer was a former member of the French Foreign Legion. Vietnam was the next stop for most of the careerists, and many were looking forward to it.

If you were a career soldier, and most of the West Pointers and senior noncommissioned officers (NCOs) were, combat assignments were the quickest and surest routes to promotion or advancement.

It was different in my case. I was a reserve officer, having earned my commission through a college Reserve Officers Training Corps program, and I was obligated to serve only 2 years on active duty. I could have opted to end my military service after my tour in Germany. But Vietnam was on everybody's mind back then, and I had little

1

trouble convincing myself that I would later regret this once-in-a-lifetime experience.

U.S. military history has always fascinated me; I grew up watching World War II movies, and my college major had been American history. Also, I guess I have always strongly believed that service to our country was the duty of all Americans, with no price too high to pay. I volunteered to extend my military service and looked forward to a tour of duty in Vietnam. What the hell, I told myself, if I did not go it would have been like dropping out of college after 3 years and never getting my degree. Plus, I had come this far in my military experience. Why not see the obligation all the way through?

I was buoyed somewhat by the degree of training I had received in Germany. We were constantly on combat-like maneuvers that included plenty of live-fire exercises at such historic World War II training grounds as Wildflecken, Hohenfels, and Grafenwöhr. How much more realistic could Vietnam be?

I left Germany in June of 1967, just as my unit was being put on alert for possible duty in the Middle East in what became the Seven-Day War. After reporting in to Fort Jackson, South Carolina, a few weeks later, I flew to Panama for a 2-week jungle warfare course. A canary-yellow Braniff jet transporting about 200 company-grade officers and senior NCOs landed at Howard Air Force Base outside Panama City in the dead of night. A 2-hour bus ride across the isthmus brought us to Fort Sherman, a small U.S. military base across the bay from Colón on the Caribbean side of the country.

The training was intense and comprehensive. Parts of it were even fun, like the time a 15-foot snake was passed around among class members seated outdoors on some bleachers. One of my classmates jerked his hands away from the snake and let its head bounce off a wooden plank. The docile critter did not seem to mind at all.

An emphasis was placed on living in the jungle. And though the training grounds were well trodden in many areas, there was still plenty of jungle to give you a feel for what it must be like in the bush country of Vietnam.

The temperature soared past 100 degrees every day. What did I expect in July in a place that was less than 10 degrees from the equator? Leeches were in every stream, and the mosquitoes were particularly nasty. The instructors told us to hang onto something or the mosquitos would lift us right off the ground and carry us away. The place even had scorpions.

We rappelled down cliffs, traversed fast-moving streams, and even participated in an amphibious landing. There were search-and-destroy missions, night ambushes, and an overnight road march that left us all exhausted. The coup de grace was a 2-day escape-and-evasion exercise through some of the wildest terrain in Panama.

There were marine and air force personnel in our class as well as a team of Navy SEALS, an independent bunch that ran rings around the rest of us with their zany and reckless behavior. I was glad they were on our side.

The best news of our 2-week adventure came on graduation day, when we were told our 1-year Vietnam tour had commenced the day we reported in at Fort Sherman. Along with our Jungle Expert badges we received our orders. I was assigned to the 9th Infantry Division, which operated in the Mekong Delta region of Vietnam, south of Saigon.

After a brief leave, I reported to Travis Air Force Base near San Francisco and then, a couple of days later, boarded a military C-141 for the 20-hour journey to Vietnam. Because the seats of the military aircraft faced to the rear I thought, "Great, I'll get to see where I've been but not where I'm going." I bought two TV turkey dinners and five martinis for the trip. The plane stopped at Wake Island for an hour to refuel and then again at Clark Air Force Base near Manila before finally landing at Bien Hoa in Vietnam. It was 0745 hours when I first set foot on South Vietnamese soil.

One of the first things I noticed was that most of the Vietnamese I saw were women. Before I could ask the obvious, a U.S. security guard at the airport told us: "I know what you're thinking. Where are the men, right? They're not here. They're in the jungle with the Vietcong. They are planting mines and sharpening their bayonets, getting ready for fresh meat like you."

Very funny, I thought. But, for all I knew, the guard's comments were probably true.

Vietnam was hot, dusty, and noisy. The "whap whap" sound of helicopters flying overhead was almost continuous. Another constant was the crush of traffic. The buses taking us to a replacement center had to fight their way through truck convoys, motorbikes, and bicycles. Everybody and everything seemed to be on the road at the same time, hurrying somewhere with a me-first attitude. It was like New York City at rush hour, only a lot of these people were carrying guns.

The roads were also lined with hustlers, either begging for handouts or trying to sell you anything from candy and cigarettes to radios and televisions. Many of the buildings were covered with netting.

"That's to keep the VC from throwing grenades through the windows," our bus driver said. "Sometimes it doesn't work very well, though. The VC wrap the grenades with string and fishhooks. When they throw the grenades, the fishhooks hang the grenade on the netting and blow out the windows and anything else in the way."

New sounds replaced the old at night. Sporadic gunfire interspersed with artillery could be heard from dusk to dawn. None of the noise bothered me on that first day; I was so exhausted after my long journey across the Pacific that I fell fast asleep without any problem at all. Ah, yes, the sleep of the innocent.

We got acclimated quickly. After only 2 days in country, the new men were taken outside the defensive perimeter at Bear Cat, the 9th Division's homebase, for some live-fire exercises. We ran into another group on a similar mission and a brief firefight broke out. Luckily there were no casualties. Later that day, during a demonstration of the Claymore mine, a young sergeant standing next to me was hit in the leg by a stray pellet from the mine. A cynic in the back quipped: "At this rate we'll all have Purple Hearts by the end of the first week." The incountry orientation concluded with an overnight patrol through a nearby rubber plantation, which proved uneventful because the area was a relatively secure one.

It did not take us long to learn the Vietnamese language—or enough of it to ensure some form of effective communication. If something was good it was "number 1" and if it was bad it was "number 10." In Vietnam, I was to learn, things were either very good or very bad. There was nothing in between. In my entire tour of Vietnam I never heard of anything that was "number 2" or "number 9."

My specific assignment came through later that first week: I was to report to the 9th Division Information

Office at Bear Cat. I guess the paper shufflers had noticed that I had experience in that area. My first military assignment in 1964, after completing Infantry School at Fort Benning, Georgia, had been as an information officer with the 1st Army at Governors Island, New York. I did not mind reprising that assignment at all.

The information job allowed me to travel throughout the Mekong Delta region, visiting each of the units of the 9th Division. In the first week I visited the 1st Brigade headquarters in Tan An and battalion outposts in Tan Tru and Bien Phouc. At the latter, I ran into a friend who had served with me in Germany, Capt. Tom Russell. He was now a company commander with the 5th Battalion, 60th Infantry Regiment (Mechanized). It was good to see a familiar face, even if he did look a lot older than the last time I had seen him.

While we toured his encampment I pumped him for information on what it was like in Vietnam. I asked him about rumors I had heard concerning atrocities in his area of operations, particularly the taking of ears from dead enemy soldiers and carving the number 9 into the victims. He did not confirm any of the stories, but he did not deny them, either.

"They snipe at us all the time and once in a while drop mortars on us," he said. "We shoot back. We hardly ever see them because they fade away into the jungle or swamps. It gets frustrating sometimes. It's awfully tough to lose men who never get to see the person they are fighting."

Russell's encampment at Bien Phouc was located in a flat, open area and was completely surrounded by barbed wire, with guardposts at the corners. There was an impermanence to the place, as if everyone was ready to pick up and move at a moment's notice. Tents served as barracks, and each was surrounded by sandbags 5 feet high. The motorpool where the M113 armored personnel carriers (APCs) were parked was a muddy swamp. Several of the M113s were dug in as fighting positions.

"We don't have any down time here," Russell said, looking over his encampment. "Nobody is very far from a bunker or his weapon. We're ready to go at all times."

My job was to gather information for stories I would write about 9th Division personnel. The stories were printed in our own unit newspaper and also sent to an individual's hometown paper. Often they would get picked up by *Stars and Stripes*, the U.S. armed services newspaper published in Tokyo.

I put in a lot of chopper time in the Mekong Delta, and it always amazed me how young and cool the pilots were. On one trip to the delta, the engine suddenly quit and we dropped what seemed like 1,000 feet before the engine restarted. One of the fuzzy-cheeked pilots turned to the other, smiled, and shrugged his shoulders; there was not the slightest hint of panic from either of the young pilots. I could not say the same for myself.

Another helicopter pilot, who couldn't have been more than 20, had blessed himself in the best Catholic tradition before liftoff and then turned to me and said: "I sure hope we make it."

Gathering up all the bravado I could muster, I looked him right in the eye and replied: "That makes two of us."

The door gunners were awfully young, too. They were also a colorful bunch, some donning cowboy hats in flight, and some regarded the entire landscape below as a free-fire zone, shooting at anything that moved, human or otherwise.

In late August I visited all the wire services and broadcasting agencies in Saigon, a trip I made several times. I sat in on the daily afternoon military press briefing that the civilians derisively called the "five o'clock follies" or "jive at five." The briefings were very slick, complete with oversized maps, charts, and even film clips. They were delivered by a cadre of officers and NCOs in crisp, freshly starched uniforms to an audience of civilian correspondents, some of whom looked as if they had just slithered out of a delta swamp, which, in fact, some indeed had.

Many of the civilians and even a few military personnel had long since come to view these briefings as nothing but a propaganda session, a kind of dog-and-pony show designed to put the best possible face on the U.S. war effort. Even generals weren't spared the cynicism of the audience. One civilian journalist sitting next to me, after hearing a briefer state that in his opinion "the enemy no longer maintains a capability to mount, execute, or sustain a serious offensive action," not so quietly whispered to a nearby colleague: "Mount this."

Escorting press members and VIPs on fact-finding missions was also one of my assignments, one that would later become a primary one. During my 6 months in the Mekong Delta I went on numerous military missions and visited many battle sites to assess damages. I also conducted dozens of interviews, often with a reporter or film crew in tow. I spent 3 days with the Mobile Riverine Force, participated in leaflet drops, and attended a multitude of awards ceremonies in the field. I even got to meet Charlton Heston, Gen. William Westmoreland, and Raquel

Welch, the latter during Bob Hope's 1967 Christmas tour. I endured the ubiquitous mortar attacks and sniper fire but at no time did I feel particularly endangered. All that was about to change.

In early January, my boss called me back to Bear Cat to tell me I was being reassigned as an information advisor to the Vietnamese 1st Infantry Division, up near the demilitarized zone (DMZ), in the city of Hue, which was pronounced "way." The Military Assistance Command, Vietnam, or MACV (pronounced "mac vee"), was apparently unhappy with the increasing number of published reports of incompetence and personal greed in the Army of the Republic of Vietnam (ARVN). The U.S. brass had decided to assign U.S. information officers to Vietnamese units as advisors in a public relations move, one that would hopefully lead to better and more consistent coverage by the press in the United States.

The 1st ARVN Division was regarded as the country's best division, and Westmoreland, according to my boss, wanted our best U.S. information officer assigned there. If true, that was very flattering. But I wasn't buying any of it.

In my diary that night, I took note of my new job, ending with this pithy sentence: "It should be a most interesting assignment." How little did I know just how "interesting" my life was to become—or how close I would come to losing it.

CHAPTER TWO

The Lotus Flower

The city of Hue, according to Buddhist myth, was a lotus flower that had sprung from a mud puddle. In early 1968 it was an island of peace in a country wracked by war.

A city of 140,000, Hue was the former imperial capital of Vietnam long before the country's division. The city radiated the past glories of the Nguyen dynasty and the more recent French colonial era and had a haunting charm that is difficult to define or fully explain. While a savage and destructive war raged throughout most of the country, Hue was regarded almost as an open city, seemingly protected by its past and present grandeur. Its location, just 100 kilometers south of the demilitarized zone, only added to its allure as a vacation spot and tourist attraction.

Hue was also the cultural and intellectual center of Vietnam. Hue University was the country's best. The city's famed Quoc Hoc High School boasted such graduates as former South Vietnamese President Ngo Dinh Diem, as well as Ho Chi Minh, Vo Nguyen Giap, and Pham Van Dong. The city was fiercely independent. In the spring of 1966 it had been a hotbed of antigovernment protests. The current military regime of President Nguyen Van Thieu and Vice President Nguyen Cao Ky, who were elected in September of 1967, viewed the citizenry of Hue with wariness and suspicion. The flamboyant Ky, who was the nation's air marshall and served as president from 1965 to 1967, had sent troops to Hue in 1966 to put down a Buddhist rebellion.

Hue's role in the history of Vietnam is a long and colorful one. In 1687 the city became the capital of South Vietnam. Just over a century later, in 1789, a patriot and one of Vietnam's greatest heroes, Nguyen Hue, defeated both the Trinh warlords in the north and the Nguyen warlords in the south and unified the country. He set himself up as emperor of all Vietnam, ruling under the name Quang Trung.

A decade later, a 16-year-old nephew of the deposed Nguyen rulers, Gia Long, decided, with help from the French, to avenge his ancestors. Starting from Saigon, he drove north, reconquered Hue and took Hanoi in 1802, reestablishing the Nguyen dynasty. Long executed the surviving members of the previous royal family as well as all the generals and their families. He reserved a special fate for the deposed ruler, Quang Toan, who was Nguyen Hue's son. Toan was forced to watch while the bones of his father were exhumed so that a group of common soldiers could urinate on them. Then Toan's hands and feet were bound to four elephants and the beasts were driven in different directions, tearing him apart.

In Hue Gia Long began building an impregnable fortress, the Citadel, modeled after the Imperial City at Peking, complete with towers and ramparts, moats, and high stone walls on every side. The outer walls form a square about 2,700 yards on a side. Three sides are straight, while the fourth is rounded slightly to follow the curve of the Perfume River. The corners face north, east, south, and west. The walls are 26 feet high and up to 40 feet thick in some sections. Many areas of the wall are also honeycombed with bunkers, which were constructed by the Japanese when they occupied the city in World War II. The three walls not bordering the river are encircled by a zigzag moat that is 90 feet wide at many points and up to 12 feet deep.

Within the Citadel is another enclave, the Imperial Palace compound where the emperors ruled in isolated peace until 1883, when the French returned to take control of the court. The emperor's audience hall with its gilt throne and red, dragon-decorated pillars was considered a national shrine. The entire enclave was surrounded by a wall 20 feet high.

The French held power over the emperors until 1945, when the last of the line, Emperor Bao Dai, surrendered his authority to the Viet Minh revolutionaries. The French were back within a year, however, and left only when they were defeated at Dien Bien Phu in the spring of 1954 during the First Indochina War, which caused a division of the country and the establishment of a demilitarized zone.

Ngo Dinh Diem, a native son of Hue and one of the leaders in the old imperial court, returned from exile in the mid-1950s to become president of South Vietnam. Diem, a Catholic, soon came into conflict with Buddhist leaders, and an uprising led by monks in Hue in 1963 was the beginning of the end for him. Three years later, another Buddhist-led rebellion centered in Hue threatened to bring down the Saigon military junta, until the rebellion was crushed, this time with the assistance of the United States.

Not even the ongoing Second Indochina War would damage Hue's independent and aloof spirit, however.

In 1968, Hue was the country's third largest city, behind Saigon and Da Nang. Strategically, Hue was located in the narrowest part of South Vietnam. Five kilometers to the east is the South China Sea and 5 kilometers to the west are the foothills of the Annamite Cordillera. Another 50 or so kilometers to the west is Laos. In between are the Ashau Valley and the famed Ho Chi Minh Trail, which had been one of the busiest infiltration routes from North Vietnam into South Vietnam. The city is divided by the Perfume River, which snakes up from the south, turns east just before Hue, and then curls north along the eastern edge of the city before emptying into the South China Sea. (See Map 1.)

The Citadel, which sits on the north bank of the river, was crowded with narrow streets and buildings, but there were open areas as well. Inside the fortified walls were oriental gardens, temples, pagodas, and ancestral burial grounds. There was even a small airstrip inside the Citadel that could accommodate light observation aircraft. In the northern corner was the headquarters of the 1st ARVN Division. It was a fortified site formerly used as a base of operations by the French Foreign Legion. The headquarters compound was protected by 6-to-8-foot walls, topped by barbed wire.

Other population areas in Hue were to the east in the Gia Hoi section and along the outer edges of the fortress walls.

About a third of the city's population resided south of the Perfume River in the newer, residential part of Hue. Among the complexes on the so-called right (south) bank of the river were the Thua Thien Province headquarters, the U.S. Consulate, internationally regarded Hue University, Hue Hospital, the city's high school, the treasury and post office buildings, and the city's power station. Thousands of graves dot the rolling hills south of the newer portion of the city, including six royal tombs. These royal tombs, which attract thousands of tourists and pilgrims annually, are located in parklike settings, protected by massive gates.

Also on the south side was the MACV U.S. advisory (Team 3) compound, a lightly fortified rectangular encampment that was once the site of a transient hotel. Its southwestern wall bordered Route 1, the main concourse through the city. A block and a half north of the MACV compound on Route 1 was the six-span Nguyen Hoang Bridge that crossed the Perfume River to the Citadel. Near the base of the bridge's southern end was Doc Lao Park and a U.S. Navy boat ramp. These two sites were to become vital to the survival of both the Vietnamese and U.S. forces in the coming weeks.

Modern Hue was actually a collection of fiefdoms. Each section of the city had its military and civil governments with much overlapping. The province chief, for example, was also a lieutenant colonel in the army. Then there were the Catholic and Buddhist hierarchies and a large population of students and Europeans. The French still exerted a huge influence, and Germans had a presence as sponsors of the city's medical school. Even the Communists were free to roam the city, though mostly in an invisible manner.

The Americans had found the city a bit perplexing; as a result, Hue was one of the few cities in South Vietnam that did not have a U.S. combat presence.

* * *

Most of the ARVN 1st Division's combat forces were scattered throughout I Corps at the time of the Tet offensive. Other than a depleted company of the division's reaction force in the Citadel and a company of ARVN tanks in the southern portion of the city, Hue was virtually defenseless.

The nearest U.S. combat base was at Phu Bai, 11 kilometers to the south astride Route 1. Phu Bai was a major Marine Corps headquarters and support facility, one that was in a state of flux in late January of 1968. At the time, Phu Bai was the home of Task Force X-Ray, a sub-headquarters of the 1st Marine Division, which had just begun the process of relocating from its old headquarters near Da Nang to replace the 3rd Marine Division, which had moved north to Dong Ha near the DMZ.

Exactly 17 kilometers northwest of Hue on Route 1 was the headquarters of the ARVN 1st Division's 3rd Infantry Regiment. The unit operated out of a former French army base called PK 17 ("PK" from the French *poste-kilometre*). A little farther north on Route 1 was Camp Evans, where elements of the 3rd Marine Division were in the process of turning over the facility to the arriving U.S. Army's 1st Cavalry Division.

Although it would appear Hue could have been reinforced with ease from either north or south, the truth was that no plan was in force for such relief because an attack wasn't expected. Also, because both Phu Bai and Camp Evans were going through a transfer of command, neither base had sufficient available reaction forces to put down a large attack.

The two brigades of the 1st Cav had their helicopters scattered over a wide area from Phu Bai in the south to

Landing Zone (LZ) Jane just south of Quang Tri in the north. In addition, the 1st Brigade of the 101st Airborne Division that arrived at Camp Evans had come north with a bare minimum of support assets and no helicopters. The airborne troopers were also unfamiliar with the Cav's way of operating.

The marines moving into Phu Bai were also new to the area and would need time to get acclimated. The III Marine Amphibious Force expected that the 1st Marine Division would be only partially effective in its new tactical area of responsibility by the middle of February and not completely effective before mid-March.

Also moving into Phu Bai at this time was a newly created MACV Forward headquarters, which would enable General Westmoreland to have a more hands-on presence with operations in northern I Corps, an area previously left to the Marine Corps. MACV Forward was to directly oversee all Marine Corps and army actions in Vietnam's two northernmost provinces of Quang Tri and Thua Thien, an arrangement that the Marine Corps brass looked upon with an almost paranoid suspicion.

January was a month of extreme confusion around Hue as the number of U.S. forces doubled and then tripled in the area. Massive influxes of men and supplies clogged the roads that ran through the city. The confusion helped mask the intentions of the enemy, who used this time to quietly slip troops and supplies into the city for the coming attack.

One of the first people I met when I arrived in Hue on 24 January was Brig. Gen. Ngo Quang Truong, the commanding general of the ARVN 1st Division. Truong, who spoke excellent English, made me feel like a VIP with his personal welcome. He also took the time to introduce me to many members of his staff.

The 38-year-old Truong was about 5 feet, 7 inches tall and weighed a gaunt-looking 130 pounds. Truong always seemed to have a Salem cigarette dangling from his lips. There was a pinched quality to his face, with deep lines around his mouth and eyes that made him look like he was squinting. Maybe the squinting came from all the cigarette smoke that hovered around his head. He also had hunched shoulders and walked with a kind of shuffle, very purposeful yet seemingly in no hurry to get where he was going.

A 1954 graduate of Dalat Military Academy, Truong had spent 12 years as a front-line commander with the ARVN Airborne Division, rising from platoon leader to assistant division commander. He had assumed command of the 1st Division in June of 1966 during the Buddhist insurrection in Hue and was generally regarded as the man who had orchestrated a peaceful resolution of the difficulties.

General Truong was tough, disciplined, and dedicated to his military profession. Unlike many of his contemporaries who had climbed the ranks through political influence, nepotism, or cold, hard cash, Truong had earned his star on the battlefield. He was viewed as a self-starter, without any hint of corruption or ego. He was regarded by the Americans as unquestionably the finest senior combat commander in the South Vietnamese army.

Gen. Norman Schwarzkopf, in his book *It Doesn't Take a Hero*, called Truong "the most brilliant tactical commander" he had ever known. Schwarzkopf served as an advisor to the Vietnamese Airborne Division as a newly promoted major in late 1965. Truong, then a colonel, was the division's chief of staff.

"[Truong] was revered by his officers and troops—and feared by those North Vietnamese commanders who knew of his ability," Schwarzkopf later wrote in his 1993 bestseller. "Any time a particularly tricky combat operation came up, [division commander Brig. Gen. Du Quoc] Dong put him in command. Simply by visualizing the terrain and drawing on his experience fighting the enemy for 15 years, Truong showed an uncanny ability to predict what they were going to do. . . . Col. Truong's greatest regret was that he'd never had a chance to attend [the Command and General Staff College]. I never met anyone who needed Fort Leavenworth less than Truong—he could have written the textbooks."

Truong was a master in utilizing U.S. firepower that was made available to his command, and he used it wisely. He believed that the jet fighters and the huge B-52 bombers gave him a big edge over the enemy. It gave him a comfort factor that only added to his natural aggressiveness.

He was also impressed by the professionalism and dedication of the U.S. advisors in his division. Privately he wondered why these Americans were so committed, while some of the officers he had seen in his own army clearly were not. General Truong was under no illusions about his power base. He knew that the Americans held the key to the future of his command and his country, and he was prepared to do whatever it took to maintain the highest level of cooperation with his benefactors.

The spotlight was on the 1st Division because it had the reputation of being the best unit in the Vietnamese army—and because President Thieu was a former commander of the division. The unit had maintained its level of excellence in recent years partly because it operated in an area with the U.S. Marines. The marines were not shy in claiming to be the best soldiers on the planet.

Truong was uniquely qualified to operate in this military fishbowl. He was different from many other ARVN generals who often seemed more interested in building their own personal fortunes than in conducting a war. Truong was anything but a hedonist. He was a dedicated career soldier and a patriot. He was also a realist. And the reality of the situation was that he had to establish and maintain good military rapport with the Americans or risk losing everything he had worked so hard for.

Truong was different in another way, too. He enjoyed being a hands-on, no-frills division commander. He loved being in the field and participating in the kill. While other generals spent much of their time increasing their own personal wealth, Truong was busy killing the enemy. And that was just fine with him. Because he was different, Truong's superiors sometimes viewed him with suspicion, sensing that he could become a potential rival. Their feelings were born of envy and perhaps guilt over their own shortcomings.

If the Vietnamese general staff was somewhat reluctant to sing Truong's praises, the U.S. brass was not. His division was called the "first and the finest" by the U.S. advisors. Even the marines, who rarely even tolerated their own countrymen in other branches of the service, were generally positive toward the ARVN 1st Division. It was the only ARVN unit they would willingly go on joint maneuvers with.

So, when the North Vietnamese decided to attack in Hue, they ran into a South Vietnamese unit that not only knew how to fight but one that was more than willing to do so. More than that, the enemy's attempt to encourage defections, a key element of its Tet strategy, had little chance of success. Much of the credit for that belonged to General Truong, a man who commanded not only the respect of his soldiers but their loyalty as well.

I found Hue a startling contrast to Saigon. Although parts of the Citadel were just as crowded as the nation's capital, Hue seemed much more relaxed and genteel. There were no honkytonk bars, neon lights, and strip joints, and only a minimum of street hustlers peddled their black-market wares.

Hue was, in a word, beautiful. It was also clean, when compared with Saigon. The courtyards, gardens, ornamental lakes, pagodas, and temples were right out of a travelogue. The traffic was stifling, however. It took almost 15 minutes to drive my jeep across the main bridge over the Perfume River on my first day in Hue. It was a fight for space on the road in a steady stream of military vehicles, three-wheeled Lambrettas, Peugots, cyclo-cabs, and motorbikes of every make and color that darted in and out of traffic with reckless abandon. I used the time to drink in the sights and smells of the city.

Both banks of the river were lined with flowering "flame" trees, and the edges of the river were filled with aromatic lotus plants and palm trees. The river swarmed with slow-moving sampans filled with vegetables and flowers for the market. Water taxis ferried officials and schoolkids back and forth across the river. I made a mental note to myself to take a ride on one of those water taxis the first opportunity I had. Sad to say, I never got the chance.

Off to the west along the southern bank of the river I

could see what looked to be an elegant clubhouse, its stately veranda overlooking the water. There were several tennis courts and a gleaming white concrete driveway leading up to the building. It was the former French Cercle Sportif, a popular social and sports hangout for the rich and famous. I never got to take a closer look.

When we reached the south side of the bridge we had to stop briefly while a parade of schoolgirls pedaled their bicycles to and from class along the wide Le Loi Street. Their long black hair and white ankle-length *ao dai* dresses, which were split up the side, billowed in the gentle breeze coming off the river. It looked as if the war had not touched Hue at all.

A couple of hundred yards farther on, we came upon the main gate of the MACV compound. Two marine guards waved us through, and I reported in to the duty officer. I was assigned a temporary bunk in a dirt-floor tent in the rear of the compound and given a brief orientation and tour.

The MACV compound was home to all but a few U.S. advisors. One of those who lived outside the compound was U.S. Marine Lt. James V. DiBernardo, who was in charge of an Armed Forces Radio and Television station just a few blocks away on Le Loi Street along the river.

I met DiBernardo my first night in Hue at the MACV officer's club. He invited me to visit his station and quarters the next day and I did. Most of my early contacts were made at the officer's club, which was a popular gathering place for all the advisors when they were not in the field with their units.

The Australian advisors were a particularly gregarious bunch. A close-knit group, the Aussies could fight, drink, and play darts with the best of them. They also loved to sing and tell tall tales. Warrant Officer Terry Eagan, who was an advisor with the 1st Division's Reconnaissance Company, loved telling the story of why none of his troops ever fell asleep on guard duty.

"When I first came here and caught a bloke sleeping, I'd creep up on him with my pistol and slowly cock the hammer right next to his ear. It's guaranteed to make him piss his pants, or worse," Eagan said as his audience burst out in laughter.

Then, when the laughter died down, Eagan resumed in that lilting down-under accent: "You know, you'd be surprised how an experience like that stays with you."

I made another mental note right then and there: my R and R vacation would be spent in Sydney, Australia. I got to keep that one.

I remember thinking to myself that this assignment had the potential to be an enjoyable one. Everything seemed so peaceful and friendly. The chow was excellent, and the beer was cold and plentiful at the officer's club. Everybody so far had gone out of their way to make me feel welcome. They seemed genuinely happy to have me aboard.

Yes, I told myself, I had really lucked out with this assignment.

There were also some mysterious types in Hue, shadowy figures who seemed to exist as half-civilian and half-military. One of them was a fellow named Johnson, though I suspected it was not his real name. One of my friends at MACV told me he thought Johnson worked for the CIA but he did not know for sure. After I had met him at the

MACV officer's club, Johnson invited me to visit his compound a couple of blocks away.

This Johnson guy lived like a prince. He had his own guards, a maid, a jeep driver, and a coterie of Vietnamese characters who responded to his every whim. When he greeted me at the gate, he was wearing a pistol on each hip and a bandolier of machine gun ammunition across his bare chest. He looked like a Mexican bandit.

He ordered a couple of beers from his well-stocked bar and took me to an outdoor patio. When the drinks came, he had one of his flunkies put some empty bottles on the top of the wall opposite his chair. Sure enough, Johnson stood up, drew one of his .45-caliber pistols from his belt, and fired off a clip, spattering the wall with bullet holes and even destroying one of the bottles.

"Want to try it?" he asked while one of his servants cleaned up the mess and put a couple more bottles on the wall. I gave him a wild-eyed look and finished my beer.

Johnson was definitely playing a role here, but I wasn't sure what it was. He looked to be in his late twenties. He was wearing a Rolex watch, and underneath the bandolier were a couple of gold chains. On a table in plain sight was a wad of U.S. money. He had a military uniform hanging over a chair that indicated he was a captain. I could not see the name tag. I asked him what he did.

"A little bit of this and a little bit of that," he answered, shrugging his shoulders. I quickly realized he was not going to volunteer any more information to me than he had to.

Another round of beers was delivered, and just as I was about to take a slug, Johnson rose from his chair and blasted another beer bottle off the top of the wall. "Yahoo!" he shouted and then sat down.

I left soon afterward, smiling to myself. I never saw Johnson again, if that was his real name.

Much of my first week in Hue was spent getting to know the U.S. and Vietnamese personnel. The latter were gearing up for the Tet holidays, a very special time to the Vietnamese. It is their Christmas, Fourth of July, and birthday all rolled into one. The celebration dates back some 4,000 years out of ancient religious beliefs in China and takes place during the full moon prior to spring planting. The early Tet observers were seeking a good harvest. In modern times Tet became a holiday to review the past, enjoy the present, and plan for the future. It is also when debts are repaid, mistakes corrected, forgiveness asked, and family and ancestors remembered. Gifts and food were left in little boxes near the graves of deceased loved ones as a means of having them share the holiday as well.

The roads were crowded with holiday traffic streaming into Hue for the Tet holidays. Some of the travelers proved to be undercover Vietcong and North Vietnamese agents, who, disguised as civilians or ARVN soldiers returning home for the holidays, used the occasion to smuggle in weapons and supplies for the coming siege. The weapons and ammunition were stashed throughout the city. Some of the infiltrators even got a chance to test-fire their weapons amid the noise of holiday firecrackers.

Everyone in Vietnam celebrates Tet regardless of religious beliefs. It is the custom for children to return to their parents' home, bringing food and gifts. Homes and shops are gaily decorated with red and gold paper and fancy lanterns. Fragrant branches from the symbolic peach tree are put in vases in the homes, and firecrackers light up the sky each night—and the louder the better to scare off evil spirits. The markets are flooded with goods. Everyone is out shopping, and the fragrance of flowers permeates the air. In all of Vietnam, nowhere is the annual week-long festival of Tet celebrated as intensely as it is in Hue.

The U.S. advisors were guests at many house parties, where Vietnamese delicacies were endured with the bravest of smiles. The smell of *nuoc mam*, a thick, pungent, fishy sauce, permeated everything, and most dishes included spicy red and green peppers. Just one little bite set my taste buds on fire. I also remember being asked to sample a pork dish that was green.

The guest of honor at the party I attended was General Truong. It seemed that every taste of food was followed by a toast of rice wine, or scotch whisky if you preferred. There was music and laughter and much smiling and bowing. Children ran in and out of the ceremonial room with the same playful joy American children have during birthdays or at Christmas. With General Truong in attendance, U.S. advisors felt obliged to participate in tasting all the delicacies the host offered, no matter what they looked or smelled like. (It is funny what the mind's eye sees. I could swear I saw some of the food moving.)

"Think of it as a kind of survival-of-the-fittest exercise," one advisor told a young lieutenant, who appeared to balk at sampling one of the more unusual dishes. "You've got to eat this food before it eats you." A short while later, that same lieutenant could be heard loudly retching outside against a compound wall.

Another ritual at Tet was a ceremonial flag raising at the Citadel's main flagpole opposite the entrance to the Imperial Palace. General Truong, his three regimental commanders, and the mayor of Hue officiated at this ceremony shortly after dawn on Tuesday, 30 January, the first day of Tet. The division's band played the national anthem, and the elite Hac Bao (Black Panther) Company served as the color guard. It was a beautiful day, surely the harbinger of a good year.

Even though some intelligence estimates predicted that the enemy would try to interrupt the Tet holiday with some kind of military action, no one expected an all-out, nationwide attack. Nor did anyone expect Hue to be a primary target. In fact, General Truong and his superiors believed that Hue would be spared, as it always had been. Hue, in fact, was regarded as such a safe and prestigious assignment that officers would often offer bribes to get stationed there. Even the North Vietnamese regarded Hue with a special reverence because of its historical significance to the country as a whole.

The Americans were a lot more suspicious of North Vietnam's plans for the Tet holidays than were the South Vietnamese. Evidence of something big had been mounting for several months. On 18 December, Gen. Earle G. Wheeler, chairman of the Joint Chiefs of Staff, warned that "it is entirely possible that there may be a Communist thrust similar to the desperate effort of the Germans in the Battle of the Bulge in World War II." Two days later, General Westmoreland told his superiors in Washington that he expected the enemy "to undertake an intensified countrywide effort, perhaps a maximum effort, over a relatively short period."

There was also a curious announcement from North Vietnam changing the start of the Tet holidays. Because of an unusual conjunction between the moon, the earth, and the sun, North Vietnam's leaders said the Tet holiday would begin not on 30 January, as indicated by the lunar calendar, but on 29 January. Hanoi, the Allies later learned, wanted the North Vietnamese people to have an opportunity to celebrate the Tet holiday before an anticipated U.S. retaliation.

Westmoreland's main preoccupation in I Corps continued to be at Khe Sanh, where an estimated 20,000 to 40,000 North Vietnamese Army (NVA) regulars were believed to be massing against the 5,000 U.S. Marine defenders. Convinced that the enemy intended to overrun the base as the first step in an all-out effort to seize the two northernmost provinces of South Vietnam, Westmoreland was determined to hold Khe Sanh at all costs. His decision was endorsed by the Joint Chiefs and a nervous President Johnson, who told his field commander that he didn't want "any damn Dien Bien Phu."

Westmoreland had repeatedly urged President Thieu to cancel the Tet cease-fire, but Thieu had demurred, claiming that it would damage ARVN morale and only benefit enemy propagandists. Thieu did agree to reduce the official cease-fire to 36 hours, but he also authorized holiday leaves for half of all ARVN troops.

General Truong had an uneasy feeling on the morning of 30 January. Rather than heading to his home south of the river after the flag raising, Truong drove back to his division headquarters to check on any intelligence updates. On his desk were reports of widely scattered enemy attacks on eight Vietnamese cities by large forces, all flagrant violations of the Tet truce.

General Truong called his staff together, minus those already given Tet leave. They went over local intelligence reports of the past few weeks, and the more they talked and read the more Truong was certain something was planned for Hue. How big? was the question. The intelligence seemed to indicate that the enemy did not have sufficient forces for a major attack on the city, but estimates of enemy troop strengths could be wrong. He checked with higher headquarters and was told they had no information on large enemy troop concentrations in the area.

Nonetheless, Truong sensed something big was brewing. A week earlier, the Vietnamese 2nd Airborne Battalion had uncovered a large weapons cache of regimental size about 5 miles west of Hue. Despite any other hard intelligence, his instincts as a field commander told him that he had to take some action. He put what was left of his division on 100 percent alert and canceled all holiday leaves of personnel who had not yet left for home. This latter decision was a tough one to make because Tet was such an important event in the lives of all Vietnamese. He realized fully that canceling the well-deserved leaves was not good for the morale of his staff, who had worked so hard during the year, but in his mind that risk was worth taking.

The order was given and immediately carried out. The division staff officers and headquarters troops were to remain at their posts. The regimental commanders were told to return to their command posts and put all their battalions on full alert. Truong also tried to reach those already on leave to have them return to their units at once, but those efforts were generally unsuccessful because most of the units were in the field.

General Truong ordered the commander of his division's reaction force, 1st Lt. Tran Ngoc Hue, to report to the division CP for orders. Lieutenant Hue's force, the

all-volunteer Hac Bao Company, was garrisoned in the
Citadel near Tay Loc Airfield, and its six platoons numbered almost 200 men. Lieutenant Hue sent three of his
platoons south of the river to act as security at the provincial headquarters, the power station, and the prison. Two
more platoons were split up and dispatched to guard
the gates entering the Citadel. That left Lieutenant Hue
with one platoon and his headquarters complement, a
force of about 50 men, to deal with any attack in the
Citadel.

Truong also dispatched his 36-man Reconnaissance
Company to vigorously patrol the western approaches
to the city, the most likely route the enemy would use to
attack Hue. The rest of the day was spent taking inven-
tory of supplies and ammunition, checking defenses, and
keeping tuned to the radio for orders or information.

Truong's actions were far greater than those taken by
most Vietnamese commanders and spelled the difference
between life and death for his command. Many of his
staff lived in the southern part of the city, as he himself
did, and had they been given leave they would not have
been able to make their way to the division headquarters
once the battle started.

The South Vietnamese government issued an order later
that day canceling the Tet truce, but it took relatively few
precautions. Other units canceled some leaves but only
put their troops on a state of increased readiness. President Thieu himself had departed Saigon to spend the holidays with his wife's parents in the Mekong Delta city of
My Tho.

General Westmoreland declared a 100 percent alert for
U.S. troops on 30 January, but the word never reached us
in Hue. While MACV was expecting a "show of strength"

by the enemy during Tet, it had no clue just how big a "show" it would be. Westmoreland's intelligence officer, Brig. Gen. Philip B. Davidson, candidly remarked a few months later: "Even had I known exactly what was to take place, it was so preposterous that I probably would have been unable to sell it to anybody. Why would the enemy give away his major advantage, which was his ability to be elusive and avoid casualties?"

The answer to General Davidson's question, which he obviously did not realize at the time, was to achieve surprise, even though it would cost enemy forces dearly in manpower.

"It did not occur to us that the enemy would undertake suicidal attacks in the face of our power," Davidson said. "But he did just that."

The Allies were also lulled into believing that because of the massive scale of the diversionary buildup of enemy troops around the Khe Sanh base near the DMZ, the enemy simply would not have enough manpower to attempt a countrywide offensive. Allied intelligence was wrong on this count, too.

I was at Lieutenant DiBernardo's compound on 30 January and declined an invitation to spend the night. As fate would have it, DiBernardo's compound was overrun a few days later and he was captured. He would spend the next 5 years in a North Vietnamese prison camp, enduring the harshest of treatment but thankful to be alive. Other U.S. advisors in his compound were not so fortunate.

I went to bed that night at the MACV advisors' compound to the sounds of firecrackers and M16 fire intermingling in the cool night air. ARVN troops, who were home on leave, emptied their magazines into the air at midnight to celebrate the end of the first day of the lunar new year, the year of the monkey. The bursts of fire, coming from both sides of the river, sent tracers streaking across the sky. A few minutes later, it became deathly quiet.

Patrolling several kilometers west of the Citadel just before midnight, the ARVN 1st Division's 36-man Reconnaissance Company, the unit General Truong had dispatched to the west earlier in the day to act as his eyes and ears, found itself right in the path of the enemy invasion.

The recon commander, Lt. Nguyen Thi Tan, quickly saw that his unit was much too small to engage the large enemy force. He ordered his troops to stay still and remain quiet while he radioed General Truong to alert him that large numbers of enemy troops were infiltrating past his position toward the Citadel. Lieutenant Tan had to whisper his report to keep from being detected.

The enemy units proved to be the 800th and 802nd Battalions of the NVA 6th Regiment. The North Vietnamese unit, augmented by area Vietcong troops, infiltrated through the Reconnaissance Company screen toward the Citadel's southwestern wall, where they waited for the signal to storm the city. When the signal came, they were aided by confederates inside the Citadel who dispatched any ARVN guards and opened the gates for them.

Meanwhile, the enemy positioned a third battalion, the 806th, outside the northwestern wall to form a blocking position astride Route 1 to prevent any reinforcements from reaching the city. The battalion's best company, which included a hand-picked sapper unit, had the mission of attacking the 1st Division Headquarters in the Citadel directly over the wall. The invading force was also bolstered by the NVA 12th Sapper Battalion.

According to a prisoner taken a couple of weeks later, the attacking forces were served a specially prepared Tet meal of dumplings, cakes, dried meat, and rice before moving into position. They were also given a propaganda speech on how they were about to inaugurate "the greatest battle in the history of our country." It would be a "flash of lightning that would split the sky and shake the earth," they were told.

Some of the invading troops took the time to change out of their jungle clothing into khaki uniforms, complete with unit designation and decorations so that they would look their best during an expected victory parade. In a display of solidarity with their Vietcong comrades, some NVA regulars wore armbands with the inscription "Born in the North, Died in the South."

The invading force never got to hold that victory parade because of the heroic efforts of the 1st Division's Hac Bao Company, the bravery of the staff and support personnel who were on duty at the division headquarters compound, and the cool leadership of General Truong.

The Hac Bao Company was commanded by one of Truong's favorite young officers. Named for the city of his birth, 1st Lt. Tran Ngoc Hue had spent almost his entire life in the city. He knew every street, building, and tunnel in the Citadel. Called "Harry" by his U.S. advisors, Lieutenant Hue was an inspiring figure. Taller and stockier than the normal Vietnamese soldier, Hue was a bold and fearless commander with a style and flair most of his contemporaries lacked. His men held him in esteem usually reserved for deities and were prepared to die for him on command.

Enemy forces continued to bunch up outside the western edge of the Citadel awaiting a prearranged signal to jump off in a coordinated attack. The North Vietnamese commander had ordered the attack to begin at 0230 with a rocket barrage from the mountains to the west, but there were unforeseen delays. One of his forward observation posts reported: "I am awake, I am looking down at Hue . . . the lights of the city are still on, the sky is quiet and nothing is happening."

The signal, which came at about 0340, was a rocket barrage on the city from the mountains to the west. The 800th and 802nd Battalions overwhelmed a depleted force of ARVN manning the western entrances to the Citadel and fanned out to begin a coordinated attack from west to east.

Lieutenant Hue was at home in bed when the first explosions occurred inside the Citadel. The first rocket traveled right over his house, which was just inside the Citadel's western wall. Also in the house were his wife, their 4-week-old daughter, and his parents.

"I jumped up and quickly put on my clothes and web gear and went outside," Lieutenant Hue said. "I remembered I had given my jeep to one of my platoon leaders across the river, so I jumped on a bicycle to head to my headquarters on the other side of the airfield. There were VC running all around me. I'd watch them go down one street and I would head the other way. I knew where I was going. They didn't."

Under the cover of darkness, Hue easily managed to mingle with the enemy troops, who were obviously confused by the narrow streets and many houses. He could hear firing from the airfield straight ahead and knew it was his unit engaging the enemy. As he got closer he called out to his Hac Bao troopers that he was coming in.

Taking charge, Hue grabbed one of the new U.S. light

antitank assault weapons (LAAWs) his unit had received and sent a volley into a dozen enemy soldiers on the other side of the airfield. The blast sent three NVA soldiers flying in the air. The rest of the Hac Bao platoon opened up with machine gun and M16 fire. Also firing at the enemy was a platoon from the ARVN 1st Ordnance Company, which was manning an ammunitions and weapons storage depot near the airfield.

The unexpected heavy volley stopped the NVA attack cold and further disoriented the NVA troops. The enemy then tried a flanking movement to the right to skirt the fire coming from the ordnance compound and ran straight into the heart of the Hac Bao platoon. Hue's troops caught the enemy crossing the runway and inflicted heavy casualties. The action forced the 800th Battalion to veer to the south and held up the 802nd, which was trying to push its way toward the ARVN 1st Division HQ along the northwestern wall. Later, the Hac Bao and ordnance units were withdrawn into the division headquarters just in time to help stave off a second attempt to overrun the compound.

While the battle was raging at the airfield, Lieutenant Hue spotted two U.S. Marines, who had been on guard duty.

"I told my soldiers to stop firing and waved them to our lines," Hue said. "They were just a couple of scared young kids. I also captured a couple of prisoners right away. One of them had on a North Vietnamese uniform with a star on the collar. My soldiers were all excited because they thought we had captured a general."

Lieutenant Hue got one of the prisoners to tell him he was from North Vietnam and that he had been in the area for the past 7 days. He also told Hue they had expected to be met by guides who would help them navigate the city and that there was a victory parade scheduled for later that day.

Another interesting thing Hue noted was that the prisoners had K ration packs on them. There were three small packages inside, each wrapped in tin foil. One package contained rice, and the other two contained eel and fish. Each package was labeled in English. There was also an accessory pack with a vitamin pill, a bag of sugar, bags of salt and pepper, an envelope with two small hot peppers, and some chewing gum. The box containing the package revealed that it was "packed in Okinawa."

Hue later told his U.S. advisor, U.S. Marine Capt. James J. Coolican, who had spent that night across the river in the MACV compound, that it was the LAAWs that had disoriented the enemy troops so badly that they were never able to regroup and mount an effective attack on the 1st Division compound.

"We had picked up the LAAWs on our way back from an exercise near the DMZ and when we got back to Hue we held several classes on how best to use them," Coolican said. "There is no doubt in my mind that their effective use on that first day saved Gen. Truong's headquarters."

Truong also helped himself with several timely decisions. The first was sending his Reconnaissance Company on a scouting mission to the west the day before the attack, and the second was alerting the Hac Bao Company to be ready for a possible assault inside the Citadel. Third, his order to temporarily abandon the airfield and consolidate his forces inside the division compound came just in time. Had he hesitated, the Hac Bao and Ordnance Company personnel might have been surrounded and destroyed piecemeal at the airfield, leaving the division HQ without the means to prevent its own destruction.

The recall bought General Truong some time. While the 800th Battalion resumed its attack on the now-abandoned airfield and looted the ordnance depot of its ammunition and weapons, Truong was able to further bolster the defensive positions of his headquarters compound, which had already thrown back one attack by the 802nd Battalion. It proved just enough to hold off an expected second assault.

The compound had barely fought off the first attack, which penetrated the wall near the Medical Company. The doctors and medics, assisted by a handful of clerks, engaged in hand-to-hand combat before turning back the assault. The defenders had suffered 11 killed and six wounded, while claiming to have killed 20 enemy soldiers.

Lieutenant Hue said that it was about 0700 when he got the call to withdraw from the airfield to the division headquarters. Picking out the quickest and safest route, Hue gathered his forces together and rushed to the division command post (CP) with impressive speed. On the move, Hue picked up additional men from the Ordnance Company and other ARVN soldiers who had remained in their homes during the fighting. He took the group, which now numbered about 150 men, through many of the back streets in which he had played hide-and-seek as a kid and came upon the main gate of the division CP from the south.

"I could see some bodies outside the wall. I also saw that the enemy had set up three machine guns overlooking the main gate to support an attack," Hue said. "I brought up some LAAWs and we blew away the machine guns. Then we threw down a smokescreen and dashed into the compound. We were very lucky. If I had arrived 1 hour later, there would have been no more headquarters."

Now well behind schedule and operating in broad daylight, enemy forces set out to seize the lightly defended Imperial Palace area. Even here, the enemy encountered unexpected resistance, this time from the 36 men of the Reconnaissance Company, which had somehow worked its way into the Citadel after its scouting mission several hours earlier to the west. By 0700, however, the enemy overwhelmed a delaying force and poured into the palace compound.

The invaders took turns sitting on the imperial throne while having their pictures taken. And then, at about 0800, a platoon from the 800th Battalion seized the main flag platform in the center of the Citadel's southeastern wall, the same area where General Truong and the mayor of Hue had presided over a flag-raising ceremony 24 hours earlier. The NVA pulled down the gold and red flag of the Republic of Vietnam and hoisted a huge 6-by-9-foot, yellow-starred National Liberation Front (NLF) flag.

While this was going on, the handpicked 40-man sapper unit of the 806th Battalion was foiled in its plan to overrun General Truong's CP from outside the Citadel to the north. The enemy unit found that a moat bridge leading to the ARVN 1st Division HQ had collapsed and in its place was a thick barricade of barbed wire. Forced to regroup, the enemy force decided to soften up the compound with a barrage of nearly one hundred 82mm mortar rounds.

When a second ground assault on the division head-quarters finally came, Lieutenant Hue and his reinforcements were ready.

Capt. Ralph Bray of Olathe, Kansas, was one of several U.S. officers on duty that night at the 1st Division head-quarters. At about 0100, after receiving Lieutenant Tan's report of enemy activity to the west, General Truong ordered the launch of an L-19 light observation plane from the Citadel airfield to check it out. According to Captain Bray's log, the plane returned at 0300, with the pilots reporting that he had seen nothing suspicious. Less than an hour later, the airfield came under heavy attack, and mortar fire began raining down on the division headquarters.

One of Bray's jobs was to monitor all the radios and try to make sense of all the chatter going on.

"I was trying to keep a log of what was happening but things were happening so fast that I had to get an ARVN translation," Bray said. "My first priority was to communicate to other units what was going on because when we get hit, usually they [were] next."

Like everybody else in the division compound, Captain Bray had to stop what he was doing and pick up a rifle when the enemy assault came.

"With all the B-40s and mortars we were taking I knew the enemy was close," Bray said. "When we had to stop them at our wall I knew they had the whole city."

General Truong had been on the radio seeking help since the attack began. He ordered the four battalions of his 3rd Regiment, which were scattered to the west, south, and east, to come to his aid. He also asked his boss, Lt. Gen. Hoang Xuan Lam, the ARVN I Corps commander, to request from Saigon the transfer of the

ARVN 1st Airborne Task Force, a strategic reserve force that was on duty north of Hue, to his direct control. The Airborne Task Force consisted of three battalions (the 2nd, 7th, and 9th). Other units ordered to Hue were the ARVN 1st Division's 4th Battalion, 2nd Regiment, and the 3rd Troop, 7th Armored Cavalry, both stationed to the north.

Truong also ordered the 7th Armored Cavalry's tank unit, which was garrisoned in the southern portion of Hue about a mile down Route 1, to proceed to the Citadel with haste. The unit commander, Lt. Col. Phan Huu Chi, barely got out of his own compound gate when his column of 26 M41 light tanks and a dozen M113 APCs were ambushed before they had a chance to get going. Enemy forces turned back the armored column with a barrage of B-40 rockets and heavy machine gun fire. Several of Colonel Chi's tanks were captured by enemy forces, which later used the 26-ton vehicles against the U.S. Marines. One of the tanks actually made it across the Perfume River, where it was destroyed by fire from the Citadel.

None of the reinforcements were able to come to Truong's rescue the first day. Until they arrived, the headquarters was defended by elements of the Hac Bao Company, the division's tiny Reconnaissance Company, and noncombat staff personnel, including the division band. All were pressed into duty as riflemen and put under the operational command of Lieutenant Hue. Every one of them was needed to ensure the survival of General Truong's command.

Another factor that unnerved the defenders at the division CP was the absence of any heavy weapons. The most potent weapons available were a couple of .30-caliber machine guns mounted on jeeps and a few LAAWs in the hands of the Hac Bao Company. On that first day, there was no artillery or air support. There would be no resupply of anything for a week.

Looking out his office window, which faced west across a huge parade ground, General Truong could actually see enemy soldiers in the early morning light climbing the walls with grappling hooks. Truong's aide emptied his pistol at the enemy from his office window.

"I never had to fire my weapon, but it was close," Truong said many years later.

One of the early heroes that day was 1st Lt. Nguyen Ai, a member of General Truong's intelligence section. Even though he was shot through the shoulder, Lieutenant Ai and his makeshift unit of clerks killed five of the enemy, the rest of which fled over the wall. Later, Lieutenant Ai helped repulse a sapper attack on the main entrance to the compound.

"I knew that we had dodged a big bullet," Bray said of the ground assault, "but I didn't realize how big until later that morning when I saw several dead VC bodies and a couple of satchel charges by the front gate."

General Truong made a quick assessment of the situation and realized that his position was still very tenuous. Yes, his eclectic bunch of soldiers had stopped a superior force at the very gates of his compound, and yes, they had been lucky. But unless help arrived soon, it was just a matter of time before they would be overrun. He did not know it then, but he would have to hang on throughout the entire day and another night before the first relief troops would arrive on the morning of 1 February.

General Truong had been given time to get his headquarters together and was very fortunate to have a young, dynamic field leader in Lieutenant Hue to take charge of the actual defense of the compound. The enemy would attack three more times that first day but were repulsed each time. Each attack became weaker, as the enemy had to divert some of its resources to deal with ARVN reinforcements coming down Route 1 from the north. There would be one more attack on the 1st Division compound the night of 31 January, but it proved to be the last one.

The enemy pulled back from the division CP and strengthened its defenses at the airfield. Other enemy troops set up a headquarters in the Imperial Palace compound, while others moved to the southeast to put pressure on Truong's garrison from the south.

Captain Bray, who was 2 weeks away from rotating home, and the rest of the noncombat support personnel at the division CP found themselves in a life-and-death struggle none of them had expected. Bray would get just 3 hours' sleep until he was relieved on 4 February. A week later, he headed home a very lucky man.

A year and a half later, Bray returned to Vietnam as a company commander and was killed in action during an operation near Chu Lai.

CHAPTER THREE

Staying Alive

At the same time that elements of the NVA 6th Regiment were moving into position to attack the Citadel, the NVA 4th Regiment came out of the mountains to the west and began infiltrating the area south of the Perfume River. Darkness and a heavy fog hid the movements of both enemy forces.

Other than a few marines on guard duty at the main gate of the MACV compound and a guard detail at a tower in the northern corner, the U.S. billet was sound asleep and unprepared for any attack.

Captain Coolican, a native of Carbondale, Pennsylvania, had been an advisor with the ARVN 1st Division since April, moving to the unit's elite Hac Bao Company in October. At 6 feet, 5 inches, he towered over his Vietnamese troops. Proficient in Vietnamese, Coolican had great respect for his little troopers and their culture.

Normally, Captain Coolican would have spent the night with his unit, which was garrisoned in the Citadel. At the last minute, however, he decided to visit his marine buddies at the MACV compound and let the Hac Bao Company enjoy the holidays on their own. Just after midnight on 30 January 1968, Coolican packed an overnight bag, jumped into a jeep, and drove himself toward the Nguyen Hoang Bridge that spanned the Perfume River to the southern section of the city and the MACV compound. (See Map 2.)

"I remember stopping the jeep just before the bridge and looking back at the city. I could see the lights of the Citadel. It was like Christmas," Coolican said. "It was a very pretty sight. I spent a moment or two admiring the lights before driving across the bridge."

Coolican arrived at the MACV compound just before 0200, 31 January. A couple of marine guards had to open the main gate to let him in. He parked the jeep against a fence by the main gate and walked to his room in the hotel annex, which he shared with another marine officer. Coolican was lucky there was a bunk available. The compound was crowded with advisors who had come in from the field for a bit of downtime while their units celebrated Tet.

There did not appear to be any extra security at the compound even though Captain Coolican knew that General Truong had put his Vietnamese troops on full alert the day before. Coolican did not think anything of it as he went right to sleep.

MACV's senior advisor, Col. George O. Adkisson, had assumed his new duties just a few days before, after returning from his home in Texas on a stateside leave. Adkisson, a 43-year-old West Pointer (class of 1945), was a tall, regal-looking gentleman who spoke softly but with authority. He was quite a contrast to his predecessor, the cigar-chomping, hell-raising Col. Pete Kelley. Kelley had kept his advisors jumping, I was told, and had built a close relationship with General Truong during his tenure with the ARVN 1st Division.

Adkisson knew, of course, that Truong had put his

troops on 100 percent alert, but he was unaware that General Westmoreland had ordered the same alert for the U.S. forces. As a result, no extra precautions had been taken or warnings given at the MACV compound the night of 30 January.

The MACV compound was not equipped to withstand much of any attack. Located in a heavily residential area, the compound was basically occupied by noncombat personnel. Other than a few marines pulling guard duty and perhaps a dozen advisors with recent combat experience, the compound was inhabited by clerks, jeep drivers, cooks, and other support personnel. However, on the night of 30 January, there were more combat advisors in the compound than usual.

The compound was rectangular in shape, about 300 yards wide by 200 yards deep. It was surrounded by a six-to-eight-foot wall, except at the main gate, which was blocked by a 10-foot-high chainlink fence. Adjacent to the main gate was a heavily sandbagged security booth manned by at least two marines who checked all traffic, military and civilian, in and out of the compound. The entire perimeter was topped by barbed wire, trip flares, and a dozen or so Claymore mines placed atop the walls at critical spots.

There was a large open field to the southeast toward Tu Do Stadium, but the surrounding houses and compounds in the other three directions offered plenty of cover and concealment for an attacking force.

Just inside the main gate was a two-story hotel annex, with about 20 rooms on each floor. The annex ran parallel to the main gate at a distance of about 30 feet. There was a 10-foot-wide pathway between the annex and the main part of the hotel, which bordered Route 1 on the west. The mess hall was on the first floor. Behind the annex was an athletic court, but its high chainlink fence prevented its use as a helicopter pad. Behind the athletic court were three rows of sleeping quarters, some with tin roofs and others with canvas coverings. The accommodations along the southeastern edge or back half of the compound, which looked over the open field, also had defensive bunkers. There were two machine gun towers, one on top of the main hotel looking up and down Route 1 and down on the main gate and another above the command bunker, which also covered the main gate. (See Map 3.)

The compound also had an officer's club (adjacent to the annex), a chapel, a barber shop, and a small dispensary. The latter was more like a first-aid station with two tiny office areas and an operating room, also very small.

Basically, the compound was a typical rear-echelon billet, heavy on the steaks and shrimp and light on the heavy weapons. The occupants were advisors and support personnel, not killers.

The one-room officer's club was a hot spot in the evenings. The larger mess hall in the main hotel served as an entertainment center when USO shows came around. I remember one Filipino touring group, Tito and his Playgirls, that performed to a standing-room-only audience in the mess hall and that even had the chaplain rocking and rolling.

Most of us in the compound used a native laundry service. The locals, mostly women, had to pass inspection every day coming in and out of the main gate but otherwise had complete freedom to move around the compound. They did a great job with the laundry, and I never heard of even one case of thievery or sabotage.

I was initially assigned to a small tent not very far from the dispensary. I believe there were five or six other officers in the tent with me. My cot had an air mattress and mosquito netting. It was not someplace you would stick a VIP.

One of my roommates was Maj. Joe Gunter, a brand new liaison officer from the U.S. 1st Cavalry Division. Another was a young marine captain who had just come down from Khe Sanh to be an advisor with an ARVN unit. One of the first things he did was move his bunk away from the wall.

"I like to be able to roll off either side of the bed when the mortar rounds come in," he smiled. Obviously he had some experience in these matters.

I had a cheap radio next to my bed and a flashlight that allowed me to read before falling off to sleep. The latrine was about 30 feet away in a sandbagged building. It was a one-holer with an adjacent piss tube. The nearest bunker was 30 feet in the other direction, leading some cynic to speculate that in the event of a mortar attack we could go either way to cover our ass.

It was just before midnight when I got back to my bunk on 30 January. I had had a fun night playing darts at the officer's club; I had even beaten a couple of Australians at their own game. What a great bunch of guys the Aussies were. They reminded me of college fraternity guys. I remember that as I walked back to my quarters I was pleased with my new assignment. The people I had met so far were very outgoing, colorful, and friendly.

My tent was dark when I entered. I quietly took off my

boots and hung my pants and shirt on a nearby chair.
I heard a burst of M16 fire and what sounded like firecrackers. Somebody was celebrating the end of the first
day of Tet. Nobody in the tent stirred. I drifted off to
sleep with a smile on my face.

BAM! . . . There was no mistaking what this noise was.
The sound and the vibration from the blast jolted me upright in my cot. A 122mm rocket, one of the enemy's
largest missiles, had landed not more than 50 feet from
where I was sleeping.

Instinct took over. I threw on my pants, put on my
steel pot, grabbed my boots and M16, and stumbled barefoot out the door toward the bunker, bumping against
my tentmates on the way. There were about 12 of us in
the bunker as two more booming explosions shook the
compound. We spent the first few minutes getting dressed
and checking our weapons. Only one or two remembered to bring their flak jackets. I checked my watch. It
was 0345.

Beads of sweat trickled down my side and gathered on
my forehead. Something pretty big was happening out
there, but for now none of us knew exactly what. One
of us peeked outside and reported seeing green tracer
fire racing across the sky. A bad sign, I was told. The VC
use green tracers. The high-pitched noises were AK-47
fire, and the louder sounds were B-40 rocket-propelled
grenades (RPGs), two of the more common weapons
employed by the Vietcong. We could also hear the "pop-
pop" of M16 rifle and M60 machine gun fire as well as
the "whump" of the M79 grenade launcher.

Nobody said anything, but we were all thinking that
we could not stay where we were. We were all an easy

target if an enemy sapper broke through and tossed a satchel charge in the bunker.

Then another rocket exploded much closer than the first three. We heard some yelling and then a cry for a medic. It was still very dark. We waited in that bunker for what seemed like a half hour before we were directed to individual guard posts throughout the compound. There we waited at the ready. For what, nobody knew.

Captain Coolican rolled out of his bed at the sound of the rocket explosion and immediately sprang into action.

"There was no doubt in my mind that it was an incoming round," Coolican said. "The first thing I did was hit the deck and turn my radio on. Then I went outside and started making the rounds. I went over by the dispensary to see about any casualties. There was a lot of fire coming from the back of the compound and I went to investigate. A bunker took a direct hit, injuring five people, all helicopter pilots. I grabbed a stretcher and helped move the injured to the dispensary."

While Coolican was coordinating the defense at the back of the compound, he was told that his radio operator, Sp4c. Frank Doezema, Jr., was taking fire in a guard tower in the northern corner of the compound. Coolican ran to the scene.

"I got some guys to lay down a base of fire and I climbed the tower," Coolican said. "Doezema was hit in both legs and was bleeding heavily. I gave him a shot of morphine and then carried him down."

Coolican then climbed back up the tower with an M79 grenade launcher and about 30 rounds of ammunition, directing most of his fire in the vicinity of the main gate.

Specialist 4th Class Doezema, a native of Kalamazoo, Michigan, had directed M60 machine gun fire toward the area of the main gate, blunting the initial sapper attack. He killed six enemy soldiers before he was wounded. Coolican, who was later awarded the Navy Cross for his actions, was credited with four kills after silencing an enemy bunker directing fire at the main gate.

While Coolican delivered fire from the tower, marine Maj. Frank Breth, the 3rd Marine Division liaison officer, led an ad hoc group of marine and army advisors to the top of the main hotel, from where they spotted more sappers and enemy troops coming up Route 1 toward the compound. One of the NVA soldiers stuffed a grenade into a ground-floor bunker, killing one of the marine guards, but the rest of the enemy force was cut down before reaching the main gate. Quick reaction by Major Breth and his helpers sent the NVA running.

Specialist Doezema, meanwhile, was badly hurt. He needed immediate medical attention or he would die. There were a couple of other wounded who could use immediate attention as well.

Coolican, as he had done dozens of times before, prepared to call for a medical evacuation (medevac). First, however, he had to find a suitable helicopter landing site. The MACV compound did not have the necessary open space to land a chopper, so Coolican checked his map and picked a location about 200 meters away at Doc Lao Park on the southern bank of the Perfume River.

Nobody knew whether the site was secure. There was no reason to think it was, but the situation was critical. Coolican had difficulty raising the marine base at Phu Bai to the south, so he tried the 1st Cav headquarters some 25 kilometers north of Hue. There simply were no medevacs available, but Coolican kept trying.

In the meantime, Coolican had to figure out the best way to get the wounded to the landing zone (LZ) without getting the rest of them shot up. As far as he knew, the enemy not only controlled the LZ, they controlled all the streets leading to it.

It was midafternoon before a medevac was available: a flatbed truck was commandeered, and the wounded were loaded aboard; two jeeps were assigned to go along as security. As soon as the chopper reported it was inbound to Hue, the truck and jeeps dashed out of the MACV compound gate and ran a hail of fire to the LZ. While some advisors made sure the wounded did not fall off the back of the truck, others manned machine guns on the jeeps or provided M16 fire.

Arriving safely at the LZ, Coolican calmly talked the chopper down. The big bird, which came in under a barrage of small-arms fire, landed quickly, took on the wounded, and was airborne in less than 30 seconds. The advisors hustled back to the MACV compound without any further injuries, which was miraculous in itself.

Doezema, who had 20 days left on his tour, was dead on arrival when the chopper landed a few minutes later.

Sp4c. James Mueller arrived in Hue as a clerk typist in May of 1967 and went home with a Bronze Star for Valor for his heroic deeds at the MACV compound in the first couple of days of the siege. He had thoroughly enjoyed his tour in lovely Hue until the early morning hours of 31 January.

"I screamed 'incoming' as I always did when the enemy

lobbed mortars and rockets into our compound. By now it was automatic," Mueller said many years later.

I scrambled out of my cot, ripped away the protective mosquito net, donned my helmet liner and steel pot and slipped on my flak jacket. In a matter of seconds I had my carbine and ammunition and was out the door with my shower shoes on. My fellow hootch mates always made fun of me because I never took the time to put on my uniform. So there I was in combat gear in my underwear and shower shoes. To me, speed was the most important thing—I wanted to stay alive.

This was not the first time Mueller had been mortared at the MACV compound, but it was by far the worst.

Usually Charlie would lob some mortars or fire rockets into the compound and we would be on alert for about half an hour. After we got the all-clear signal, we would return to bed to get some rest. But not this time. All hell broke loose after we were all safely in our bunker, which held five or six men. Small-arms fire could be heard from every direction, and more loud explosions continued after the mortars and rockets.

The sergeant came by and instructed us to fire at anything that moved. When we opened up with a barrage we hit the trip wires, and the flares on the barbed wire were ignited. Our entire corner of the compound was lighted up like it was daytime. We heard intensive small-arms fire coming from the school on our right and automatic weapons fire coming from the direction of the commanding officer's quarters. ARVN soldiers in billets directly in front of us fired a few rounds at our position, but we thought it was an accident so we did not return fire. After a minute or two, the fire from the ARVN billet stopped. But the explosions, the flares, the small-arms fire, the loud noises, the yelling, the screaming, and the chaos seemed to go on forever. We did not realize what was going on around us. We stayed in our bunker, followed the sergeant's orders to defend the corner, and prayed that we would survive this hell.

This was my first combat guard duty assignment, and, though I could tell by the level of gunfire that there were a lot of enemy soldiers out there, I never felt in any real danger. I do not know how to explain that. Actually, my feelings were more of exhilaration than fear.

There is a lot of time to think while your eyes scan an area looking for people who want to kill you. I remember thinking, "I hope I see something to shoot at, something to hit." My eyes were the size of baseballs that first night. I wasn't going to miss anything, especially somebody trying to shoot me.

I was paired up with a marine captain named Bob Williams in a second-floor room of the hotel annex overlooking the main gate. We talked some over the next couple of hours but mostly we watched in silence. I do not remember being scared, probably because it was all so new to me that I did not know any better.

I kept moving my eyes from side to side, as I had been taught during a night-fire exercise at Fort Benning almost 4 years before. Suddenly it became very quiet. The sky to the east began to lighten, and then it was morning. Right in front of me was a big hole in the ground where an enemy rocket had landed earlier. A jeep was upside down, and another was on its side up against the fence. There were two little bodies in the street by the main gate, and at first I thought they were children. They were enemy sappers.

"Everybody OK? Everybody all right?" came the call down the line. One by one we answered from our guard posts.

It was 0600, and a damp chill hung over the compound. There was absolutely no movement to our front. We sat and waited for somebody to tell us what had happened. At the same time, there did not seem to be any urgent need for information, because, except for some random mortar fire, nothing was going on.

I left my window post briefly to take a piss. What a relief that was. When I stood up I also checked for any wounds from shattered glass that filled the room. Everything looked and felt all right.

A little while later, my partner and I took turns returning to our billet to get the rest of our clothes and gear. I jogged in a crouch past a couple of buildings that were riddled with bullet holes. Bigger holes were made by B-40 grenades. I could see other MACV personnel moving around performing the same tasks. Sniper fire zinged overhead.

As I looked to my right over the compound wall I could see across the street the top of a steeple, which I was sure the enemy was using to shoot down on us. The steeple was part of the Jeanne d'Arc school complex. The building itself was a yellowish stucco structure with a colonnaded front. The school was next door, as was a small dispensary building marked with a red cross. As long as enemy snipers occupied the steeple, all our movements within the advisors compound would be quick and in a crouch.

I entered my tent quickly, put on a shirt and my flak jacket, and grabbed my shaving kit. I also took my flashlight and radio and double-timed back to my guard post, ready for anything. Someone had come by and dropped off some C rations and M16 ammunition. I turned on the radio and someone on the Armed Forces Network was saying that Saigon was under attack. Other cities were also being hit. Nothing was said about Hue.

Colonel Adkisson called his most senior advisors together for a situation report at first light. Though the land line to the 1st Division headquarters in the Citadel had been cut, Adkisson had talked to General Truong by radio. It had become clear to both men that large forces of NVA and Vietcong troops were at work throughout the city. Truong described his situation as desperate, but Adkisson felt that the worst was over at the MACV compound.

"I quickly came to the realization that the North Vietnamese could easily have overwhelmed us," he said. "Since they had not, it seemed most likely that they were simply not interested in us or our compound. For this reason I did not believe subsequently that the compound was in great peril."

Nonetheless, Adkisson did not hesitate to call for help.

The nearest point of relief for the MACV compound was the marine base at Phu Bai, which was also under attack. Phu Bai, which straddled Route 1 only 11 kilometers south of Hue, was the site of Task Force X-Ray, or the 1st Marine Division forward headquarters. Until 13 January, Phu Bai had been the headquarters of the 3rd Marine Division. Different units from both divisions were still coming and going at the base at the time of the Tet offensive.

On 31 January, Task Force X-Ray consisted of the regimental headquarters of the 1st and 5th Marines and four infantry battalions, each with its full quota of supporting arms. When orders came down to provide assistance to Hue, X-Ray commander Brig. Gen. Foster C. LaHue decided that he could spare only one company. What La-Hue and everybody else did not know at the time was that Hue was currently under attack by a division-sized enemy force that had enough supplies, ammunition, and reinforcements to keep them in business for a long, long time.

As the morning wore on, the advisors hunkered down in the MACV compound and collectively took a deep breath. We reflected on our good fortune that the enemy had never followed up its initial attack with a determined ground assault. Stopping the enemy forces was one thing. Getting them to leave Hue would prove to be one of the toughest assignments of the entire war.

Personally, I had the sense that it was over. I took out my pocket diary and wrote my first words of the battle:

Wednesday sure came fast today. Somebody out there doesn't like us. I lost track of the mortars. The first one was sure loud. [I later learned it was a 122mm rocket.] Dawn couldn't come soon enough. I was so nervous you couldn't have shot a BB up my ass with a bazooka. I wasn't scared though. I don't know why. There were a couple of bodies on the road in front of the main gate, not more than 50 feet from my guardpost. There was some yelling in the compound but mostly it's been pretty quiet, except for the machine guns and M-16 fire, and the mortars. I didn't have to fire my M-16 at all. But I was ready. I guess I'm in the shit. Oh well, I guess I had to expect it. This is a war zone.

At about 1000 on 31 January I heard my first helicopter of the battle. It flew right over the MACV compound toward the river, drawing fire all the way. A few minutes later I heard some more firing, but the helicopter never returned. We learned later that it was shot down but that the crew members had been able to escape to a nearby ARVN compound, where they were rescued a few hours later. That daring rescue mission by CWO Frederick Ferguson earned him the Congressional Medal of Honor.

Chief Warrant Officer Ferguson, a veteran chopper pilot with Company C, 227th Aviation Battalion, 1st Cavalry Division, had been in the air well before dawn the morning of 31 January. Temporarily operating a little north of Chu Lai while the 1st Cav was preparing its move to Camp Evans 25 kilometers northwest of Hue, Ferguson's company parked its choppers on a ballfield that belonged to a construction battalion just 2 or 3 kilometers from Phu Bai. Early on the morning of 31 January, the ballfield came under heavy mortar and rocket attack.

"We were concerned that the mortars would destroy our planes, so we decided to get them out of there," Ferguson said many years later.

When the mortar fire eased, the crews of the 12 choppers raced to the ballfield and took off without lights. They had decided to fly up to Camp Evans and land, but the base was fogged in. They then turned around and headed south for the airstrip in Hue Citadel, but they were told it was under attack. Finally, they raised Phu Bai on the radio and received permission to land despite the fact that the base was still under attack. By this time the choppers had to land because they had only 20 minutes of fuel left.

Shortly after daybreak the choppers were refueled and headed back to their basecamp a few miles away for further assignment. Ferguson heard on the radio that one of the choppers in his company had been shot down in Hue and that five other choppers in his unit, which had attempted a rescue, had been driven off by intense fire. Word was passed down from above to stay away from Hue.

Ferguson knew in an instant what he had to do.

"If I was there, I'd want someone to get me out," Ferguson said. "It was my duty, my job, to get them out."

Ferguson told his crew to strip the chopper of excess weight and stand by for a rescue mission. Then he convinced three other gunships to go along on the mission to provide covering fire while he attempted a rescue. Timing would be critical. He figured he had a window of opportunity of between 15 and 20 seconds to get on the ground and then get out of there. Precision flying would be required because the only area in the tiny ARVN compound where Ferguson had any chance of landing was a small space between one of the buildings and a flagpole. The area offered only a few meters of clearance on either side for the overhead rotor.

At about noon, Ferguson radioed the compound that he was ready to come in as soon as the mortar fire let up. He notified the other three gunships to stand by and then gave his crew special instructions. He planned to come in low from the east along the Perfume River, turn left just beyond the main bridge, and drop down quickly into the compound.

"I remember looking out of my right side as we went

past the Citadel and seeing the VC flag flying on the flag-pole inside the Citadel," Ferguson said. "My gunner on that side—a guy named Ford who we called Edsel or a guy named Edsel we called Ford, I can't remember—said, 'Let's fly past and get the flag on the way out.' "

Ferguson's ship swooped in through a hail of enemy fire and dropped straight down on the landing area in a big cloud of dust.

"I don't know which compound it was. It's been almost 30 years," Ferguson said in 1997. "It wasn't too far from the river, though."

After everyone was on board, he picked the chopper straight up so the blades would not hit a nearby building or the flagpole and made his escape. Just as the chopper lifted off, however, a mortar round exploded nearby, spinning the aircraft 180 degrees and forcing Ferguson to exit the compound in the wrong direction, that is, away from where the other three gunships were hovering to provide covering fire.

It did not make any difference which direction he exited because all the choppers were out of ammunition. Ferguson's chopper, riddled by small-arms fire, was the only one to make it back to Phu Bai.

"Had it not been that I had five wounded people on board, I'd have probably put mine down sooner than I did," Ferguson told author Tim Lowry in 1985.

The transmission was gone and there was zero oil pressure. It was stinking, you could smell it. It was hotter than hell in the back. The airplane was shaking so bad you couldn't read the instrument panel, but it was still flying. So I pushed it into the Hue–Phu Bai air strip and when I cleared the fence, I just slid it onto the sand out front. If that barbed-wire fence had been another strand higher, I don't think I'd have made it over.

It was a hairy mission, but we were all alive. There was a lot of slapping each other on the back. You know how it is when you have a real high like that. Everybody is real happy and excited.

It took us a day to come down, but we were back in the war the next day.

Chief Warrant Officer Ferguson, who left active duty in 1972, remained in the National Guard and retired from the army in 1997 with 39 years of service.

CHAPTER FOUR

To the Rescue

Sgt. Alfredo Gonzalez and his pal Cpl. Bill Jackson had gotten less than 3 hours of sleep before they were driven from their bunks at Phu Bai early on the morning of 31 January.

Most of their Company A, 1st Battalion, 1st Marines (Alpha 1/1), had flown in from Quang Tri north of Hue the previous day after an operation near the DMZ. Hours were spent unpacking their gear, policing up the company area, and washing out the dirt and stench of 2 weeks of combat patrolling near Con Thien, where Corporal Jackson had earned a Purple Heart. The tired grunts, who were looking forward to some rare time off, climbed into their sleeping bags just after midnight.

At 0345 the entire company, responding to shouts of "incoming, incoming," was running at full speed for the slit trenches and bunkers as enemy mortars and rockets rained down on the combat base.

Inside the command bunker, radios were crackling with reports of similar attacks throughout the region. When the situation stabilized just after daybreak, the base commander, General LaHue, received orders from his superiors in Da Nang to send some help to Hue, which was reported to be under ground attack. Lacking any specifics on the size of the attack, LaHue decided to send Alpha 1/1.

Alpha 1/1 was really only half a company. Parts of two platoons were still in Quang Tri, and the only officer at Phu Bai was the company commander, Capt. Gordon Batcheller.

Batcheller, the son of a navy admiral, was a career man who had seen more than his share of combat action, usually from a spot at the head of his unit. He was a gung-ho marine, having shaved his head to illustrate the point. His men not only trusted him but they respected him as well.

Batcheller called his NCOs together and told them they were going to Hue City, which was 11 kilometers north up Route 1. Some of the company had been through the city before on truck convoys headed toward the DMZ. The operation, he said, should take 1 or 2 days. As it turned out, it would take over 2 weeks and Batcheller, who was severely wounded, would never make it past the first few hours.

In the absence of any officers, Sergeant Gonzalez, who was platoon sergeant of the 3rd Platoon, was made acting platoon leader. The 21-year-old native of Edinburg, Texas, a town on the Mexican border, was a fearless fighter and well respected by his men. The 19-year-old Jackson, a native of New York City, was made acting platoon sergeant of the 2nd Platoon.

With only one map and hardly any reliable intelligence information, the men of Alpha 1/1 left the Phu Bai combat base at about 0830 heading into the unknown. They loaded aboard half a dozen six-by-six trucks and were augmented by two U.S. Army trucks with M55 anti-aircraft machine guns. The latter trucks had quadruple

.50-caliber machine guns (quad .50s) mounted over their cabs.

The relief column was supposed to meet up with some ARVN troops who were to help guide them into the city. They never showed. Batcheller waited almost an hour for them before heading out on his own.

Batcheller's original mission was to proceed through Hue and link up with a unit from the U.S. Army 1st Cavalry Division well north of the city. Batcheller's map extended only a kilometer past Hue. Oh, well, Batcheller thought, he'd figure it all out on the way. A few minutes later, his mission was changed. He was to proceed to the MACV advisory compound just short of the Perfume River.

Batcheller did not like the sound of this new order and asked for an intelligence update in the area. He was told that there was none. Batcheller also had an eerie feeling about what he was seeing. Route 1 was usually bustling with traffic at this time of the morning, and there was none. Normally, there would be little kids begging for food along the roadside. There were none. Added to this was a light fog that lay quietly on the countryside. He had the feeling he was heading off into the twilight zone.

About an hour later, approximately 3 kilometers short of the city, Batcheller's column caught up with a convoy of four marine M48 tanks that were halted by the side of the road. The tanks, which belonged to the 3rd Marine Division, were on their way to the Hue U.S. Navy landing craft, utility (LCU) ramp for further shipment to the DMZ. They had halted near the wreckage of a burned-out ARVN tank. The convoy commander had radioed back to Phu Bai reporting the enemy activity and requested infantry support to proceed.

Batcheller's force quickly joined up with the tanks and made plans to get under way again. Batcheller had his troops dismount from the trucks to provide security for the tanks. Sergeant Gonzalez's platoon fanned out to the right and Corporal Jackson's platoon took the left.

It was only a few minutes before the convoy was taken under fire from a building 50 meters away at a fork in the road. Machine gun fire whistled over their heads as the company's men dove for cover. A minute later, the firing stopped. Gonzalez stepped out from the building with a smile on his face and four captured AK-47 rifles in his arms.

While the convoy halted to plan its next move, Batcheller was informed that a group of marine work vehicles was approaching from the rear. Leading the latter group was Lt. Col. Ed LaMontagne, the 3rd Marine Division embarkation officer who had decided to accompany the work vehicles to the LCU ramp. At the suggestion of Colonel LaMontagne, Batcheller decided to pick up the pace. Being the only officer in the company, Captain Batcheller had also decided to move his command group to the front of the column to exercise better control.

As the convoy approached the vital An Cuu Bridge over the Phu Cam Canal about 2 kilometers from the MACV compound, the signs of enemy activity increased. More ARVN tanks littered the side of the road, their crews burned beyond recognition. It looked as if the enemy had tried to blow up the bridge but had failed.

Batcheller was not going to wait around for the enemy to reinforce the bridge, so he gave the order to lay down a base of fire while his infantry and tanks rushed across the bridge. Batcheller and his radio operator jumped aboard the lead tank and raced to the other side without incident. The others followed.

About 100 meters past the bridge, the convoy came upon an intersection with a traffic circle in the center. Along the roadside were a half-dozen destroyed ARVN tanks that belonged to the 7th Armored Cavalry, which was garrisoned just a few hundred meters from there. The tanks had been ambushed by the enemy earlier that day when they tried to respond to a call from Gen. Truong, who had ordered them to proceed to the Citadel as quickly as possible.

The enemy opened up with a volley of B-40 rockets that struck the lead tank. Captain Batcheller escaped injury, but the barrage killed his radioman and a senior corpsman. Despite the heavy fire the entire convoy made it across the bridge.

With the early-morning fog completely lifted, Batcheller could see about 600 meters of exposed roadway ahead that crossed a sugar cane field. At the end of the tree-lined causeway was the southern edge of the heavily built-up city of Hue. Batcheller tried to get some air and artillery support before jumping off across this exposed area. But he could not reach anyone because all the radio lines were clogged with traffic, much of it Vietnamese. He did reach his boss at Phu Bai, 1/1 commander Lt. Col. Mark Gravel, who promised to lead a relief force his way immediately. In the meantime, Gravel ordered Batcheller to proceed on to Hue with due haste.

"We knew the enemy was watching us as we started down the causeway but there wasn't much we could do about it," Jackson said. "We fanned out on the right side of the road and the skipper [Batcheller] was walking behind the lead tank. I saw him dash to his right to help a wounded man. Then he was hit by a hail of fire."

The next few minutes were chaotic. It was difficult to see where the fire was coming from. The quad .50s, which had been moved forward in the column, sprayed both sides of the road as the marines hunkered down in a roadside ditch. The only marines who moved were those dragging wounded comrades out of harm's way.

Captain Batcheller was hit in both legs and his right forearm by a machine gun blast. The impact was so great that it blew him off the road and into a ditch, where he became entangled in a coil of concertina wire. Even though badly wounded and unable to move, he shouted to his most senior soldier, Gunnery Sergeant J. L. Canley, a six-foot, four-inch, 240-pound giant of a man, to take charge of the company and proceed to the MACV compound.

The marines, using the tanks and quad .50s as a shield, sprinted across the causeway but halted again when they reached a built-up area about 500 meters south of the MACV compound. It was at this time that Lieutenant Colonel Gravel's relief force, which consisted of Company G, 2nd Battalion, 5th Marines (Golf 2/5) and his operations officer, Maj. Walt Murphy, arrived on the causeway.

Capt. Chuck Meadows, Golf 2/5's commanding officer, was as much in the dark as everyone else about what was going on in Hue. His unit, which was temporarily assigned to the operational control of the 1st Marine Regiment, was the "palace guard" at Phu Bai. The unit spent the night of 30 January on a hill about 1 kilometer to the west of Phu Bai and had a ringside seat for the rocket attack on the combat base that occurred about 0330.

After returning to the base shortly after daylight, Captain Meadows was called to the 1st Marine command post and told he was being attached to 1/1 commander Lieutenant Colonel Gravel for a relief mission in Hue. The exact mission was to proceed to the ARVN 1st Division CP in the Citadel and escort General Truong back to Phu Bai. The convoy left Phu Bai at 1030. Lieutenant Colonel Gravel's jeep was at the head of the column, and Captain Meadows was in the cab of the second truck.

All was fairly quiet until the convoy crossed the An Cuu Bridge and started across the 600-meter causeway toward the southern outskirts of the city. An NVA machine gun opened up on the left of the column, and Meadows ordered his men to disembark from the trucks and move to the right side away from the fire. Abandoning the trucks temporarily, Golf 2/5 quickly crossed the cane field by hugging the right side of the causeway berm. Off to the left, the troops could see khaki-clad NVA soldiers heading north on a parallel course to the city just out of small-arms range. For many of the marines it was the first time they had actually seen enemy troops in the open.

As Golf 2/5 left the causeway it ran into wounded marines from Alpha 1/1 who were being attended to by corpsmen. One of the wounded was Captain Batcheller.

Lieutenant Colonel Gravel and Major Murphy directed efforts to police up the wounded marines from Alpha 1/1, including Batcheller, and sent them all back to Phu Bai on a couple of the trucks. Batcheller, who was later awarded the Navy Cross, would need 10 months in a stateside hospital to recover from his wounds.

Sending the wounded back virtually defenseless over hostile territory was a gamble, one Gravel felt "was a terrible long shot." He decided that it was worth the risk if the wounded were to be saved. "We weren't going to get any helicopters in there . . . so we took them back," Gravel said. The trucks completed the return trip to Phu Bai without incident.

It was noon and the relief convoy had now reached a crossroads. It couldn't afford to hunker down where it was or its vehicles might be picked off one by one. Bold action was called for, and Lieutenant Colonel LaMontagne had a plan. While the bulk of the convoy directed heavy fire on the surrounding buildings, he would lead a breakout dash with two tanks and a couple of squads the last 500 meters to the MACV compound. LaMontagne had been to the compound many times in the past few months and knew exactly where it was.

We in the compound could hear the force coming up Route 1. We started yelling and cheering. One advisor, a captain, lifted his head above the sandbags atop the compound wall to get a good view of the marines coming up the street and was struck in the head and killed by a bullet, probably a ricochet. He was standing right next to me.

There was a lot of yelling and firing from the marines as they seemed to be spurred on by the sight of the U.S. flag flapping in the breeze over the MACV compound. The noise echoed off the buildings as we tried to hunker down to avoid any more stray bullets. Finally, the small force of marines, led by Lieutenant Colonel LaMontagne, turned the corner off Route 1 and entered the front gate of the compound.

Pausing to catch his breath, LaMontagne reported to Colonel Adkisson and began making plans to return back down Route 1 to police up the remaining marines and guide them to the compound. Several advisors, including Major Breth and Captain Coolican, located some trucks and joined LaMontagne on the mission.

The entire marine force, including two truckloads of wounded and dead, was inside the compound by 1500. The compound was now bolstered by nearly 300 marine infantrymen, four marine M48 tanks, two army trucks with M55 quad .50s, and two ARVN M41 tanks. The rescue mission had come at a big price, however, because the marines had suffered 10 killed and 30 wounded. Little did they know it was only the beginning.

Marine Maj. Wayne R. Swenson, a liaison officer to the ARVN 1st Division from Task Force X-Ray, spoke for many of us at the MACV compound when he told a journalist several days later: "I have little doubt that many of us would not be alive today had those marines not arrived when they did."

As happy and relieved as the advisors at the MACV compound were, the marines were equally happy to get off the streets and away from the gauntlet of small-arms fire and B-40 rockets that had tormented them on their rescue mission up Route 1.

I went out to visit with a couple of the marine grunts to welcome them to Hue and get a story or two about their journey to the city. I brought along my camera, a notepad, and several pens. I walked up to a couple of grunts who had slumped against a fence by the main gate. They had loosened their flak jackets to get at some soggy cigarettes. They were drenched in sweat, and their hands shook so badly they could barely strike a match.

"How was it coming up here? What's going on out there?" I asked.

The marines told me they had come up Route 1 from their base camp at Phu Bai. It was only 11 kilometers and they were under heavy fire much of the way. The last few clicks (kilometers) had been a bitch. They spoke with a rush, still feeding off the adrenaline used on the journey. They looked so young.

"You know what it looked like when we hit the outskirts of the city?" one of the grunts said in a burst of words. "It looked like an old western town, like Dodge City. Some of the buildings had wooden fronts with porches on the second floor. There were these narrow alleyways between them. There were even wooden sidewalks."

Minutes later a sergeant walked by and shouted, "Saddle up, saddle up!" in his best John Wayne imitation. There was no bitching or griping. They put out their cigarettes, tightened up their flak jackets, slung on their packs, and got ready to go. Headquarters at Phu Bai had called, and they were to proceed on their original mission, which was to cross the Perfume River, enter the Citadel, and escort General Truong back to Phu Bai.

The most immediate priority, however, was the evacuation of the wounded and a resupply of ammunition. While the compound's lone doctor, Capt. Stephen Bernie, did his best to patch up the wounded marines, a patrol secured a helicopter LZ a block from the compound near the LCU ramp on the Perfume River. It was the same site that Captain Coolican had mapped out earlier in the day.

As the marines of Golf 2/5 filed out of the compound I walked to the fence to see where they were going. Less than a minute later, the sounds of machine gun fire filled the air. It was not long before the stretchers arrived. I stood by the gate with my M16 at the ready and waved the stretcher bearers through on their way to the dispensary. They kept coming and coming.

A group of four marines jogged toward the main gate, each of them holding a corner of a poncho with a wounded comrade inside.

"Where's the doctor, where's the doctor?" one of the lead bearers shouted on the run.

"Follow me," I said as I led them behind the hotel annex to the dispensary.

There were at least two dozen wounded either sitting or lying on the ground outside the dispensary.

A marine corpsman told the group with the poncho to put the man down near the door and the doctor would be right with them. When they put the poncho down a gush of blood washed over one of the bearer's boots. The wounded marine had bled to death.

The noise of the battle grew in intensity. There was no mistaking the AK-47 fire and the green tracers that identified enemy machine gun fire. The bad guys were out there in force.

As young as the marines looked going out the gate, they looked even younger coming back on stretchers. They were just kids, really. Many of them were teenagers, barely out of high school. They called themselves "snuffies," and they wore it as a badge of distinction. Anyone not a marine, rear-echelon types, and generally anyone that went by the book were "poges," definitely not a badge of distinction. "Poges" were "number 10."

Young or not, they bled just as much as any other combat veteran. I was struck by their stoicism and their pride. Although some of the wounds looked gruesome, I do not remember any whimpering or yelling. They seemed

to bear their wounds with an almost calm detachment.
Lit cigarettes hung from blood-stained lips. Some were
smiling as if they had just returned from a shootout at the
OK Corral. Others flashed the OK sign with their thumb
and forefinger or gave the thumbs-up sign. Others were
so badly wounded they could not make any sign at all.

The stretchers were stacked up outside the dispensary. The most serious would get the quickest attention.
Dr. Bernie would get to everyone, but it would take
awhile. An occasional mortar round dropped in the compound, one coming awfully close to a direct hit on the
dispensary. Even the dead and wounded were not safe in
this place.

Just inside the dispensary, on the floor along a wall,
were a couple of body bags. As the day wore on the body
bags multiplied. One of the dead was an old friend of
Captain Williams, the man I shared my guard post with.
I went with Williams to the dispensary to pay his last re-
spects. He knelt by the body bag and, gathering all the
courage he could summon, unzipped it so he could see
his old comrade's face. He began to weep, and I could
not find any words to make him stop.

It was my first experience with a body bag. It would
not be my last.

Lieutenant Colonel Gravel was in a particularly foul
mood. Soon after arriving at the MACV compound, he
had a shouting match with the senior advisor, Colonel
Adkisson. Gravel, acting the part of a conquering marine
hero, felt that Adkisson, an army man, was being less
than cooperative. The two men could be seen jawing at
each other near the command bunker.

Gravel later told a reporter he felt that Adkisson had

a plentiful supply of ammunition, weapons, and equipment and that "he wasn't too willing to part with it until he saw that if he wanted to keep his hat and ass together, he'd better be nice to us because we were all that he had."

Gravel was now being ordered by his superiors in Phu Bai to take his exhausted marine force across the Perfume River and try and link up with General Truong in the Citadel. In the absence of any specific intelligence about enemy strength, he believed it made no sense to jeopardize their precarious foothold at the MACV compound by an attack into unknown territory. If the enemy across the river was as strong as what he had seen en route to the city, it would be suicidal. After voicing his concerns, he was told to "proceed."

Fearing the bridge might not be able to support the weight of his tanks, Gravel decided to leave all five of the vehicles and an infantry platoon at the helicopter LZ, where they could support the attack with covering fire. The tanks would also ensure the safety of the LZ, which was now getting heavy use as a medevac and resupply point.

The operation nearly turned into a disaster.

Ten marines were mowed down crossing the bridge, and another 40 would be wounded before the ill-advised mission was called off.

Second Lt. Steve Hancock's 2nd Platoon was assigned the point. His job was to cross the 400-meter-long bridge, turn left along Route 1, and proceed about 300 meters to the Thuong Tu Gate, the nearest entrance to the Citadel. He was to continue into the Citadel and head about 2,000 meters due north and link up with General Truong in the ARVN 1st Division CP.

NVA machine gunners opened up just as the platoon reached the crest of the bridge, forcing a temporary halt to the mission. Marines scattered to the sides of the bridge looking for cover. Others dashed out to drag their wounded comrades to safety. While bullets zinged overhead and caromed off the steel structure above his head, Lieutenant Hancock reached his company commander, Captain Meadows, on the radio and asked, "What now?"

Lieutenant Colonel Gravel, who was observing from the base of the bridge, decided that the first thing to be done was to get the wounded men off the bridge. He called back to the MACV compound and asked Colonel Adkisson to send up some vehicles to help him evacuate his wounded. Allegedly told that there were no vehicles available, Gravel flew into another rage against Adkisson, threatening to pull all his troops out of the MACV compound.

In the end, it was Gravel's operations officer, Major Murphy, who scrounged up the assistance needed to evacuate the wounded, a mission that would cost him his life.

"Murphy was the man who drove the effort that first day and he took chances he probably shouldn't have," Captain Coolican said.

Murphy watched on the southern end of the bridge as an Army M55 machine gun truck sped across the other side and started hosing down suspected enemy positions with its quad .50s. Suddenly two enemy soldiers ran out of a nearby building and threw what looked to be satchel charges in the back of the truck. The explosion lifted the truck into the air.

Murphy dashed across the open bridge to try and pull

a couple of wounded marines from the truck. Even the chaplain, Lt. Richard Lyons, rushed to the bridge to help. Both were knocked to the ground by a B-40 rocket. Lyons suffered a leg injury and limped off, but Murphy did not get up. He was hurt seriously. Both of them were immediately evacuated to the MACV compound dispensary, where Captain Coolican was busily trying to arrange a medevac.

"I went over to Murphy and told him to hang in there, that he'd be on his way to a hospital shortly," Coolican remembered. "He told me his back was hurting him but otherwise he seemed in control. He was comforting the other wounded marines. When I came back to get him for the medevac, he had bled to death."

Chaplain Lyons, who was on a nearby stretcher, was carried to Murphy's side just before he died so that he could administer the last rites.

The loss of Murphy, who was posthumously awarded the Silver Star, was a particularly bitter blow. Coolican, Breth, and Swenson had each served with Murphy before. All of them had tremendous respect for his leadership qualities. Gravel was devastated: Murphy was more than just his right-hand man, he was one of his best friends.

The mission, meanwhile, continued. The first platoon of Golf 2/5, under Lt. Mike McNeil, took over the point and, after knocking out a bunker guarding the north end of the bridge, reached the other side without meeting much resistance. The rest of the company followed. McNeil's lead squad turned left and proceeded along Route 1 in the shadow of the Citadel wall. The troops passed a movie theater that displayed a poster of *Gone with the Wind*.

McNeil's point squad turned right toward the Thuong Tu Gate and paused for a moment. Ahead of them was an arched gate leading into the Citadel, and high above them to the left and flapping in the breeze was a huge NLF flag. The point squad stepped out into the street toward the gate and was met with heavy machine gun fire, stopping the marines in their tracks.

It was decision time. If the lead element remained where it was, it could be wiped out—and there was no guarantee that it could execute a successful withdrawal without suffering equally high casualties.

Gravel knew what had to be done. He ordered Golf 2/5 to pull back, all the way back across the bridge. Using smoke grenades to mask their movement, the advance units slowly withdrew, picking up their wounded as they went. When they reached the northern end of the bridge they were aided by covering fire from the tanks and mortars from across the river. By 1900, 4 hours after they started, the whole company was back on the south side of the river.

As ill-conceived as the excursion across the river proved to be, it could have been a whole lot worse. Had the enemy force allowed the two platoons of Golf Company to move into the Citadel, it might have easily wiped out both platoons, which would have then left the MACV compound without the necessary troops to defend itself.

"We were no match for what was going on across the river," Gravel admitted later.

Golf Company commander Meadows was equally critical of the mission.

"I had 49 casualties the first day, and almost every one of those was going across that one bridge and then getting back across that bridge," he said with obvious bitterness.

Gravel and his marines had learned an enduring lesson on that nearly disastrous foray across the bridge. Never again would marines be sent against an enemy in fortified positions without the accompaniment of tanks. The mission also cleared up any doubt that the NVA had come to Hue City with a lot of first-line, well-armed troops who were prepared to stay until they were physically pushed out.

Having barely escaped from a near-disaster, the marines were called upon for yet another mission this first day. Another order came down from Phu Bai to try and rescue some U.S. civilians who were believed to be hiding in a building a couple of blocks away from the MACV compound. A squad from Alpha 1/1, accompanied by two tanks and a few MACV volunteers, was sent on a mission that would be repeated time and time again over the next couple of weeks.

The expedition moved less than 100 meters before it was stopped in its tracks by overwhelming enemy fire. No Americans were rescued, but the mission opened the door for the first trickle of frightened refugees, who, under the cover provided by U.S. forces, made their way to the safety of the MACV compound. The trickle would become a flood in the next couple of weeks, creating a logistical and security nightmare for the U.S. forces in Hue.

One of the last acts of the first day was a late-night medevac from Doc Lao Park. Eight marines were scheduled to be air lifted to Phu Bai, but the total rose to 12 when four more were wounded transporting the stretchers to the LZ.

Other than the relief of the MACV compound, the

biggest success of that first day had been the establishment of a relatively secure LZ by the Perfume River. Much of the credit for that belonged to the MACV advisors, who helped establish the site while the marines were off on their foray across the river.

Despite the fact that the LZ was open to enemy fire from the Citadel across the river, it was one of the few easily identified open areas within a short distance of the MACV dispensary. Advisors took turns ferrying the wounded from the compound to the LZ that first afternoon, and it was Captain Coolican who called in most of the medevacs and resupply choppers.

At first, the choppers attracted heavy fire. The big marine twin-rotor CH-46 Sea Knights would hover out of small-arms range until they got the word the LZ was ready. Then they would swoop down like giant prehistoric birds and discharge their cargo of ammunition and supplies as fast as possible, while stretcher bearers stood by to quickly carry the wounded aboard. Rarely was a chopper on the ground for more than 30 seconds.

The choppers were most vulnerable just before landing and just after takeoff, when they were silhouetted against the sky above the buildings or trees. As extra security during these dangerous periods, two U.S. Navy riverine patrol boats from the nearby LCU ramp positioned themselves out in the river to train their twin .50-caliber machine guns on enemy positions on both banks. It proved just the touch to give the LZ much of the security it needed.

Night evacuations were especially tricky, calling on all the coordination the advisors and marines could muster. Flashlights were used, but the ground personnel had to be very careful that the beams of light were directed straight up in the air so that only the helicopter pilots could see them.

My second night of guard duty at the MACV compound was less anxious than the first because we now had the security blanket of 300 combat marines and four tanks. But I still did not get much sleep. The arrival of the marines had increased the level of firing and made everyone a little more jumpy to noises around us.

The advisors huddled in small defensive groups and talked about the near-miss we had experienced. The size and identity of the enemy forces was still unknown, but no one doubted that they were big enough to have easily overrun our compound. That they did not was viewed by many of us as a miracle.

The temperature dropped to about 50 degrees as I covered up in my guard post. I looked out toward the Citadel from my second-floor perch and watched as flares lit up the pitch-black sky. The flares, attached to tiny parachutes, floated slowly to the ground, casting eerie shadows on the skyline. Machine gun and mortar fire resonated throughout the night, spooky reminders that the neighborhood was full of bad guys.

Across the river in the Citadel, General Truong's small garrison in the division HQ was barely hanging on, still awaiting the arrival of reinforcements that had fought their way from bases to the north down Route 1 to within a few meters of the fortress wall. They would have to wait until the next morning to move inside the Citadel, where they would give General Truong enough strength to start turning the tide.

In retrospect, the enemy forces had made three costly mistakes that first day. First, they had failed to overrun

General Truong's headquarters, and second, they had not followed up with a ground assault on the MACV compound when they clearly had more than sufficient manpower to accomplish both missions. Third, they failed to destroy the An Cuu Bridge south of the city on Route 1, leaving open an avenue for the marines to effect a rescue mission to the MACV compound and then continue to use the highway for resupply and reinforcements in the coming days. Had the bridge been blown, it would have delayed the arrival of the marines. Who knows whether the MACV compound could have waited any longer to be rescued.

Later it was learned that the enemy's timetable for overrunning the MACV compound had been disrupted when one of its key units was held up by an allied artillery barrage south of the city. By the time the enemy unit had regrouped and proceeded to Hue it was behind schedule. So, when the signal for the attack came—the barrage of rocket fire from the western hills—the unit was not in position to follow up with a ground assault.

Also, there are indications that there was a significant delay in the commencement of the rocket attack, perhaps by as much as an hour. When it did come at 0340 it was much too close to daylight, giving enemy forces insufficient time to take full advantage of the darkness.

It had been a close call for those of us in the MACV compound, and we were indeed fortunate that the enemy chose not to exploit our weakness.

Before grabbing a little sleep, I made my second diary entry:

What a full day. There was no time to be scared. There was no time to eat, piss or shit, either. These Marines are terrific, the bravest bastards I've ever seen. I can't get over how young they look. Everyone gets his orders and off they march, right into the face of almost certain death. As bad as it was today, I have the feeling the worst is over. I hope so.

CHAPTER FIVE

Help for the Citadel

Capt. Ty Cobb had one very important mission to accomplish on 29 January. That was to scrounge up some American chow for his Vietnamese counterparts to enjoy the following day at Tet. Cobb, no relation to the baseball Hall of Famer by the same name, was the senior advisor to the ARVN 2nd Airborne Battalion that was temporarily stationed north of Hue at Quang Dien, which is about 15 kilometers east of PK 17. He took a jeep and a small truck over the back road to PK 17 and then traveled down Route 1 through Hue to Phu Bai.

The road was crowded with military and holiday traffic, but no more than usual. Passing through Hue, Cobb couldn't help noticing how beautiful and peaceful the city was. Cobb, a native of Sparta, New Jersey, had served briefly as an airborne liaison officer to the ARVN 1st Division a couple of months before being sent to the 2nd Airborne. There were smiles on the faces of the people he passed. Why should they not be happy? Most of them were home for the holidays.

Although he had been in Hue many times during his tour of duty, Cobb always marveled at the sheer size of the Citadel each time he saw it from a distance. The structure seemed to jump out at him as he approached the city. The Citadel just dominated all the other buildings on the outskirts of the city, rising like a huge medieval castle.

As the two-vehicle convoy approached the main bridge over the Perfume River, Cobb thought about the mission his unit went on the week before. The 2nd Airborne was lifted into an area about 8 kilometers west of Hue to investigate reports of enemy activity.

"We discovered a huge cave dug into the side of a hill. It was filled with all brand-new stuff, much of it still in boxes," Cobb said many years later. "We found dozens of machine guns, six 60mm mortars, 27 brand new SKS rifles with bayonets, surgical equipment, and 3 tons of rice. It was obviously a regimental headquarters."

What they did not find were any enemy troops.

"It's a good thing because we would have been badly outnumbered," Cobb said. "I think many of them were already in Hue disguised as civilians and reconnoitering the city."

The entire cache was brought back to the 1st Division HQ. The following week, many of the captured weapons and equipment were used against the enemy when they attacked the Citadel.

"Looking back on it, I'd like to think that confiscating that cache might have helped the defenders in Hue weather that first assault," Cobb said. "Maybe we played a role in helping them hang on."

Cobb quickly dismissed all thoughts about the enemy cache on the ride to Phu Bai. Since the intelligence people at the 1st Division HQ apparently did not think too much of the find, Cobb was not overly worried that the enemy was planning a big offensive in the area. Besides, he had a very important mission of his own to fulfill that day.

The convoy pulled into Phu Bai and Cobb loaded up the truck with as much food as he could bargain for. The haul included 60 pounds of sugar—the Vietnamese loved their sweets—10 pounds of coffee, two cases of canned peaches, some canned corned beef, and a couple of boxes of cookies. The return trip north was slow but uneventful.

The next day, Cobb and his counterpart, Major Thach, visited all four companies and divided the goodies. There was also a ceremonial Tet dinner at the battalion CP at noon. The celebration continued into the night, and at midnight a few of the troops fired their M16s into the air. Others set off firecrackers.

Then all was quiet.

Capt. Jack Chase had similar duties to perform on the day before Tet. Chase, of Jericho Center, Vermont, was the U.S. advisor to the ARVN 3rd Troop, 7th Armored Cavalry (3/7) stationed just outside PK 17 northwest of Hue.

"I managed to scrounge up some supplemental packs that often came with C rations," Chase said. "The soldiers liked the gum and candy but they didn't have any use for the shaving gear. They preferred to pluck the hairs from their face."

The 3rd Troop, 7th Cav had recently undergone a change of command. First Lt. Tran Van Minh had succeeded Capt. Nguyen Van Thi the month before and was still feeling his way around his new unit.

"Thi had been highly respected by his men," Chase said. "He was regarded as one or two ranks below God, while

Minh had only been on one mission as commander, so he still had to make his reputation."

The unit had a sit-down dinner the afternoon of Tet, with much ceremony and exchanging of gifts. Minh gave Captain Chase a lacquered photo album that he still cherishes. The table was full of traditional and exotic foods, and there was much laughter and good fellowship.

"They had killed a water buffalo," Chase remembered. "As I recall, it was the stringiest, toughest thing I ever ate."

Everybody went to bed that night with full stomachs and happy hearts.

One of Capt. Chuck Jackson's main duties at Tet was to make certain that his unit, the ARVN 7th Airborne Battalion, had enough American-supplied booze for the celebratory feast.

"The preferred drink was Black Label scotch," Jackson said, "but we'd drink Red Label in a pinch. The other favorite drink was Hennessy Cognac."

Jackson's unit had just moved to An Lo, a few kilometers north of PK 17, a day or two prior to Tet for security reasons and was scattered around the countryside. Captain Jackson, of Macungie, Pennsylvania, made the rounds of all four companies with his counterpart, Maj. Le Van Ngoc, on Tet, sampling various holiday goodies at each of the stops.

"I didn't much care for most of the Vietnamese food. It's kind of hard to swallow a piece of pig with the hairs still on it," Jackson said. "But I did like the little cubes of what I thought were caramel wrapped in a palm frond. They were delicious. Later I found out they were fermented raw pork cubes."

Jackson, like Cobb and Chase, went to bed that night without any thought of an impending major enemy offensive. Less than 6 hours later, fate would bring all three units together in a bloody clash against a superior enemy force that sought to deny them access to Hue Citadel, where they had been summoned to rescue the beleaguered 1st Division HQ.

General Truong's call for help went out about 0430. After calling his scattered 3rd Regiment and 7th Cavalry to rally to him in the Citadel, Truong put in a request through channels to have the three battalions of the 1st Airborne Task Force (the 2nd, 7th, and 9th) put under his operational control. After getting approval from his superiors, all three units were alerted to move to Hue. The 9th Airborne and 2nd Troop, 7th Cavalry were under heavy ground attack at their base in Quang Tri, about 50 kilometers north of Hue, and were unable to comply with the orders until they finished dealing with more urgent matters.

"We got the call at about 0430," 3/7's Chase said. "We weren't under any attack and thought it wasn't terribly major. We prepared for a 3-day operation."

Eight kilometers north of PK 17, the 7th Airborne was awakened by sporadic mortar fire at 0300. An hour and a half later, a message came in to join up with Chase's outfit and proceed to Hue to "help relieve some 1st Division troops."

The two units joined up at PK 17 and embarked down Route 1 toward Hue at 0920. The sun was shining brightly as 3/7's 12 APCs took the lead. The 375-man 7th Airborne spread out, with two companies on each side of the road. A railroad line, which paralleled Route 1 to the west, was on the right flank. Many of the airborne troops had taken off their helmets and donned their trademark red berets.

About five kilometers from Hue, the railroad line narrowed to about 100 meters from Route 1, forcing the "Red Hats" to spread a little to the right to cover the other side of the tracks. At about noon, with the walls of the Citadel in sight, the lead APC took a direct hit from an RPG round, igniting all the ammunition on board and killing all eight occupants. The convoy stopped in its tracks.

"The shot had come from a spot between the road and the railroad tracks. They let the APC get right on top of them, perhaps 15 or 20 feet away before firing," Chase said. "You would never think anybody could hide in that terrain, but all they needed was a little clump of bamboo."

The convoy stared in horror as the APC continued to "cook off" with secondary explosions. Nobody could get near the vehicle to help those trapped inside. When another APC ventured close to get a better look, it too was struck by a rocket. Several of the crewmen jumped off the vehicle and headed for cover. The rest of the APCs opened fire with their .50- and .30-caliber machine guns, raking both sides of the road.

"When we finally got to the first APC there wasn't enough left of the crew to put in a helmet," Chase said.

Moments after the second track was hit, the 7th Airborne's lead company on the left flank started taking fire from a large cemetery to its front. After a brief conference with Lieutenant Minh, the CO of 3/7, it was decided the 7th Airborne would make a frontal attack on the cemetery while the remaining APCs of the 7th Cav, which could not maneuver in the graveyard because of all the burial mounds and headstones, would provide supporting fire.

The enemy let the airborne troopers get halfway through the graveyard before cutting down the lead elements with deadly machine gun and small-arms fire and a hail of mortar rounds. Then it got worse.

"A hundred and fifty men rushed across the cemetery and after they had gone about 300 yards there was virtually nobody left standing," said Chase, who had watched the charge from an APC on the road. "I can still see them dropping one by one. It was like what you would imagine happened during the Civil War. Pickett's charge comes to mind."

A stunned and shocked Jackson, who was back at the battalion CP, remembered it as a "bad day, a real bad day."

"Number 10" to the max.

The 2nd Airborne Battalion, which had been alerted early that morning to prepare for duty in Hue, was held up by a blown bridge on its way to PK 17. After fighting its way through a couple of enemy roadblocks, the 350-man battalion arrived at PK 17 around noon after a 5-hour march.

"Nobody knew what was going on in Hue. We didn't know how serious it was," Captain Cobb said. "We were told basically that they needed help and that it shouldn't take very long to complete the mission."

By the time they scrounged up some trucks for the ride down Route 1, the 2nd Airborne did not leave PK 17 until 1400. Because they were told it was going to be a short mission, most of the troopers took off their packs and left them at PK 17, along with any extra gear.

"The first thing I saw when we got near Hue was a pile of equipment by the side of the road," Cobb said. "It was 5 feet high and 10 feet around. It was all the equipment taken off the killed and wounded ARVN soldiers earlier that day. I had a feeling in the pit of my stomach that it would be a bad day. I grabbed some grenades from the pile. I thought I might need them."

The 2nd Airborne Red Hats then made plans for their own attack through the cemetery, only they would be making a flanking run instead of a frontal assault. The unit's assistant senior advisor, Capt. Donald C. Erbes, was in the lead company with the battalion executive officer.

"We hadn't gone more than 100 yards when the exec took an AK-47 round right through the helmet, killing him instantly," Erbes remembered.

Momentarily stunned, Captain Erbes pulled the exec's body behind a gravestone and urged the rest of the troops ahead. Another company, this one with senior advisor Ty Cobb and the battalion commander, saw what was happening and raced out to continue the attack.

"A funny thing happened running across that graveyard," Cobb said. "I thought it was all over for Captain Cobb. I was maybe 100 yards behind the lead element, and, as I was running, I saw a little puff of white smoke as a 60mm mortar round landed right between my feet. I guess I was fortunate that the ground was soft and it buried itself pretty deep. The next thing I know I was doing a 360-degree flip in the air, landing on my feet. Other than a slight concussion and a little piece of shrapnel in my nose I was all right.

"I then looked over at the command group and they were laughing at me. Here we were right in the middle of a battle and people being killed all around and they are laughing at me. I had to laugh, too."

Meanwhile, Captain Erbes was trying to get some artillery fire on the area but could not reach anybody. He also tried to get some helicopter gunships from the U.S. 1st Cavalry Division. Finally, he was able to contact a lone gunship that was in the area to come in and see if he could help the situation.

"The pilot said he wanted to make a dry run over the area to see where the friendly troops were," Erbes said. "Then he was shot down. It was the last helicopter gunship I saw while I was in Hue."

A decision was made to stay the night and not try to enter the Citadel until the next morning. Guards were posted, and the three units spent hours policing up the dead and wounded from the battlefield and trying to catch their breath.

"Many of the enemy we killed were wearing civilian clothes, which I guess made it easy for them to infiltrate the city," Chase said. "Another thing I noticed was that they didn't even bother to police up the weapons and ammunition from our troops. This made me believe they had everything they needed. They didn't need any of our weapons. They came to Hue well armed and with all the supplies they could carry."

It was not until midnight that anybody could think of getting a little sleep. Cobb, Erbes, and Jackson lay down in the cemetery but had a difficult time closing their eyes.

"It was really cold, and there still was a lot of noise going on," Cobb said. "I was thinking we sure could use our packs that we had left behind at PK 17. I shivered the whole night."

Just after midnight, Jackson said he thought he heard somebody trying to start up one of the damaged APCs just off the highway.

"All I could think of was that the enemy was going to take one of our APCs and turn it against us," Jackson said. "We didn't need any of that."

Erbes, of Gainesville, Florida, said he remembered hearing dozens of explosions going off in the Citadel during the night. He assumed that the enemy was blowing up stuff it had captured.

All was fairly quiet the next morning, 1 February. The rescue force had been in touch with the 1st Division HQ, which said it would send out a platoon from the Hac Bao Company to guide the force to a secure gate. The three shaken units, led by their Black Panther guides, swept east along the northwestern wall, carrying their dead and wounded with them. There was very little enemy resistance. They ate what food they could find along the way. All three units were safely inside the Citadel by noon.

The rescue force reported casualties of 40 killed and 91 wounded, most of them in the ARVN 7th Airborne Battalion. The rescue force also claimed to have killed 270 of the enemy. It had captured five prisoners, 71 individual weapons, and 25 crew-served weapons. Captain Chase also reported the loss of four APCs from his original total of 12. Captain Cobb said he could tell by the looks on the faces of those in the ARVN 1st Division compound that something big was happening.

"Everybody looked scared," Cobb said. "An American advisor walked up to me and said the shit was pretty deep here."

Two hours after reporting in, all three units were sent into action to expand the friendly perimeter around the division compound.

Perhaps the most heroic journey to the Citadel was undertaken by the ARVN 1st Battalion, 3rd Regiment (1/3), which had been cut off and surrounded several kilometers east of Hue. The unit's commander, Capt. Phan Ngoc Luong, a 1960 graduate of Dalat Military Academy, was another of General Truong's outstanding line officers. Luong was a strict disciplinarian who ran his battalion with an iron hand. Displeased by the lax behavior of some of his troops, Luong had ordered a sweep operation the night of 30 January as a form of punishment.

"We ran into the tail end of a Vietcong battalion and found ourselves in a pitched battle," Captain Luong said. "We were soon down to only three clips of ammo per man, and the enemy was all around us. We had to get out of there."

Luong's advisor, U.S. Army Maj. Gary Webb, managed to contact some helicopter gunships soon after daylight, and the helicopters provided covering fire while 1/3 broke the enemy encirclement and fought its way farther east toward the coastal town of Ba Lang. There, Webb called in a resupply and medevac helicopter.

"We killed over a hundred of the enemy and captured so many weapons we couldn't carry them," said Luong, who later reported friendly casualties of 15 killed and 33 wounded.

After being resupplied, the 1st Battalion bypassed some

enemy strongpoints the next day and finally reached Ba Lang. There, the battalion boarded three Vietnamese junks and motored up the Perfume River to the Citadel, arriving at 1500. The unit was immediately dispatched to an area along the northwest wall. Major Webb, who had served an earlier tour in Vietnam as an advisor to a Montagnard outfit, was later awarded the Distinguished Service Cross.

Other ARVN troops arriving in the Citadel on 1 February were two companies from the 4th Battalion, 2nd Regiment. They were air-lifted into the Citadel from their base near the DMZ at Dong Ha at 1500 and immediately deployed to the southeast sector of the city along the northeast wall. The rest of the battalion, along with a company from the 1st Battalion, 1st Regiment, arrived late the next day by airlift. Also arriving on 2 February was the ARVN 9th Airborne Battalion, which had been engaged in heavy fighting to the north at Quang Tri. The 9th, which had been flown in by U.S. Marine helicopters, joined up with the 2nd and 7th Airborne Battalions to help retake the Tay Loc Airfield that day.

The 9th Airborne had just moved into temporary quarters at Quang Tri the day before Tet. Most of the men of the 650-man battalion, like its sister units, the 2nd and 7th Airborne, were disappointed that they were not allowed to return home to Saigon for the holidays. But they had resigned themselves to make the best of the circumstances.

"As best as I can recall we didn't have much in the way of a Tet celebration," said Capt. Dick Blair, the 9th's senior U.S. advisor. "I remember some of the troops dancing in the streets under one of those dragon costumes, but we didn't have a sit-down ceremonial meal or anything. We all went to bed kind of early on January 30."

Part of Quang Tri is a walled city much like Hue but on a smaller scale. The city, which sits astride Route 1 about 50 kilometers northwest of Hue, served as the headquarters of the 1st ARVN Division's 1st Regiment and the 2nd Troop, 7th Cavalry. It was also home to MACV's Advisory Team 4.

The Headquarters Company of the 9th Airborne and two of its line companies bedded down inside the walled city of Quang Tri. A third company camped out south of the town, and another was positioned to the north. The 2nd Troop, 7th Cav (2/7) was encamped about one kilometer to the west.

On the night of 30 January, 9th Airborne advisors Sgt. Mike Smith of Dahlonega, Georgia, and Sfc. John Church, old friends from their days together with the 82nd Airborne Division, met at the NCO club in Quang Tri for a few beers. The two advisors reminisced about the old days and raised a glass or two of beer to celebrate the Vietnamese New Year. It was the last time Smith saw Church alive.

At about 0300 on the morning of 31 January, Captain Blair was roughly awakened by his counterpart, Maj. Nguyen Te Nha, and told to get up and get in gear because NVA forces were attacking the city.

"The first thing I did was grab the radio and try to reach Sergeant Church, whose company was guarding the northern approaches to the city. I couldn't get him and I knew something bad was happening," Blair said.

The NVA, moving under the cover of darkness and through a heavy fog, walked right through Church's company, effectively wiping it out. The paratroopers had 40 killed and 65 wounded. Church was one of those killed in action.

Captain Blair, of Centerville, Virginia, had his radio on and could hear brief snatches of conversation from the company. One of the things he heard was the company commander telling his troops to forget about firing their weapons and just throw grenades. The company commander, according to Blair, also requested artillery on his own position, but it was denied because it was too dangerous.

The enemy apparently just missed running into the 2/7 Cavalry, skirting to the north of their encampment. The unit's U.S. advisor, Capt. Jim Zimmerman, was at the MACV compound inside the walled city when the enemy struck. Within an hour the unit had sent an APC for Zimmerman, and he was in the fight.

Over the first couple of hours, the NVA had dropped about 200 mortar rounds on the city, forcing everybody to seek cover. As it began to get light, Captain Blair and Major Nha went up on the roof of a building in the walled city to get a better view of what was happening. As the fog lifted they could see khaki figures moving out of the treelines and heading toward the city.

Blair turned and asked Nha what he was going to do now.

"We are going to attack," Blair said Nha told him. "Paratroopers don't die fighting in holes. They die attacking."

That's exactly what the ARVN 9th Airborne Battalion did. Smith's company led one charge into the enemy, and, even though the NVA force had the greater numbers, it backed off. Later in the day, gunships from the U.S. 1st Cav appeared on the scene and started hosing down everything and anything in sight, including friendly troops.

"I was looking up at the gunships and then they turned in our direction. I yelled for everybody to get down," Smith said. "Most of the troops hunkered down in holes or behind berms. It was hairy. I got on the radio and asked Captain Blair to see if he could call them off. But they kept shooting."

The 9th Airborne, with help from the 2/7 Cavalry, fought off the attackers all during the day on 31 January. That night the enemy, which had committed two regiments to the attack on Quang Tri, sent in reinforcements from the west for a final push. As they massed in a big graveyard outside the city, Blair made radio contact with a Douglas AC-47 gunship, an airborne killing machine the grunts called "Spooky" or "Puff the Magic Dragon" because of its terrifying array of rapid-firing Vulcan machine guns.

"We put Spooky on them all night long," Smith said, "and in the morning there were so many bodies in parts of the graveyard that you couldn't see the ground. I don't know how many we killed. I never did count them."

When conditions stabilized somewhat on 2 February, the 9th Airborne turned the defense of the city over to the 2/7 and made arrangements to leave for Hue. The unit embarked for Hue Citadel in two shifts aboard U.S. Marine Sea Knight helicopters. The entire battalion was in the city by dusk. General Truong immediately sent it to the western section of the city, where it helped in recapturing Tay Lock Airfield.

It would be 4 more days before the 2/7 could leave Quang Tri for Hue. After 1 week of heavy fighting, some of it house by house inside the walled city, Quang Tri was finally declared secure. The ARVN defenders in Quang Tri claimed to have killed 1,450 of the enemy and captured 485 weapons.

CHAPTER SIX

Facing the Unknown

The situation around the MACV compound in southern Hue had eased somewhat after the first day, but enemy forces still controlled everything else in the area.

From my guard post in a second-floor room of the hotel annex overlooking the main gate of the MACV compound—which the marines had dubbed "the Alamo compound"—I had a panoramic view of the airspace over the Citadel on the night of 31 January, and, despite overcast skies, the sights were truly spectacular.

Flares dropped by low-flying aircraft literally turned the night into day—all night long. The flares drifted slowly in a swaying motion over the Citadel and the river, and, when they eventually burned out, others took their place high above the city to begin their own death spiral. The shadows bounced off the low clouds, casting eerie images over the entire landscape on both sides of the Perfume River. When the flares approached the ground the shadows moved among the buildings, causing more than one machine gunner to develop an itch in his trigger finger.

While my eyes focused on the flares, my ears tuned into the distinctive sounds of machine gun, M16, and AK-47 fire. Occasionally you could hear an enemy mortar round leave a tube and then hear the explosion only a few yards away. Once during the daytime, I looked up and saw a mortar round in flight just before it crashed into the roof of an adjoining building. Members of the advisory staff shuttled from guard post to guard post keeping everyone's morale up. They passed out information, ammunition, and C rations. I would have to get used to C rations because there would be no hot chow for a month.

While the advisors stayed put, the marines manned two- and three-man outposts on the street corners and nearby buildings. They also bolstered our defenses in the compound: just having them around was a tremendous security blanket. But it did not stop the mortars and it did not guarantee we would not have to fight off a ground attack.

While the marine brass huddled in their new CP at the MACV compound to plan the next day's action, the grunts caught what little sleep they could, knowing that at sunup they would be putting their lives on the line again in completely unfamiliar surroundings. None of the marines had had any training in street fighting. Neither had the ARVN forces in the Citadel, for that matter. The last time U.S. Marines had experienced sustained house-to-house combat was during the Korean War, in Seoul, back in 1951. That battle was against an enemy that was fighting a rear-guard action, and Hue was different, much different. The enemy forces in Hue were well dug in, well supplied, and prepared in some cases to fight to the finish.

The marines quickly realized that "Operation Hue City," as they had dubbed it, would take a lot longer than anticipated. It would take much longer than a couple of days. It might even take a week, or longer.

What the marines needed most that first night was rest, because it seemed clear they would need all the strength they could muster to stay alive in the coming days. But the flares and machine gun fire would not permit much more than a catnap. And smoking was definitely not a good idea. An enemy sniper could easily pick up the glow of a cigarette, and the result could be fatal.

One of the first decisions made by the Allied command was that Hue would be divided into two spheres of influence. Retaking the Citadel and other areas north of the Perfume River was to be an ARVN job. The area south of the Perfume River, or the right bank, was assigned to the U.S. Marines.

Originally, there was no thought given to using any other U.S. forces even though elements of the army's 1st Cavalry Division and the 101st Airborne Division were on duty barely 25 kilometers north of Hue at Camp Evans. General Westmoreland was initially reluctant to commit those forces to Hue because, first of all, he thought he would not need them. Besides, many of them were green troops and new to the area. If he was going to be forced into using them it would be to reinforce areas along the DMZ, particularly at Khe Sanh, which he still believed was the enemy's main objective.

The marines made the MACV compound officer's club their CP and took full charge of all operations south of the river. The marines consulted with Army Colonel Adkisson and his advisory staff as a courtesy, but the latter had no tactical or strategic authority whatsoever in clearing the enemy from the city.

"There was never any doubt who was in charge," Adkisson said later. "[The marines] did the fighting and took terrible casualties. The Battle of Hue is primarily a Marine Corps story."

"We've gotten ourselves into a fine mess," Sergeant Gonzalez said to himself as he hunkered down next to a tank and tried to grab a little rest.

Gonzalez had been in the Marine Corps almost 3 years, rising quickly in rank because he was a born soldier. Others looked up to him. His elevation to acting platoon leader on the trip up to Hue had come as no surprise to anyone in the 3rd Platoon of Alpha 1/1.

Even though only 21, Gonzalez acted much older. The other grunts, many of them in their teens, also acted older than their years; they had become men in an awfully short time. Months of sleepless nights, wincing at sniper fire, and the constant strain of looking for tripwires and booby traps had forced them to grow up fast or not live to grow up at all. One thing that was for sure, there would be a lot more aging before this operation was over.

Lieutenant Colonel Gravel, the senior marine officer in Hue over the first 3 days, had his orders for the following day (1 February). He was to force the enemy out of his area of operations, which included everything south of the Perfume River. Gravel's area of responsibility was basically 11 blocks wide by nine blocks deep. To do the job he had two understrength companies (Alpha 1/1 and Golf 2/5), a force of 300 infantrymen, and four M48 tanks, two army trucks equipped with M55 quad .50 machine guns, and two ARVN M41 light tanks.

Gravel, who was still seething from having had to send Golf 2/5 across the bridge the day before, was limited in experience as a line officer, but he knew how to follow orders. He was a kick-ass type of officer whose bark was as loud as it gets. In typical "can-do" spirit, he sent his marines into battle on 1 February not knowing what was out there but determined to blast his way through any obstacle.

Gravel huddled with his brain trust, which included Majs. Frank Breth and Wayne Swenson and Capt. Jim Coolican, all marine MACV advisors or liaison officers. The absence of Major Murphy was almost painful. Gravel did most of the talking and all of the yelling. He did nothing to hide his disdain for MACV's senior advisor, Colonel Adkisson, with whom he had had two run-ins the day before. Marines, being marines, often had little use for military personnel in other branches of the service. Usually it was not anything personal; it was just the way they were.

Lieutenant Colonel Gravel also railed against his own superiors back in Phu Bai for issuing orders without any reliable intelligence information to back them up. Most of all, he was apprehensive about his situation in Hue: he believed that without the customary artillery and air support, frontal attacks in Hue were suicidal. The one thing he had learned from the previous day's assault across the bridge was that the enemy force in Hue was much larger and much stronger than anyone thought. He wanted more men and more heavy weapons, and he would keep yelling at higher headquarters until he got them.

His booming voice could be heard throughout the compound.

"Don't those people back there know what is going on up here?" Gravel screamed while pacing in his CP. "We were lucky to make it up here in the first place. Now they want us to wrap this thing up in a day or two. If I don't get more men and equipment, they are going to wrap us up."

Higher headquarters wanted Gravel to attack westward to relieve a garrison of government troops believed to be holding out at the Thua Thien Province Prison. That objective was 1,200 meters or eight long blocks from the MACV compound.

Being the career marine he was, Gravel was not about to say no. But he knew before his troops set out that the mission could not be accomplished. He issued the orders and was not at all surprised when his men were stopped in their tracks only 50 meters outside the gates of the MACV compound.

The marines could not get past the first block.

"Every building was a fortress, and each building had interlocking fires with another," one of the grunts told me. "You couldn't show your face for more than a second or it would draw fire. We moved inch by inch, and then it got dark, forcing us to return to the MACV compound."

One of the first priorities was the main campus building of Hue University at the foot of the Nguyen Hoang Bridge over the Perfume River. Only a block north of the MACV compound, it overlooked the crucial helicopter LZ in Doc Lao Park and the navy LCU ramp. By noon the gravity of the situation was apparent to everyone. For every marine who tried to go forward, it seemed that another one was carried back to the dispensary at the MACV compound with a ghastly wound of some kind.

"It was like fighting a hive of bees," a private told a reporter. "Fire was coming from street level, from windows on the second floor and from the roof of every building. We had to crawl everywhere and then call in the tanks so we could retrieve our wounded. It was obvious the enemy had plans to stay where they were and fight for every square foot of territory. It also looked like they had plenty of ammunition, too."

Even some of the advisors were pressed into combat action. Sp4c. Jim Mueller, a clerk typist by trade, and a couple of his army buddies at the MACV compound joined up with a marine squad that was trying to rescue a group of civilians who were believed trapped in a house less than a block away from the compound.

"I was scared. I had never done anything like that before," Specialist Mueller later wrote. "The sergeant had told us that the enemy would shoot at anything brightly colored, so we took the time to rip off our shoulder patches and stripes. I loaded up my uniform with extra carbine ammunition, .45 clips and grenades. We then helped the Marines load the tank with as much ammunition as it could carry."

The tank, with the mixed squad following close behind, left the main gate and slowly moved out onto Route 1, hugging a wall across the street from the MACV compound.

"Suddenly I came under fire from a sniper in the house facing the compound," Mueller said.

The fire was coming from a slatted window in the attic area. I did not return fire because I had to ask the sergeant for permission to shoot. So I said, "Sarge, there's someone up there shooting at me." He asked, "Where?" I pointed and said, "There." He said, "Well, they're not shooting at you now." "Well, no," I said. "Do I have permission to shoot back?" He said, "If he starts shooting again, call me and then shoot." I thought, how crazy this war was—a soldier needs permission to defend himself.

A little later, Mueller and his buddies carefully entered the house, which appeared to have been used as a small hospital.

"There were many beds around the room, but in the middle was a bed with a curtain around it," Mueller wrote further.

Our job was to secure the room, so we had to make sure that no one was in the bed. I really started to wonder about killing someone. Do I shoot first and ask questions later? Or do I wait until they open up the curtain and in a split second decide to kill the person who is there? Or do I not pull the trigger? All that was going through my head as I approached the bed, ready to shoot. One of the guys crept up to the curtain and quickly yanked it open. There was no one there. I took a deep breath.

By noon of 1 February, Dr. Bernie's tiny dispensary was overflowing. Bodies in plastic bags covered much of the floor space, and there was a line of walking wounded waiting to get into the building. There were over a dozen marines on stretchers outside the building waiting for a medevac. Corpsmen were running in and out of the area all day long. Every once in a while a mortar round would explode in the compound. Hardly anybody noticed.

If there was a man pushed to his limit it was Dr. Bernie. Bernie, whose specialty was ophthalmology, had earned his medical degree from Ohio State University in 1966. Since coming to Hue in the fall of 1967, his main duties had been holding sick call and administering inoculations. His small dispensary was not equipped to handle major surgery, nor did it have sufficient accommodations for seriously wounded patients. It did not take long for him to run out of surgical thread, morphine, bandages, and body bags.

From a health and morale standpoint, the situation at the dispensary became critical on the first day.

Mueller, the clerk typist who had tried his hand as an infantryman, was assigned to help out at the dispensary. For 3 weeks, he helped keep records of those treated, passing out cigarettes to the wounded and basically trying to lift the spirits of everyone who needed it. Later he found time to write of his experiences.

I remember the first Marine wounded by an enemy AK-47 rifle who was carried into the dispensary. He had a nasty head wound, and the blood would not stop flowing. The doctors bandaged the soldier and did a tracheotomy, but that was about all they could do. I was instructed to hold his legs during the treatment because his body quivered and shook. The doctors commented on the fact that the AK-47 bullets really tore up human flesh.

To say that the doctors were amazing would be an understatement. Without much sleep and under enormous stress, they worked long hours to care for the wounded. One day a Vietnamese civilian whose penis had been partially severed was brought into the dispensary. He was treated with respect and care just like everyone else. The doctor operated and the Vietnamese man had an excellent prognosis for a complete recovery. You never saw such a grateful person.

On another afternoon, a badly wounded Marine was brought into the dispensary after a street battle. Shrapnel had taken off most of the young man's foot; only a few ligaments were holding his foot to his ankle. The doctors administered a shot of morphine, then cut off his foot—still in its jungle boot—and put it into a body bag. An army chaplain was by his side during the whole operation. After the operation, the wounded Marine looked up at the chaplain and asked: "Padre, how can God love them and us?" The chaplain was speechless.

Golf 2/5, which had barely survived the foray across the bridge the first day, jumped off the morning of 1 February with the unrealistic mission of relieving ARVN forces believed holding out at the province prison. The marines managed to cross the street outside the MACV compound and advance all of 15 meters before they were pinned down by sniper fire. As the day wore on, the mission was scaled back. Still, the marines found themselves bogged down less than a half-block from their line of departure.

Lieutenant Colonel Gravel, who spent much of his time at the CP monitoring the radios and keeping in touch with Phu Bai, was incredulous that his marines could advance no farther than 15 meters. He ranted and railed but, in the end, all he could do was accept the fact that he was asking his tired troops to do the impossible. He could tell it was impossible by the steady flow of casualties he saw coming back from the battle.

Gravel's superiors in Phu Bai continued to think otherwise, however, and kept pressing him to move forward.

If Gravel had had access to artillery and air support, it might have been a different story. But both were denied him by low, overcast skies and an agreement by the Allies to try and limit the destruction of this historic and symbolic city.

Shortly after noon on 1 February, Gravel was ordered to return all the trucks that had been used to transport troops from Phu Bai to Hue the day before so that they could be reloaded with fresh troops and ammunition for a return trip. Route 1 was hardly secure, and troops would be needed to ensure the convoy's safety. Gravel put Lt. Bill Rogers in charge of a reinforced platoon that would act as an escort. Rogers also had a second mission. Not only was he to ensure that the convoy got through, he was to personally convey to the brass at Phu Bai just how serious the situation was in Hue. Then he was to lead the resupply convoy back to Hue to help in defense of the city.

Gravel had seen the effectiveness of his two companies (Alpha 1/1 and Golf 2/5) cut in half in 24 hours of action. Fully 150 men had suffered some kind of wound or had been killed. Many wounded were patched up on the spot by corpsmen and continued fighting, but there were about 75 casualties who needed immediate evacuation either because they were seriously wounded or dead.

An emotional Lieutenant Colonel Gravel put it all on the line when he gave Lieutenant Rogers his marching orders to Phu Bai. Laying it on as thick as he could, Gravel told Rogers that the lives of everybody in Hue depended on his ability to convince the brass in Phu Bai that the situation in Hue was an emergency and far worse than what was being described in military press conferences.

Rogers loaded the trucks with the most seriously wounded, lined them up outside the MACV compound, and told the drivers not to stop for anything. The boldness of the move and the convoy's speed apparently caught the enemy by surprise. The convoy roared across the open 600-meter causeway and across the An Cuu Bridge, drawing only scattered sniper fire. One truck broke down, but the wounded were quickly transferred, and the convoy reached Phu Bai without a single casualty.

Of equal importance, Lieutenant Rogers, who was shaking in his boots in front of General LaHue, had apparently convinced the Marine Corps brass that the enemy force in Hue indeed deserved more attention and resources than it was getting. He was instructed to tell Lieutenant Colonel Gravel that things would be changing.

Later that afternoon, Company F of 2/5 (Fox 2/5) was airlifted to Hue aboard marine twin-rotor CH-46 Sea Knights. On the next day, 2 February, Company H of 2/5 (Hotel 2/5) ran a gauntlet of fire up Route 1 aboard a 12-truck relief column. This "Rough Rider" convoy also included five Ontos vehicles, each equipped with six 106mm recoilless rifles. They were the building busters the marines had ordered to blast the enemy out of Hue.

But it was not until 3 February that the marines totally got their act together. That was when 1st Marine Regiment commander Col. Stanley Hughes and 2/5 commander Lt. Col. Ernest C. Cheatham arrived. Colonel Hughes took overall command and coordinated a plan that would slowly sweep the enemy from the south side of the Perfume River over the next week.

Arriving with Fox 2/5 the afternoon of 1 February was the first batch of civilian reporters and photographers. Among the first on the scene were Gene Roberts of the *New York Times*, Skip Troelstrup of *Time*, and George Syverste of CBS. Among the arrivals the next day were Al Webb, Dick Oliver, and Dana Stone of United Press International, George McArthur and John Lengle of the Associated Press, Jack Lawrence and Don Webster of CBS, Bill Brannigan of ABC, Wilson Hall of NBC, and Bill Tuohy of the *Los Angeles Times*.

By the time the first resupply convoy arrived from Phu Bai on 2 February, the replacements had heard all kinds of horror stories about the bloodshed in Hue. They had seen and talked to the casualties who had either been trucked out or flown out of the city to the triage center at Phu Bai. The stories they heard had scared the shit out of them.

Esquire correspondent Michael Herr, who rode up on one of the early Rough Rider resupply convoys from Phu Bai, captured the mood perfectly in his highly acclaimed book *Dispatches*, when he wrote: "All the grunts were whistling and no two were whistling the same tune. It sounded like a locker room before a game that nobody wanted to play."

The influx of more troops, an expanding press corps, and a flood of refugees had the MACV compound bulging at its seams. Other accommodations had to be found for the refugees, which included many ARVN soldiers trapped at home on leave during the Tet holidays. The refugees were eventually moved to quarters at Hue University, but the media correspondents, after checking in at the MACV compound, fanned out with the marine units throughout the city, and were basically free to come and go as they pleased.

Many of the correspondents bedded down on the floor of the mess hall in the MACV compound. A lot of marines had also staked out the same area and were not shy about throwing their weight around. Some of the reporters and cameramen came to me from time to time asking my help in sorting out the sleeping arrangements. I could only shrug my shoulders. This was clearly one case where the pen was not mightier than the sword.

A fully-complemented Fox 2/5, commanded by Capt. Mike Downs, began landing troops at Doc Lao Park at about 1500 on 1 February, and the entire company had reached the city by helicopter 2 hours later. Most of the big Sea Knight choppers, which were designed to carry 25 combat-equipped troops or 5,000 pounds of cargo, came in under heavy sniper fire, forcing the marines to exit the rear ramp on the run with their heads down. The choppers took many hits, but the airlift was completed without a single casualty.

The troops ran off the big choppers and immediately sought cover. Some turned to watch the empty Sea Knights climb into the overcast sky, wondering forlornly what they had let themselves in for. The platoon leaders quickly got their troops up and into a defensive perimeter. Captain Downs and his staff reported in to Lieutenant Colonel Gravel at the MACV compound and were issued orders to relieve Golf 2/5 at Hue University.

Golf 2/5 had sustained 64 casualties, including seven dead, in its first 24 hours in the city. It did not take long for the new arrivals from Fox 2/5 to get their noses bloodied, either.

The 2d Platoon of Fox 2/5 passed through Golf 2/5's front lines, and its point man was immediately shot down. Corpsman James Gosselin, a 26-year-old former Green Beret, charged into the open trying to get to the wounded marine and was shot dead. Two more fell in the next 5 minutes.

Two marine tanks were called up to help provide protection for those trying to rescue their comrades. The 50-ton monsters sprayed the buildings on both sides of the street with .50-caliber machine gun fire and inched up the street, offering more cover fire as marines quickly dashed out to retrieve the bodies. The bodies were dragged or carried back to a second tank and stacked on the rear deck behind the gun turret for removal to the rear. Just as the second tank started to back up, a B-40 rocket slammed into its side, tossing two of the wounded back into the street. Stretcher bearers rushed to the scene to gather up the wounded, and the entire force withdrew to its line of departure.

In less than 2 hours, the 2nd Platoon of Fox 2/5 had suffered four killed and 16 wounded, including its leader, Lt. Rich Horner.

Welcome to Hue City.

As darkness fell on 1 February, there was little to show for an entire day's fighting except a stream of casualties that taxed the MACV compound's medical facility and damaged morale badly. Two emergency medevacs were carried out at Doc Lao Park, this time with a tank leading the way to the LZ.

The marines were not through for the day just yet, however. Higher headquarters in Phu Bai, obviously still not fully grasping the severity of the situation in Hue, ordered Lieutenant Colonel Gravel to send Captain Downs's fresh Fox Company on a night attack westward toward the province prison. Gravel was astonished at the directive and went off on another tirade. How could higher headquarters expect his troops to traverse 1,200 meters in a night maneuver when they were unable to go 15 meters during the day? Gravel successfully petitioned his superiors to reconsider and the order was canceled—but only for that night.

More personnel and supplies arrived the next day when Hotel 2/5 under Capt. Ron Christmas trucked up from Phu Bai on Route 1. Christmas, who would rise to the rank of lieutenant general before he retired, also brought along two army Dusters and two Ontos vehicles. Also hitching a ride was the remainder of Alpha 1/1, which had been stranded in Quang Tri 2 days earlier when the rest of the company was airlifted to Phu Bai.

Most of the replacements in Christmas's convoy had left Phu Bai scared out of their wits. Having heard stories of the fury going on in Hue and worse, many of them had witnessed the truckloads of casualties that had come back on the first day. The triage center at Phu Bai was crammed with wounded, some of whom were friends of the replacements. Word spread quickly that Hue City was one badass place.

"Charlie really has his shit together up there," one of the wounded veterans warned the replacements. "They are everywhere and loaded for bear. Keep your ass down and don't try to be a hero."

Any doubts about the veracity of the warnings disappeared shortly after the replacement convoy crossed the An Cuu Bridge and raced across the 600-meter causeway into the built-up section of the city's outskirts. Bodies and wrecked vehicles littered the roadside, and smoke drifted out of pockmarked buildings. The buildings, hard by the road, turned Route 1 into a narrow alleyway and a shooting gallery for the hidden snipers. The replacements could sense the danger. It felt like death.

The convoy was late leaving Phu Bai because Captain Christmas hoped to get some artillery and air cover. The overcast weather never cleared, and the convoy did not get underway until 1400. By the time the convoy reached the built-up outskirts of the city and started taking heavy fire, it was 1500.

About 300 meters short of the MACV compound, the convoy had halted briefly when the lead truck rolled into a crater caused by a command-detonated mine. A heavy fusillade of .50-caliber and small-arms fire poured down on the stalled convoy, and the marines answered back as best they could. The marines dismounted and, knowing they had to move quickly or die, fought the rest of the way on foot.

The Alpha 1/1 stragglers joined up with their outfit, and, for the first time since arriving in the city, the company had an officer in its complement. Second Lt. Ray Smith relieved Gunnery Sgt. J. L. Canley as company commander. Gunnery Sergeant Canley had held the job for 2 days after taking over from Captain Batcheller, who had been severely wounded on the first rescue mission only 48 hours earlier. Captain Christmas's Hotel 2/5 was ordered to relieve Alpha 1/1, which had established its CP at Hue University. Less than an hour after arriving in Hue, Hotel 2/5 moved out and established contact on a sweep operation to the west along Le Loi Street paralleling the Perfume River.

For Pvt. Peter Hoban, one of the Alpha 1/1 stragglers, the journey to Hue was everything he was warned it would be. Hoban, a 19-year-old from Milton, Massachusetts, had been in country 2 weeks. Stranded at Quang Tri while the rest of his company flew into Phu Bai on 30 January, Private Hoban had missed his unit's original deployment to Hue on 31 January; he arrived at Phu Bai on 1 February and had only a few hours to get ready to rejoin his unit.

"On the way up to Hue we passed a lot of bodies on the side of the road, civilians," Hoban said. "The first time I saw marine casualties was when we got to the MACV compound. There were 30 or 35 bodies in ponchos in the courtyard. They'd been there for a couple of days. The dead weren't a priority medevac."

Hoban and the rest of the Alpha 1/1 stragglers rejoined their unit and were reassigned to duty around the MACV compound and in support of Hotel 2/5. Hoban, too, was in action less than an hour after arriving in the city.

"You couldn't stand up. You had to crawl everyplace," Hoban remembered many years later. "There was a red-headed kid in our outfit. I don't know his name, but he had the M79. He got a bullet right between the eyes, and the captain told me to get the M79. By the time I got to him, he had a death grip on it and I had to pry his fingers off the thing to get the gun out of his hand. There isn't a day that goes by that I don't think of the marines and Hue."

Just after 1800, the men of Hotel 2/5 had their first baptism in the struggle going on in the city when they helped beat back a fierce counterattack by the enemy, one that was aided by supporting fire from enemy troops across the river in the Citadel. The firefight, which continued throughout much of the night, lit up the sky like a Fourth of July celebration and kept everyone wide awake for another night.

Incredibly, another order came in from Task Force X-Ray in Phu Bai to send Fox 2/5 on another rescue mission at the provincial prison. Once again, the marines could move only half a block. Ironically, that very night the prison was overrun by NVA forces, resulting in the release of some 2,200 inmates, some of whom would later take up arms against the Allies.

The first 3 days had been a mighty struggle as the marines went through on-the-job training in house-to-house fighting. The weather—overcast, cold, and misty—greatly restricted both air and artillery support, which allowed the enemy complete freedom to evacuate its casualties and resupply itself with fresh troops and ammunition from the west without interference. In addition, the marines were inhibited by a political decision that forbade the use of heavy weapons in order to minimize damage to the historic city. That policy, which the marines generally obeyed, was later abandoned when the Allies argued successfully that adhering to that standing order was causing unacceptable casualties.

The marines were also slow to grasp the size and scope

of the enemy attack in Hue. Intelligence estimates over the first few days were often guesses, and it wasn't until a significant number of prisoners were questioned that the marines knew precisely what they were up against.

One of the first official press briefings of the situation in Hue came from General Truong's boss, I Corps commanding general Hoang Xuan Lam. Lam, who was obviously ill informed, told the media late on the afternoon of 31 January that communist forces had been ejected from all cities in his area of responsibility except for Hue, where a "platoon" was still holding out at the Citadel airfield. It was a strange statement because General Lam was speaking from Da Nang, which was more than 100 kilometers to the south.

The truth, of course, was that there was a multibattalion enemy force on both sides of the river that was showing no signs of giving up the territory it had captured. Furthermore, the enemy troops occupying Hue appeared determined to stay as long as they could and milk as much publicity as they could.

General LaHue at Task Force X-Ray in Phu Bai was just as uninformed about the enemy's disposition as General Lam. In response to a question from a UPI reporter on 1 February on the status of the fighting in Hue, Hughes replied: "Very definitely we control the South Side of the city. I don't think [the enemy] can sustain. I know they can't. I don't think they have any resupply capabilities and once they use up what they have brought in, they're finished."

As 2 February came to a close and a heavy firefight lit up the sky, it was clear that the marines would have to earn every inch of ground in the city and that initial intelligence reports had greatly underestimated the enemy's strength and resolve. It would take much more than "a couple of days" to take care of the "little problem" in Hue.

CHAPTER SEVEN

Total War

When the North Vietnamese swept into Hue they brought with them political officers armed with photographs of and dossiers on the city's anticommunist leaders and government officials. Working door to door, like pollsters of death during their 25-day occupation, the Communists hunted down and systematically slaughtered hundreds of victims: young and old; men, women, and children; Vietnamese and foreigners; and generally anyone who was unfortunate enough to be in the wrong place at the wrong time.

The brunt of this deadly assault fell mostly on the little people. The powerful and wealthy usually managed to either flee or hide themselves in fortified areas.

The most intense political activity occurred in the southern portion of the city and in the densely populated section called Gia Hoi, an island area just east of the Citadel. Gia Hoi was the seat of a working revolutionary government ruled by a Communist mayor in conjunction with local revolutionary councils and policed by Vietcong and NVA soldiers. The area was left virtually undisturbed by the Allies for over 3 weeks while the military focus centered on retaking the Citadel.

All citizens in Gia Hoi were required to fill out ques-

tionnaires describing their life, work, and political atti-
tudes. Those who had expressed acceptable political ideas
were then assigned such tasks as disseminating propaganda, organizing political cells, and setting up local defense groups. Those with unacceptable or "erroneous"
views were called in for further interrogation. Some were
then visited by propaganda teams or sent to reeducation
classes, where they received instruction in the history and
goals of the revolutionary struggle. Others were dealt
with more harshly, often in full view of their families or
friends.

The population of the Citadel underwent less of a propaganda barrage because the enemy was kept busy trying to defend itself. Later, however, civilians in the Citadel
suffered alongside the enemy as the Allies brought more
and more firepower to bear on that stone fortress. Some
were executed, while others just fell victim to the fortunes of war.

Many victims of Vietcong and North Vietnamese terror were government officials, those who worked for U.S.
organizations, and police or security forces. The majority,
however, were ordinary citizens. Teachers were a favorite
target because they were people with a profound understanding of politics and had a strong influence over the
young. They were often viewed as people who might be
called upon to assume anticommunist leadership in their
area. Teachers were therefore labeled as "very dangerous" and classified as "traitors."

Political officers would roam the streets with bullhorns,
exhorting the population to come out of hiding and join
in the so-called uprising against the puppet Saigon regime
and the Americans. If this method of flushing out suspected enemies did not produce results, enemy troops

would go door to door with guns, dragging away anyone who remotely fit the descriptions on their enemies list.

Among those killed over the course of 3 weeks were numerous government officials and civil servants, ARVN officers and enlisted men, local leaders, local militiamen, priests, Germans, Filipinos, Koreans, and Americans, and a whole lot of ordinary citizens who had no loyalties to either side.

It has been estimated that 6,000 civilians were rounded up at Hue. The number of bodies reported found is almost half that figure.

According to Vietnamese custom, the fortunes of an individual for each new year are foreshadowed by the first visitor to call at Tet.

Mr. Vinh, who lived a few blocks from the MACV compound in the southern section of Hue, heard somebody knocking on his front gate very early on the morning of 31 January. When he went out to see who was there, it turned out to be an old friend he had not seen in many years. His friend, who was a member of the Vietcong, told him in hushed tones that victory was near and then abruptly left.

Unable to get back to sleep, Vinh soon heard other noises and, when he looked outside, he could see Vietcong and NVA soldiers moving around his neighborhood on foot and in vehicles. They were setting up machine gun emplacements and mortar positions, running back and forth with ammunition. He could hear the soldiers shouting into bullhorns and going door to door trying to rally the people against the "puppet" Saigon government and the U.S. "imperialists."

Communist agents had actually infiltrated Hue 6 months

before, organizing political cells and drawing up maps of
Allied defenses. They also began compiling names and ad-
dresses of suspected "counterrevolutionaries" throughout the city. A sympathetic Hue University professor was
named head of the Alliance of National, Democratic, and
Peace Forces in the city. A former chief of the city's National Police became the new mayor. The old mayor
went into hiding the first day, abandoning his wife and
six children.

People were ordered to take down all South Vietnamese flags and replace them with NLF flags, if they had
them. If not, the flags would be provided. Political meetings were held to encourage the citizens to join the revolutionary government. At one rally, a group of young
men and women were handed weapons and acclaimed as
the uprising troops for their area. A theatrical show was
even staged by a North Vietnamese drama troupe to de-
nounce the South Vietnamese and Americans.

Soon, however, the revolutionary fervor turned grim.
Vietcong and North Vietnamese cadres marched through
the streets summoning all civil servants, military personnel, and anyone who worked for the Americans to report
immediately to designated areas. They were assured that
nothing would happen to them. Most elected to flee or
hide out in bunkers that had been recently constructed
inside their homes.

As the days went by the invaders increased their pressure to find those still in hiding. Houses were revisited
and thoroughly searched. Angry voices, amplified by bullhorns, warned that anyone found hiding would be sum-
marily executed. Those flushed from their homes were
marched to prisoner collection points, their hands tied

behind their backs. Many were never seen or heard from again.

Those who resisted and fired back at the invaders only invited an even larger attack. The Vietcong would initially back off from a point of resistance, regroup, and return a day or two later with a greater force. There would be no room for negotiation then.

On the fifth day of the occupation, enemy troops entered the Phu Cam Cathedral on the south side of the city and arrested several hundred Vietnamese Roman Catholics, all of them men or boys of military age. As they were led away, a Vietcong leader told everyone remaining not to worry. The young men were only being taken to a nearby pagoda for political reorientation sessions. Two days later, the soldiers returned and told the women still living in the sanctuary to prepare provisions for their loved ones.

None of the men of Phu Cam ever returned.

The most thorough and sadistic roundup of suspected anticommunist personnel took place in Gia Hoi just east of the Citadel. NVA and Vietcong political agents were free to conduct their house-to-house purges without having to worry about interference from Allied troops. Gia Hoi was a newer section of Hue, where much of the city's burgeoning middle class, such as teachers and businessmen, had taken up residence. Under no military pressure from the Allies, communist agents took their time checking out everybody in the region. As mentioned earlier, the invaders even set up their own government here.

At first, the Communists told the citizens in Gia Hoi to report for briefings and lectures, assuring them that they would not be harmed. Some were told to come back a second time, again with the same assurances of safety. The cadres also worked on the people to divulge information about their neighbors—then the neighbors were visited.

As in other areas of the city, civilians tried to hide from the invaders, hoping to wait out the occupation. A week went by and then it became two. Food ran short and desperation set in. One by one, many citizens came out of hiding and were taken away for questioning. The behavior of the Communists could be totally unpredictable: one day they would smile and promise that nothing would happen; the next day they would return with a vengeance and drag people away, who were never to be seen again.

Panic set in as more and more people never returned from indoctrination sessions. Gunshots were heard more frequently, and fresh graves were spotted in the northern section of the island in an area called, ironically, the "Strawberry Patch."

Gia Hoi had been designated as the final destination for many of those deemed "enemies" of the revolutionary forces. Prisoners were shipped to the area from inside the Citadel and other areas along the north bank of the Perfume River, where a court system had been set up. Justice was swift and merciless, especially in the later weeks, when it became apparent that the Communists would be thrown out of the city.

A schoolyard and an adjacent sandpit in the northern section of Gia Hoi had become a huge cemetery, filled with many innocent men, women, and children. The following month, I saw for myself the horrors committed under the aegis of revolutionary fervor. It was an experience I would never forget.

* * *

Jim Bullington, a U.S. foreign service officer on loan to the Agency for International Development, was on his second tour of Vietnam. Stationed in Quang Tri, he took an Air America shuttle flight to Hue the afternoon of 30 January to visit his fiancée and her family for the Tet holidays at their home in the southern section of the city. Bullington brought along an American guest, Steve Miller, a U.S. Information Service official based in Hue.

After the party ended around midnight, Miller dropped Bullington off at a guesthouse next to the Hue municipal power station near the Perfume River. Miller then drove to his own quarters nearby.

Bullington was awakened by small-arms fire a few hours later but went back to bed thinking that the police must be firing at a sniper. Arising just after dawn, Bullington made plans to drive to the MACV compound, which was about nine blocks to the east, to check on any intelligence reports. But when he walked outside his host stopped him and told him to get back inside the house and stay put because there were enemy troops in the area. Bullington waited and waited. Finally at about 1500, he heard a soft knock on his door. He could barely hear the knock over the pounding of his heart.

It was his host, a Franco-Vietnamese civilian who managed the power station. He offered Bullington a ham sandwich and a warm bottle of beer. He also filled him in on what was happening in the city. The NVA had occupied the power station and, for all he knew, most of the entire city as well. Most certainly, he told Bullington, they would get around to visiting his hideout shortly.

The man suggested that Bullington move to the quarters of two French priests who lived nearby, where he would be safer. The priests gave Bullington a black clerical gown to wear. Because Bullington spoke only rudimentary French, the priests had decided to tell anyone who asked that their guest was a visiting Canadian priest.

"You're welcome here as long as you need to hide," one priest told him, "but I'm sure your marines will retake the city tomorrow or the next day and you will be safe." Little did Bullington know that it was only the beginning of his ordeal.

Bullington basically kept out of sight and waited to be rescued. He did nothing to call attention to himself. He watched the streets from the second floor of the priests' house but he saw little enemy activity. He heard a lot of gunfire on both sides of the river and occasionally heard the sound of helicopters, but without a radio, he never really knew the extent of enemy activity in the city.

On the morning of 3 February, he spotted his first NVA soldiers in a courtyard of a building two blocks away. The soldiers were wearing neat khaki uniforms with some red and blue cloth as a shoulder patch on their left sleeve. They carried AK-47s and RPG launchers. Then he heard the rumble of a tank and thought for a minute the marines were coming down the street. It turned out to be an ARVN M41 tank that had been captured a couple of days earlier by the North Vietnamese.

Finally, on 8 February he heard another tank and American voices. It was not long before they reached his hideout. He walked out waving a white flag and was rescued without a shot being fired. Before he could find out about the fate of his fiancée and her family, Bullington was sent to Da Nang for a debriefing. It was not until 14 February that he returned to Hue and found out that his fiancée and her parents were all right.

Bullington also learned upon his return to Hue that the two priests who had harbored him for a week were discovered shot and killed on 10 February. They had been on their way home from a mass when they were ambushed by men in black pajamas. The motive for the killing may have been their willingness to provide refuge for an American.

Bullington discovered some more bad news. Steve Miller, the U.S. Information Services official who had joined him at the Tet dinner at his fiancée's house, was also found dead. Miller had decided to wait out the NVA invasion at his quarters, which were obviously targeted by the enemy. His body was later discovered outside, his arms bound behind him. He had been shot in the back of the head.

Marine Lt. James V. DiBernardo lived to tell a story that could easily have happened to just about any American on duty in Hue during the Tet offensive.

DiBernardo, who had spent 14 years as an enlisted man before receiving his commission in 1966, had run the Armed Forces Radio and Television station in Hue since the previous October. He was a career journalist and, like me, he was a graduate of the military's Information School at Fort Slocum, New York.

DiBernardo had his own quarters in Hue, not more than a couple of blocks from the MACV compound. His compound consisted of two small buildings, a lean-to, and a trailer, all surrounded by a 6-foot-high wall. The actual studio and transmitter for his station was two blocks away and a prime target of the enemy attack.

He had a mixed bag of people working for him and sharing his compound. There were four U.S. enlisted men and a couple of civilians. Also assigned to his compound were two ARVN military policemen, whom DiBernardo called "white mice" because of their white helmets and small stature. He enjoyed being on his own—but he really had no choice. There was no room for him in the crowded MACV compound.

DiBernardo kept in daily contact with the MACV compound and attended all the intelligence briefings he could. He took many of his meals there and was a regular at the officer's club, where he was well liked. Often he acted as host to visiting marine friends, who kidded him on his lonesome lifestyle.

The Tet offensive would change all that.

"I remember being called over to the MACV compound the day before the attack for a briefing on enemy activity," DiBernardo told me many years later. "I was told to double my guards at my compound and to expect some kind of trouble. I told them that other than the two white mice I didn't have any guards."

When the first rocket blast hit the city early in the morning of 31 January, DiBernardo knew exactly what it was.

"The first thing I noticed was that the white mice were gone," DiBernardo said. "I called the MACV compound and spoke to the duty officer. He told me they were under fire and to hold where I was until they could get back to me. The phone went dead and I never heard from them again."

DiBernardo and his staff sat tight for 3 days and 3 nights while all around them shells were exploding and enemy troops were dashing from house to house.

"It was like watching a movie," DiBernardo said.

Next door to DiBernardo's compound was General

Truong's house. DiBernardo saw that the military police guards had left the front of the house, so he went over to see if he could help Mrs. Truong and her two children, then aged two and four. She told DiBernardo they were all right and would be able to handle the situation on their own.

It wasn't until 1974, when DiBernardo returned to South Vietnam on a fact-finding tour, that he found out that Mrs. Truong and her children had managed to get away to safety. It was also the first chance Mrs. Truong had to thank DiBernardo for his offer of help 6 years earlier.

Meanwhile, DiBernardo obeyed orders and stayed put in his own compound. Helicopters flew overhead and one even strafed his compound. And then on 3 February he heard some American voices coming down the street.

"I thought it was just a matter of time," DiBernardo said, "but they never got there."

Later that day the enemy zeroed in on DiBernardo's compound and began a siege that lasted 15 hours. The enemy set fire to the roof of the main house, and then a soldier rushed the compound gate with a satchel charge. DiBernardo leveled his carbine at the invader but the rifle jammed. The explosion of the satchel charge tore into DiBernardo's right arm. Gathering his other wounded men together, DiBernardo made the decision to get out before the house crashed in on them. They charged out a back gate toward an open area in the general direction of the MACV compound.

The men were cornered by about two dozen NVA soldiers about 100 meters from the compound, and DiBernardo was wounded again, this time in his left hand. Two others in the group were killed.

DiBernardo and four others in his group were taken prisoner and disarmed. Then they were immediately taken from the area under armed guard.

"They ran us about a mile to what looked like an armored compound, and then after a couple of hours we were taken to a Buddhist temple where they were rounding up all those who had been captured," DiBernardo said.

His wounds were treated by some Red Cross personnel, which included a couple of American women.

"The women said they were Quakers," DiBernardo said. "One was Marjorie Nelson, who was a doctor, and the other was Sandra Johnson, who was a teacher. I also saw a Chinese advisor there. I know he was Chinese because he was so much bigger than the Vietnamese."

One of the first things his captors did was take his boots. He would remain barefoot until he reached a prison camp in North Vietnam a couple of weeks later.

"They kept yelling in my face that I was a CIA agent, but I convinced them I wasn't by showing them my identification card. It probably saved my life," DiBernardo said.

After about 2 days of interrogation, DiBernardo, along with 22 others, was marched out of the city toward the hills to the west and then north through the jungle to North Vietnam. Their hands were tied behind their backs with communications wire, and the group was joined together by a long rope.

"They marched us out Indian style," DiBernardo said. "We slept during the day, mostly in temples, and walked at night. We were fed mostly rice balls. It took me a year to get the marks off my wrists from the commo wire."

Unlike some captives, DiBernardo accepted his fate with a quiet resolve.

"There is no doubt in my mind that what helped me get through it was my Marine Corps training," DiBernardo said. "Hell, after basic training I felt I had nothing else left to be afraid of. I feared my drill instructor more than I ever feared any of my captors."

A sense of humor also helped him get through the indignities of life in a prison camp. There was one time when his guard, a scrawny, bucktoothed, bespectacled individual with a perpetual grin whom he called "Smiling Jack," complimented him on a trench he was digging in the prison compound.

"I'm going to dig my way all the way to the United States," DiBernardo said almost casually. "After that crack they didn't let me outside again for 6 months. I guess they had no sense of humor."

When members of a marine patrol finally reached DiBernardo's compound in Hue on 5 February, they discovered the body of Sgt. Tom Young, one of the enlisted men who worked at the radio and TV station. He was found lying in a ditch near the back gate. His hands were bound behind his back and he had been shot in the back of the head. Two marine combat correspondents, who both had been overnight guests at the compound, carried Young's body back to the MACV compound on a door they had found nearby. Tears streamed down their faces. They believed the same fate had befallen DiBernardo.

DiBernardo was one of the lucky ones, though there were times during his imprisonment when he certainly did not think so.

DiBernardo, along with 590 other prisoners, was released on 5 March 1973 as part of Operation Homecoming. His plane touched down at Travis Air Force Base just outside San Francisco on 8 March, where he was reunited with his family, which included twin girls who were born just after he was captured. Now living in Southern California, DiBernardo remained in the Marine Corps, retiring as a major in 1978.

CHAPTER EIGHT

The Tide Turns

After 2 days of intense fighting, it had become clear that more pressure would be needed to force the enemy from Hue. Under normal circumstances, the marines would try to surround the enemy, call in vast amounts of supporting fire, and then go in and mop up any survivors. Operation Hue City was proving to be anything but a normal operation.

Because the Tet offensive was a series of attacks throughout the country, there was a finite amount of resources available to the struggle in Hue—at least over the first 2 weeks. And so the Allies were unable to surround the enemy and close the western back door to the city, which had allowed the enemy free access to evacuate their wounded and bring in fresh troops and supplies at will.

To deal with this problem, it was decided on 2 February to commit the 2nd Battalion, 12th Cavalry (2/12) of the U.S. 1st Cavalry Division's 3rd Brigade, which was garrisoned at Camp Evans, about 25 kilometers north of Hue. In an action dubbed "Operation Jeb Stuart" the 650-man unit, which had been in the area less than 4 weeks, was ordered to move southeast along the western edge of Route 1, break up an enemy regimental headquarters, close the back door to Hue, and then link up with Allied troops.

One of the hoped for side effects of the operation was to divert some of the enemy forces fighting in Hue and thus alleviate the pressure on the Allies. Men of the cavalry unit, which was to be plagued by a shortage of supplies, particularly ammunition and aviation fuel, would have to fight as infantry because of a lack of assault helicopters. Most distressing, however, was the fact that this unit would go into battle without the customary artillery preparation to soften up any enemy positions.

Intelligence was still spotty, but 2/12's commander, Lt. Col. Dick Sweet, who had been an instructor at the Infantry School at Fort Benning, looked forward to getting in on a piece of the action. It proved to be much tougher than anyone had imagined. Before the mission could be completed, two more battalions of the 1st Cav and another from the U.S. 101st Airborne Division would have to be committed to enable the Allies to finally close the back door to Hue.

After establishing a new LZ just south of PK 17, Sweet's four line companies marched into battle on 3 February, heading southeast with Route 1 on its left flank. The troopers traveled lightly, leaving their cumbersome packs and extra ammunition back at Camp Evans. It was the habit of cav troopers to travel as lightly as possible and then have their packs delivered to them by helicopter after they had secured an objective.

Capt. Bob Helvey's A Company took the lead. Helvey had previously served as an advisor to the ARVN 1st Division, and he was the officer most familiar with the terrain. The first sniper shots rang out 2 hours into the march, briefly holding up the battalion. Captain Helvey called for some artillery fire but was unable to communicate with the two ARVN 105mm guns back at PK 17. It was to be a recurring problem.

Sweet's force pushed on. About 6 kilometers above Hue the battalion moved through the wooded hamlet of Lieu Coc Thuong. Even though it was deserted, the village contained many freshly dug trenches and bunkers. As the troopers cleared the village they could see many civilians fleeing across a rice paddy into the nearby village of Que Chu. They also saw NVA soldiers manning trenches just inside the tree line.

Lieutenant Colonel Sweet spent the next hour trying to get some fire support on the enemy trenchline. He was unable to contact the two ARVN 105s at PK 17 because of language problems, and the ceiling was too low for fixed-wing air support. Several helicopter gunships did come on station, but their fire proved ineffective against the well-dug-in enemy. One of the gunships fired on the wrong tree line, killing a trooper from Company A.

Sweet, not knowing what effect the gunships had had, decided to conduct a frontal attack across the rice paddy. The enemy let the troopers cover about half the distance before snipers began picking them off with uncanny accuracy. Particularly vulnerable were those who stopped along the way to help wounded comrades. The battalion regrouped and managed to push its way into the trenches. The assault had cost 2/12 Cavalry 9 dead and 48 wounded.

While the cavalry troopers rested the night of February 3–4, the enemy quietly moved forward in an attempt to surround the Americans. When men of Sweet's force began preparations to resume the attack early the next morning, they found themselves pinned down inside their own perimeter by deadly accurate sniper fire often less than 30 meters away.

By 1000 the situation was becoming desperate. U.S. forces had suffered 20 casualties, and fire was so heavy that only one medevac helicopter was able to land. Another medevac was attempted at 1350, and again only one chopper, the same one that had made it earlier, could get in and out.

Lieutenant Colonel Sweet had to make a decision. He could try and go on the offensive, he could stand and fight, or he could withdraw. Outnumbered and suffering more and more casualties every hour, there was really only one choice for him to make. And he had to make it quickly.

Sweet huddled with his officers and, rather than retreat the way they had come back to PK 17, he decided on a night move deeper inside enemy territory to a hilltop 4 kilometers to the south. Deception would be a key to the move. The enemy must believe that Sweet's troopers intended to stay another night in their perimeter.

All the wounded who needed evacuation were airlifted out by 1651, but 11 dead remained in the perimeter. Sweet had another tough decision to make. To carry out the dead would slow the march and risk discovery, so he decided to leave the dead in a temporary mass grave, an abandoned mortar pit, intending to return at a later date to retrieve them. To preclude the NVA from uncovering the bodies and mutilating them out of vengeance, a note in Vietnamese was left at the site declaring that the mound contained only the bodies of 11 soldiers and no weapons or ammunition.

A night withdrawal was a tricky operation. The men were briefed in small groups and told that there must be no noise. Sniper fire was to be ignored, but if they ran into heavy fire they were to attack through it. They must keep going and avoid getting bogged down. Many troopers left dummies and booby traps in their foxholes.

Just after dark and under the cover of a smoke barrage from a newly arrived cavalry 105 battery at PK 17, Companies A and D left their sectors and passed through Companies B and C. The entire battalion completed its withdrawal by 2020.

A little later, the troopers could hear some firing and explosions from their old position caused by booby traps and trip flares left behind. Another nice touch was provided by Lieutenant Colonel Sweet. He had ordered an artillery strike on the old perimeter to be executed 3 hours after his unit's departure.

The column swung west and, after crossing a stream, turned due south on a 4-kilometer hump over open ground. The entire force reached its new hilltop location at 0710, 11 hours after the withdrawal had begun.

The new position, which was reinforced and resupplied later that day, gave 2/12 a good vantage point to observe enemy infiltration routes and call in available supporting fires to harass enemy troops coming from and going into Hue.

The back door was far from being closed, but the Allies now formed a bothersome presence in the area.

Meanwhile, more help was on the way to reinforce Lieutenant Colonel Gravel's small, battered force of marines around the MACV compound.

The marine brass made another big commitment to Hue on 3 February by sending Colonel Hughes, the 1st Regiment commander, to the city as the on-site commander.

Joining Hughes in a convoy of replacements and supplies from Phu Bai was 2/5 commander Lt. Col. Ernest C.
Cheatham, Jr., who had three of his companies (Fox,
Golf, and Hotel) already engaged in the city. Lieutenant
Colonel Gravel, the on-site commander over the first 3
days, retained control over Alpha 1/1 and got most of the
replacements to form a second company called Bravo
1/1. The new company was formed by the command
group from the real Bravo 1/1, volunteers, and generally
anyone who could be spared from duty at Phu Bai.

Hughes, who had won a Navy Cross at Cape Glouces-
ter in 1943 and a Silver Star at Peleliu the following year
as a young platoon leader, believed in giving his subordi-
nates free rein to do what they felt the situation dictated.
After arriving in Hue at 1300 on 3 February, Hughes called
Gravel and Cheatham together and told them to do whatever they felt was necessary to dig the enemy troops out
of their defensive positions, and he would take care of
getting his units what they needed. Hughes also said he
would try and keep higher headquarters off their backs
while they did the job.

Gravel, with the smaller force of Alpha and Bravo 1/1
at his disposal, was given a supporting role and an additional mission of keeping Route 1 clear. Cheatham's three
line companies (Fox, Golf, and Hotel) were to spearhead
the attack westward along the southern boundary of the
Perfume River.

"I want you to attack through the city and clean the
NVA out," Hughes told Cheatham in a terse, one-sentence
mission statement. Cheatham stood there with a blank
look on his face waiting for anything else Hughes had
to say.

"If you're looking for any more, you aren't going to get it. Move out," Hughes barked.

As Cheatham started for the door, Hughes reached out and put his hand on Cheatham's shoulder and said softly, "You do it any way you want to, and if you get any heat from above, I'll take care of that."

Cheatham, who would earn a Navy Cross for his leadership in Hue and eventually rise to the rank of lieutenant general, stood 6 feet 5 inches, earning the nickname "Big Ernie" from his troops. He had been an unhappy camper the past 2 days sitting in Phu Bai while all three of his line companies were fighting in Hue without him.

Knowing that he would soon join his troops in Hue, Lieutenant Colonel Cheatham used the time to study the different aspects of conducting house-to-house fighting. When he finally left for Hue, he had scrounged up all the 3.5-inch rocket launchers and ammunition he could find. Also brought along in the convoy were six mule-mounted 106mm recoilless rifles and a quantity of tear gas and gas masks.

After getting his orders from Hughes, Cheatham set up his own CP at Hue University and called his company commanders together to prepare an attack plan. While the planning was underway, he received news relayed from Task Force X-Ray in Phu Bai that the South Vietnamese government had lifted all restrictions on the use of heavy firepower south of the Perfume River.

Cheatham was noticeably buoyed by the news. He was now free to call on any available supporting arms he needed without fear of creating an international incident. Much of that heavy firepower, however, including naval fire, 8-inch howitzers from Phu Bai, and tactical aircraft, would not be available until the weather improved. In the meantime, he could use his tanks, 106mm recoilless rifles, mortars, and 3.5-inch bazookas with impunity.

Cheatham peered out at the terrain from his second-story CP and tried to visualize how best to use his artillery. He would need a minimal force on his right because the Perfume River offered a natural boundary. The left flank was what worried him. The landscape consisted of one concrete building after another, each one a stout bunker unto itself. The buildings would have to be dealt with one at a time, a job he knew would not be easy.

Cheatham's three-company force of about 700 men jumped off a little after 1400. While Gravel's forces provided security on the left flank, a small company of stranded ARVN troops were to follow the marines, mopping up any isolated pockets of resistance as well as handling the flow of refugees.

From the start, things did not go well. Cheatham soon discovered what Gravel had been saying the first 3 days. Directly across the street from the university were two large buildings, the Thua Thien Province Treasury Building and the post office, each occupied by battle-tested NVA regulars who blocked any advancement by the marines. The 106mm guns and tank fire hardly made a dent in the thick walls. Over the next 18 hours Cheatham's troops attacked the same two buildings six times and were repulsed each time.

Captain Christmas, the commanding officer of Hotel Company, said later he believed the marine force just was not big enough for the job at hand. One company could maintain a frontage of about one city block. With only three companies under his command, Cheatham had two companies forward and one in reserve. This left the left flank open and exposed to enemy machine gun positions.

Gravel, who had weathered a stormy long-distance relationship with his superiors in Phu Bai the past 3 days, was not surprised that Cheatham was having a difficult time making any headway against an enemy well dug in. Although not wishing Cheatham any misfortune, Gravel did feel somewhat vindicated.

United Press International reporter Al Webb and cameraman Kyoichi Sawada and I joined up with Fox Company's second platoon as it left Hue University on its mission to attack the treasury and post office buildings barely a block away. It did not take any of us long to realize that every building, every window, every roof, and every intersection harbored potential death. Gunfire was coming from several different directions at once.

The point man stepped out onto tree-lined Le Loi Street and was met by a hail of bullets. Tanks were called up and, as the 50-ton tracked monsters inched their way down the street, they provided a screen for the infantrymen. The tanks also attracted a lot of fire. Cheatham told a reporter later in the battle that one of his tanks had taken 121 hits and went through five crew changes.

"Tankers who survived came out of their vehicles looking like they were punch drunk," he said.

The bodies of fallen marines also attracted a lot of fire. They were staked out by enemy gunners as bait, waiting for other marines to expose themselves in a rescue attempt so that the gunners could pick them off as well.

Bodies littered both sides of the street. Marines dragged them to the side of the street or behind some cover to be retrieved by others as the attack went on. Corpsmen raced back and forth between the dead and wounded, and tanks were called up to provide a screen to remove the casualties. When all the fallen had been retrieved the tanks backed up out of harm's way. In the first 30 minutes, the 2nd Platoon of Fox Company had suffered two men killed and had 19 wounded.

Other platoons of 2/5 were experiencing the same thing. When night fell on 3 February the marines again had to settle for no gain.

A frustrated and angry Cheatham called his company commanders together for a night powwow to plan the next day's action. Everyone got a chance to talk about lessons learned and what they thought should be done to rout the enemy from their strongholds. The discussions were emotional.

The first thing they all agreed upon was that more heavy weapons were needed. Tactics of fire and maneuver would not work in street fighting without the threat of heavy weapons. Objectives could be reached only by going through buildings. It was decided to employ more 106mm recoilless rifles and 3.5-inch rocket launchers. The latter, called "bazookas" in World War II, were easily the most portable and arguably the most effective. The marines were told to create holes in compound walls, rush in, clear all the rooms, and set up sniper fire of their own for the next building. If there were any streets to be crossed, they would be crossed under a smokescreen with lots of covering fire.

Different techniques were tried. One of the best utilized an eight-man team. Four riflemen covered the exits while two men rushed the building with grenades and two other riflemen provided covering fire. The team would rotate the responsibilities among the eight men on the next building.

Timing was of the utmost importance. In describing the tactics used by his infantrymen to a reporter, Lieutenant Colonel Cheatham compared them to the game of football, in that every man had do his job or the play would not work.

"We hope to kill them inside or flush them out the back for the four men watching the exits," he said. "Then, taking the next building, two other men rush the front. It sounds simple but the timing has to be just as good as a football play."

Success would have to be accomplished without artillery, which the marines had come to rely on in most of their earlier missions in open country. Most of the available artillery from Phu Bai was directed at interdicting enemy escape routes to the rear and not on buildings. The marines would have to use their own mortars for close-in support, using them as a "hammer" on top of the buildings.

"If you put enough [mortar] rounds on the top of a building, pretty soon the roof falls in. And this is simply what we did," Cheatham said.

But the proximity of the enemy, sometimes only yards away, limited the use of mortars in many circumstances. This is where the 106mm recoilless rifles came in. The 106s, with their lack of protective armament, were dangerous to operate, however: they had to be aimed first with a .50-caliber spotting round before firing the main gun, and that meant the crews had to spend a lot of time in the open.

Fire from the 106s was available in three different ways. The gun could be employed singularly, either mounted on

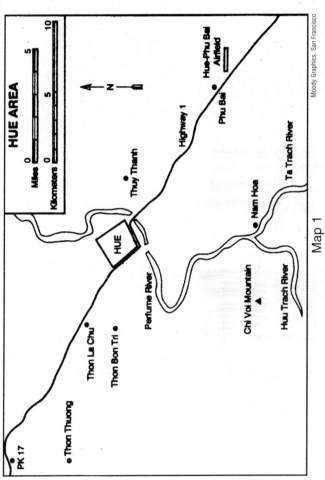

Moody Graphics, San Francisco

HUE AREA

Miles
0   5

Kilometers
0   5   10

N

PK 17

Thon Thuong

Thon La Chu

Thon Bon Tri

Perfume River

Thuy Thanh

HUE

Highway 1

Phu Bai

Hue-Phu Bai
Airfield

Nam Hoa

Chi Voi Mountain

Huu Trach River

Ta Trach River

Map 1

DOWNTOWN HUE

1. MACV
2. Doc Lao Park
3. Police Compound
4. Cane Field
5. Hue University
6. Chemistry Lab and Music Room
7. Jeanne d'Arc High School
8. Le Loi Primary School
9. Public Health Complex
10. Treasury
11. Post Office
12. Student Center
13. U.S. Consul's Residence
14. French Cultural Center
15. Cercle Sportif
16. Hospital Complex
17. Thua Thien Provincial Admin. Complex
18. Thua Thien Provincial Prison
19. Antituberculosis Center
20. U.S. Consulate
21. Hue Municipal Power Station
22. Le Lai Military Camp

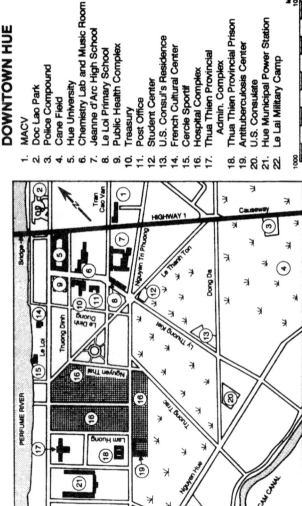

Map 2

Moody Graphics, San Francisco

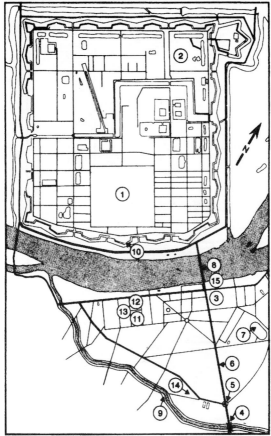

HUE

1. Imperial Palace
2. 1st ARVN Division CP
3. MACV Compound
4. An Cuu Bridge
5. Traffic Circle
6. Cane Field Causeway
7. Tu Do Stadium
8. Nguyen Hoang Bridge
9. Phu Cam Canal
10. Citadel Flagpole
11. Thua Thien Provinicial Prison
12. Thua Thien Provincial
   Admin. Center
13. Hue Municipal Power Station
14. Hue Cathedral
15. Doc Lao Park

Moody Graphics, San Francisco

Map 3

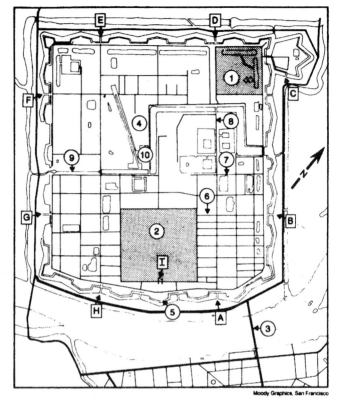

THE CITADEL

1. 1st ARVN Division CP Compound
2. Imperial Palace
3. Nguyen Hoang Bridge
4. Tay Loc Airfield
5. Citadel Flagpole
6. Mai Thuc Loan Street
7. Tinh Tam Street
8. Dinh Bo Linh Street
9. Thuy Quan Canal
10. 1st ARVN Ordnance Company Armory

A. Thuong Tu Gate
B. Dong Ba Gate
C. Truong Dinh Gate
D. Hau Gate
E. An Hoa Gate
F. Chanh Tay Gate
G. Huu Gate
H. Nha Do Gate
I. Ngo Mon Gate

Moody Graphics, San Francisco

Map 4

A 100-foot hunk of the Nguyen Hoang Bridge across the Perfume River lies underwater after a sapper attack on 7 February 1968 (U.S. Marine Corps Photo, reproduced at the National Archives)

Marines hunker down next to crates of ammunition aboard an LCU on a trip across the Perfume River to the Citadel (U.S. Marine Corps Photo, reproduced at the National Archives)

Ammunition for a 3.5-inch rocket launcher is delivered to a rooftop firing position by marines of Hotel 2/5 on the south side of Hue (U.S. Marine Corps Photo, reproduced at the National Archives)

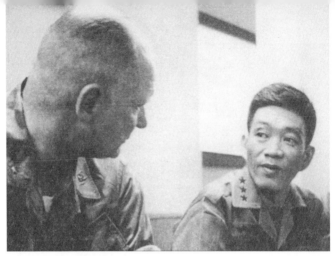

Lt. Gen. Ngo Quang Truong, right, then I Corps commander, confers with Brig. Gen. Edward J. Miller, commanding general of the 9th Marines Amphibious Brigade, on 8 September 1972 (U.S. Marine Corps Photo)

A squad of marines help carry a 106mm recoilless rifle into position during fighting on the south side of Hue (U.S. Marine Corps Photo)

A platoon from Hotel Company 2/5, wearing gas masks, jumps off on an assault (U.S. Marine Corps Photo)

Marines carry a wounded comrade in a poncho through a hole in a wall during the fighting (U.S. Marine Corps Photo)

CBS newsman Walter Cronkite conducts a walking interview with 1/1 commander Lt. Col. Mark Gravel on 10 February 1968 (U.S. Marine Corps Photo)

A wounded marine is patched up by a corpsman during a break in the action (U.S. Marine Corps Photo, reproduced at the National Archives)

jeeps or mules or carted around by hand even though it weighed 350 pounds. Or it could be used in a unit of six on a tracked vehicle called an Ontos. The Ontos was a scary looking piece of destruction, but it was also very vulnerable. The gasoline that fueled the tracked vehicle was, of course, inflammable, and the gunner often had to stand in the open to sight the weapon or to reload the six tubes, giving an enemy gunner plenty of time to line up the vehicle in his cross hairs.

The backblast of the weapon was also very dangerous. Lieutenant Colonel Cheatham's forces once used a portable 106 from a second-story room, and the backblast caved in the wall of the building. In all cases, the weapon had to be handled with extreme care or the backblast would cause injury or even death to the crew using it or to any grunt who happened to be to the rear of the gun when it went off.

I had fired a 106 before in training but I had never seen an Ontos until 3 February, when one of them rumbled down the street by the MACV compound and let loose with its six guns. The vehicle nearly rocked over backward and threw up a huge cloud of dust and smoke. I'll never forget it. As the dust settled, I could see stenciled on the back of the Ontos the phrase: "I'll Huff And I'll Puff And I'll Blow Your House Down."

The next day, Sunday, 4 February, Lieutenant Colonel Gravel's two depleted companies joined in the attack to take some of the pressure off Lieutenant Colonel Cheatham's forces. Gravel was given the mission of attacking and taking the Jeanne d'Arc school and church complex only 100 meters west of the MACV compound. I stood at the compound wall as a cloud of tear gas, unleashed by Cheatham's troops to the right, floated over Gravel's advancing troops, temporarily halting the attack.

After a delay of about 30 minutes, Alpha 1/1 crossed Route 1 and was met by machine gun fire coming from the church's steeple. Gravel ordered a tank to silence the fire. One shell from the tank's 90mm gun brought the whole structure tumbling down into an adjacent courtyard. The marines attacked through the debris and rushed into the church, tossing grenades and spraying everything in sight.

Sergeant Gonzalez and Corporal Jackson were among the first inside the church, and then they turned their attention to the adjoining school, which had several wings. The two marines led a charge into one wing of the school and then started taking B-40 rocket fire from another wing across a courtyard. Gonzalez fired off a half-dozen LAAW rounds from different windows, trying to get the enemy soldiers to show themselves so that some of the marine gunners could pick them off.

As Gonzalez flashed to another window, an enemy gunner fired a B-40 that caught the sergeant right in the lower part of his flak jacket, killing him instantly. Jackson was stunned by the sight of his friend lying in the rubble, his guts hanging out. He and another grunt put Gonzalez on a door that had been blown off its hinges and carried him to a first aid station back at the church. Gravel was standing there open-jawed as they laid Gonzalez's bloody body down on the floor.

Jackson wept and held Gonzalez's hand until a corpsman arrived. Nothing could be done for him. He was gone.

Two civilian photographers appeared at the scene and began snapping pictures. Jackson exploded.

"Get out of here, you poges!" Jackson screamed, swinging his M16 into the face of one of the cameramen. "Get the fuck out of here! Just leave us alone."

Sergeant Gonzalez, who had been an inspirational leader since the first day of the battle, was later awarded the Medal of Honor for his many acts of bravery in Hue. He was the only marine in the Battle of Hue to receive his nation's highest award.

A resupply convoy from Phu Bai arrived at the MACV compound the morning of 4 February with a couple of passengers who would play key roles in the next few days. The first was Lt. Comdr. Robert Hamilton, a navy doctor. Dr. Hamilton, who brought along four of his corpsmen, provided the first relief for exhausted MACV doctor Stephen Bernie, who, with the help of some Vietnamese medical personnel, had had to go it alone for 4 days.

Lieutenant Colonel Hamilton, 34, had spent a day off in Hue a week earlier, driving up with a couple of his friends to take in the historic beauty of the city. They had eaten in one of the outdoor cafes on the north bank of the river and taken many photographs. They had even tried to enter the Imperial Palace but were denied access by some ARVN guards. On the way back, the party stopped off at the MACV compound officer's club and had a few drinks with Dr. Bernie.

One of the few doctors at Phu Bai when the Tet offensive began, Hamilton was badly needed to help at the busy triage center. It was not until 4 February that he could be spared to help in Hue. Until then the five marine companies in Hue had had no doctor of their own.

Hamilton and his four corpsmen were part of a 30-truck convoy that left Phu Bai that morning. The medical personnel wedged themselves aboard trucks crammed full of ammunition. Security was provided by a handful of marine clerks who were pressed into duty as riflemen atop the swift-moving trucks. The security was needed, too: the convoy had to shoot its way the last 500 meters into the MACV compound.

The most relieved man in camp was Dr. Bernie. While the two doctors stood chatting for a few minutes a mortar round went off on the roof of a nearby building, spraying the two of them with shrapnel and concrete. Dr. Bernie had a cut on his arm but it was not serious. Dr. Hamilton escaped unhurt and would later laugh at the contrast between this and his previous visit to the charming city of Hue.

The second VIP arriving in Hue on 4 February was Maj. John Salvati, Cheatham's can-do executive officer. Salvati's scrounging and improvisational skills were to pay big dividends in 2/5's relentless push westward in the next few days. Cheatham turned his exec loose as a roving commander. Salvati coordinated the use of the 106mm guns, instructed troops how to employ the 3.5-inch rocket launcher, and designed new ways to utilize tear gas as an effective weapon to chase enemy troops from their bunkers and spider holes.

The marines had tried using smoke grenades on the treasury building, but what little smoke they produced was quickly dispersed by the breeze coming off the river. The ever-resourceful Salvati suggested using the E8 tear gas launcher, which he had seen stacked against the wall of an ARVN compound adjacent to the MACV compound. The launcher, about 2 feet high, could hurl as many as sixty-four 35mm tear gas projectiles up to 250 meters in four 5-second bursts of 16 each. Unlike the grenades, the E8 could flood an entire area so that every room and bunker would be permeated by the gas. As far as he knew, the NVA forces had not brought any gas masks with them to Hue.

Salvati hustled back to the MACV compound and, after cajoling and threatening some ARVN guards, loaded his jeep with four of the tear gas contraptions. But when he returned to the front and set one up, it failed to work. Undaunted, Salvati thought the launcher might work with an electrical impulse. A marine sergeant scrounged up an old crank-operated field telephone and hooked it up to the E8 launcher. It worked like a charm. Soon the treasury building was awash with tear gas.

The marines, who had already donned their gas masks, blasted the building's wrought-iron front gate to pieces with a round from a 106mm recoilless rifle. Then, a platoon from Fox Company charged through a hole in the wall into the courtyard, tossing grenades and firing from the hip on the run.

The NVA ran out the back, gasping for air. Some were picked off by marine snipers from the roof of an adjacent building, but most of them got away. Inside, marines finished off a dozen or so disoriented soldiers who were crawling around on the floor in a daze, obviously affected by the tear gas.

The seizure of the treasury building on 4 February was followed rapidly by a bloodless occupation of the adjacent post office and public health buildings.

Later that night, a platoon from Fox Company, which was occupying the post office, discovered an underground bunker that yielded the bodies of two dozen enemy soldiers, who must have been killed when an ammo cache was detonated by a LAAW rocket. Also, a platoon from

Hotel 2/5, responding to some harassing fire, overran two smaller buildings along the river, one of them the French Cultural Center. Hiding in the latter were 175 civilians, two of whom were Americans.

Just before dark, another resupply convoy arrived from Phu Bai, the last one to make it up Route 1 before enemy sappers finally got around to blowing up the An Cuu Bridge. The bridge's destruction, however, came 5 days too late to have any tactical value. Resupply would continue by air and by water until the bridge was repaired a week later.

The marine successes of the day had given everyone reason to believe that the tide had turned in southern Hue, and, for the MACV advisors, the focus began to shift to the fighting in the Citadel, which had reached a near stalemate. The first batch of advisors, including Captain Coolican of the Hac Bao Company and the liaison officers for Task Force X-Ray, Maj. Wayne Swenson, and the 1st Air Cav Division, Maj. Joe Gunter, were airlifted into the Citadel late on the afternoon of 4 February. The senior advisor, Colonel Adkisson, left the next day.

"That first flight into the Citadel was low, fast and hot," Coolican said. "We must have flown 20 feet off the deck through a hail of fire. But we made it. It was good to see Harry [Lieutenant Hue] again."

Oh, what stories those two had to tell.

CHAPTER NINE

Live, from Hue

An uneasy truce may be the best way to describe the relationship between the media and the military in Vietnam. Although there were few if any rules for dealing with the media, many commanders went through the entire war with the standard "no comment" response to questions. Understandably, the military grew rather uneasy about the news media as the war raged on, recoiling at the prospect of civilian outsiders second-guessing their efforts. On the other hand, however, many commanders were only too willing to include the media representatives in missions and freely gave press briefings whenever time allowed.

In previous wars, ones in which U.S. interests were clearly at stake, the press was considered a member of the team by the military and politicians. No such happy coexistence took place in Vietnam. Because there were so many media members in country, accredited and unaccredited, the chances of keeping anything secret or off limits was virtually impossible.

I do not know what the press was like in other wars, but the correspondents and film crews in Vietnam were—like the troops who fought the war—awfully young. I can still see a "full-bird" colonel in his mid-forties yelling

149

at a long-haired, bearded correspondent who was barely 20 years old, asking him when he planned on getting a haircut. The communications gap may have been pretty wide for the senior officers, but there did not seem to be any problem for the young grunts.

Young as they were, the reporters did an outstanding job of covering the war in Hue. And, as more and more of the unfiltered truth was absorbed by the public, it became increasingly clear that the United States was in the wrong place at the wrong time. The news media weaved themselves in and out of the action, and very often the military never knew they were there. Most of the time the grunts just wondered why the correspondents were there when they did not have to be.

By 4 February, there were at least 50 members of the media scattered with the marine forces in the southern section of Hue. Before the battle was over 3 weeks later, close to 150 media personnel would visit the battle site, many, such as CBS anchorman Walter Cronkite, flying in one afternoon and leaving later that day with their stories.

Many media members remained in Hue for the duration, filing dozens of stories and putting their lives at risk time and time again. In some ways, the correspondents were no different from the military forces in country. There were front-line types and rear-echelon types. Those who went to the front and stayed there until the action was over wore their label as combat correspondents as a badge of honor and regarded those comrades who rarely left the air-conditioned comfort of Saigon with contempt.

Veteran correspondent George McArthur, who began his journalistic career in the Korean War, covered the Vietnam War for 10 years, right up until the fall of Saigon in

1975. He flew to Hue on 3 February as Saigon bureau chief of the Associated Press and remained until the battle was over. McArthur, outspoken and often gruff, had little patience with desk-jockey reporters or media icons and was not bashful in saying so. He was not afraid to take on anyone, including Cronkite, who had acquired a reputation as the "most trusted man" in the United States. McArthur said in an interview several years after the war ended,

> Cronkite is not one of my heroes. When Cronkite broadcast in Hue during the Tet offensive, he arranged to have a shelling of the ridgeline behind him. This was his famous trip when he supposedly changed his mind. Baloney. He'd made up his mind before he ever came out there. But the Marines staged a shelling at four in the afternoon, and he was up on top of our mission building in Hue doing his stand-upper, wearing a bulletproof vest and a tin pot. And I was up there [on the same roof] doing my laundry. Crap.

Cronkite had flown up from Saigon to the south side of Hue on 10 February, and because I was in the Citadel across the river I missed his appearance. He filmed a carefully staged report and then flew home. Later that month, he stepped out of his impartial observer role to broadcast a one-of-a-kind commentary on the folly of U.S. involvement in Vietnam. Cronkite told an estimated television audience of some nine million that the United States was "mired in a stalemate" in Vietnam, one it could not win.

His skillfully crafted script touched millions of Americans who had grown disillusioned and weary with the war.

"We have been too often disappointed by the optimism of the American leaders to have faith any longer in the silver linings they find in the darkest clouds," Cronkite told his national audience, one that included President Johnson. "The only rational way out then is to negotiate, not as victors, but as an honorable people who had lived up to their pledge to defend democracy, and did the best they could."

That broadcast is largely credited with helping persuade the American people and President Johnson to give up on the war.

McArthur's assessment of Cronkite's appearance in Hue, which was shared by others in the media, conveniently overlooked the credentials of the man. Hardly a pacifist, Cronkite had been a distinguished UPI correspondent in World War II, landing with U.S. troops in North Africa and Normandy. He had also jumped into Holland with the 101st Airborne Division. He always considered himself a reporter, someone who would go out and get the news, not make it. And though he had not served nearly as much time in Vietnam as many of his colleagues, he managed to get the story right more often than not.

In Hue, the media had absolutely free rein to go where they wanted and write what they pleased. And, because there were so many of them, they were almost impossible to keep track of. They were like hobos, bumming rides on trucks and helicopters here and there and often turning up right in the middle of the wildest firefights. They ate what the grunts ate, they slept where they did, and they endured almost as many hardships.

There were times in Hue when they were just a plain nuisance.

"Who the hell are all those civilians?" Colonel Adkisson, the senior advisor, bellowed on the first day of the media's arrival.

"Media types, Colonel," I answered.

"Well, tell them to stay out of the way. And get their names," Adkisson said to me. "I want to know who they all are and if they should be here."

With notebook in hand, I went out and had them all sign in, writers, photographers, radio and television people. I'm sure I did not get them all.

Competition was keen among the reporters and photographers, and many showed immense amounts of courage. There were times when the reporters and photographers pitched in as stretcher bearers or messengers. Some even ferried ammunition to the front lines and took turns taking potshots at the enemy.

One of my favorite correspondents was a young man named Mike Morrow. He was a freelancer who had dropped out of Dartmouth to see for himself what the war in Vietnam was all about.

Sporting a full red beard, Morrow drove himself relentlessly, jumping from unit to unit throughout the country. He came to Hue early and stayed until the fighting was over. A young man of uncommon good sense and insight, his views were decidedly left of center. But he was never openly disrespectful of the military. If anything, it was just the opposite. As with many of his colleagues, it was hard not to marvel at the courage and determination of both the American and Vietnamese soldiers in this unforgiving war. He and I talked away many a night on the pros and cons of U.S. involvement in this most complex and controversial war. He was good company on a lot of scary nights.

Much has been written about Vietnam being a "living room war," and it was true. All three television networks were in Hue by 2 February, and what they shot often appeared the same day on television in the United States. The politicians and the military found it increasingly difficult to put their spin on what was happening in Vietnam and not have it challenged by television coverage of the same action. The American public could see for itself what was happening, and much of it was not very positive.

There may have been delays in getting supplies and reinforcements to some combat units in Vietnam, but the media never seemed to have any difficulty in getting their stories and film out of a battle zone. Their resources and moxie in this regard were amazing.

CBS had three camera crews in Hue within the first few days, while NBC and ABC initially had one crew each. More arrived as the battle intensified, and then it became a flood when the Battle of Hue became the only show in Vietnam. Other print media who made it to Hue included Charles Mohr of the *New York Times*, Peter Braestrup of the *Washington Post*, Don Sider of *Time*, Don Kirk of the *Washington Star*, and John Carroll of the *Baltimore Sun*.

There were also a couple of women correspondents who showed up at the MACV compound on 2 February: Isabelle von Green, a writer for a German magazine, and Cathy Leroy, an accredited French journalist and photographer.

*   *   *

Leroy was something of a legendary figure in Vietnam, though some of her colleagues viewed her with more than a tad of suspicion. Only 5 feet tall and weighing 85 pounds, she wore her blonde hair in pigtails. Born near Paris, where she became an accomplished sky diver, Leroy had made a combat jump with a U.S. airborne unit in Vietnam a couple of years earlier and was wounded in an action near Khe Sanh. She had also been banned from I Corps for 6 months for cussing out a senior marine officer, a feat, by the way, which was roundly applauded by her peers.

She and a French colleague, François Mazure, were in Phu Bai at the start of the Tet offensive. The two had managed to hitch a ride aboard a marine truck convoy leaving Phu Bai for Hue on 1 February but had decided en route to go off on their own before reaching the MACV compound. The two changed from fatigues into civilian clothes and rented a tandem bicycle. Their escapades, which can only be described as "ballsy," were published in the 16 February 1968 issue of *Life*. The issue included a full-page color photo of two NVA soldiers on the cover and a seven-page story and photo layout inside.

"The road was empty now, the people hiding in their houses," Leroy wrote, describing the scene after she and Mazure left the marine truck convoy. "We were growing nervous and whenever we did see people peering from the houses, François called 'bonjour, bonjour' very loud and friendly to show that we were French and not American."

When they reached a built-up area near a marketplace not too far from the MACV compound, they heard some shooting. They got off their bicycle and were directed to a nearby cathedral by some civilians.

"François kept saying 'Phap bao chi, phap bao chi' (French press) but the people did not look happy to see us," Leroy wrote.

A Vietnamese priest said the two were welcome to spend the night. Leroy estimated that there were 4,000 refugees in and around the cathedral.

After they had stayed the night, a priest told the pair that many of the people at the cathedral had expressed fear that the North Vietnamese might take reprisals against them for harboring foreigners. A young boy in the crowd had volunteered to try and lead them through the NVA lines to the U.S. compound, and the priest had even written a letter that might help in gaining them safe passage.

Minutes later they were apprehended by some NVA soldiers who tied their hands behind their backs with parachute cord, and they had their cameras taken from them. Their captors appeared to ignore the letter from the priest.

"In order not to seem frightened or apprehensive or guilty, François acted as if he were offended and furious at being made to suffer such indignities," Leroy wrote in the *Life* piece. "Overhead an American spotter plane and a Vietnamese bomber circled. Each time they came over, François and I dived for the dirt. The North Vietnamese seemed unconcerned—they hardly moved."

While held captive, the two correspondents met a Frenchman who managed an electricity plant in the city. The man, heavyset and about 50, told Leroy an extraordinary story.

A year earlier, while out driving at night, the man had been ambushed by the Vietcong and a bullet had severed two of his fingers. When the Vietcong rushed up to the car to finish him off he screamed, "I am a Frenchman." The Vietcong (VC) leader bandaged his wounded hand, helped him restart his car, and released him.

A year later, the North Vietnamese had come to Hue at Tet, charging in waves across the rice fields to occupy the Frenchman's house. Several VC political agents arrived to talk with their comrades, and, incredibly, their leader was the same VC who had ambushed him a year before. The VC greeted the Frenchman cordially, and since then, although the Frenchman and his family—a Vietnamese wife and two teenage daughters—were prisoners in their own home, the North Vietnamese had treated them quite well.

While Leroy was talking to the Frenchman, the door opened and in walked an NVA officer.

"He was about 25, carried a .38 pistol and he looked really rather dashing, like some of the Vietnamese university students one sees in Paris," Leroy wrote. "When the Frenchman's wife told him who we were, he ordered his men to untie us and asked whether we had our cameras."

When their cameras were returned, Leroy and Mazure decided that they might as well throw caution to the wind and act like the journalists they were. A good offense would be their best defense.

"When we asked if we could take some pictures, [the North Vietnamese officer] agreed immediately and escorted us outside," Leroy wrote. "The men seemed to be delighted at the idea of having their picture taken. The only trouble was that they always wanted to strike the phony heroic poses you see in North Vietnamese propaganda pictures. When we got back to the house, François remarked very offhandedly, 'Well, we have to get back to Paris with our story, so we'll be running along now.' "

Apparently, the officer in charge did not object at all. In fact, he seemed very happy to assist the correspondents in any way he could.

"The Frenchman passed out cigars to François and the officer and they all lit up. Then we shook hands gaily all around and said goodbye and good luck," Leroy wrote.

When the pair arrived at the MACV compound a few hours later with their tale of capture and escape—all recorded on film—some of their media colleagues raised an eyebrow or two. The cynics, who knew Leroy well, voiced the opinion that Leroy's tale of adventure owed its happy ending to her unique personality, in that she probably became such a pain in the ass that the NVA let her escape just to get rid of her.

Mazure, who worked for Agence France-Presse, also drew attention with his account of his capture and escape. In a dispatch to a French publication he filed on 2 February Mazure wrote:

At dawn, the new masters of the city went through the streets in groups of ten. In each group there was a leader who spoke to the people through a bullhorn. . . . The other members of the team . . . knocked on doors and passed out pamphlets and leaflets. Joking and laughing, the soldiers walk in the streets and gardens without showing any fear. . . . They give an impression of discipline and good training. . . . Numerous civilians brought them great quantities of food. It didn't seem that these residents were being coerced in any way.

A few days later, the Saigon government expelled Mazure from the country for "spreading procommunist propaganda."

One of the most popular interviewing areas in Hue was the helicopter LZ by the river. There, among the body bags lying in row after row, journalists had easy and relatively safe access to the walking wounded and those on stretchers awaiting a medevac to Phu Bai.

I accompanied UPI reporter Dana Stone a couple of times to the LZ. Stone would ask a wounded marine his name and hometown and then ask him to describe how he got hit. Most of the marines loved being interviewed and willingly supplied any information asked, often embellishing the responses with colorful language.

Stone was a particular favorite of the marines because of his unbridled energy and curiosity. A Vermonter by birth, Stone had reddish hair and wore wire-rimmed glasses. Only 26 at the time, he mingled well with the grunts. He had a wild sense of humor and a complete irreverence for military brass, a quality the common soldier found endearing. He was known throughout I Corps as "one crazy dude." In 1970, while on assignment in Cambodia with his pal Sean Flynn, son of movie star Errol Flynn, Stone disappeared and was never heard from again.

When the marines began a big push westward on 5 and 6 February, Don Webster and his CBS television crew were with them. The three companies of 2/5 maneuvered a full block almost unopposed on 5 February before enemy resistance stiffened at the Hue Central Hospital complex and the marines had to call it a night. That night, a U.S.

Navy barge arrived at the LSU ramp with much-needed supplies and reinforcements.

Replenished, the same three companies jumped off at 0700 on 6 February and progress was swift. The hospital complex was taken, then the prison, and finally the province headquarters complex. At the latter, the CBS cameras were rolling when the marines took down an NLF flag and raised the Stars and Stripes in its place. The U.S. flag had been pilfered from the MACV compound by a marine who was to remain nameless.

"There was no bugler and the other marines were too busy to salute, but not often is a flag so proudly raised," said an emotional Webster in his narrative during the filming.

Lieutenant Colonel Cheatham, whose marines had fought and died taking the province headquarters, knew it was a breach of protocol to raise the U.S. flag on a Vietnamese building, but he gave his approval to go ahead and do it anyway.

"We're not authorized to fly the U.S. flag," Cheatham told Gunnery Sgt. Frank A. Thomas, "but go ahead and run it up before anyone tells us not to. We're doing the fighting. We may as well have our flag get the credit. I want those NVA guys across the river to see this."

With the CBS crew and a few other photographers crouching in a corner of the compound, their cameras at the ready, Gunnery Sergeant Thomas raced out to the flagpole and, with the aid of two other marines, quickly took down the NLF flag and hoisted the U.S. colors. The marines started cheering. To some, it was almost like the famous flag raising at Iwo Jima in World War II. Lieutenant Colonel Cheatham radioed his superior, Colonel Hughes, back at the CP and said: "Be advised, we have taken the province headquarters, and somehow or other, an American flag is flying above it."

The taking of the province headquarters complex on 6 February, which the enemy had used as its command post, and the raising of the U.S. flag proved to be more than just a symbolic victory. The twin acts signaled the beginning of the end of all serious resistance by the enemy on the south side of the Perfume River.

Cheatham, who enjoyed dealing with the media, put it even more succinctly. "When we took the province headquarters," he told a bunch of reporters and a TV crew, "we broke their back."

It would take 4 more days of mopping up before the marines would officially declare the south side of the city secure. By that time, another marine force was getting ready to cross the river and try its luck in the Citadel.

Although the fighting had slackened on the south side, there were other concerns that popped up in its wake. The refugee problem had reached staggering proportions. Every turn in the fighting had flushed out hundreds of Vietnamese civilians of every age. Whole families were able to survive the shelling and street warfare by hunkering down in small bunkers they had constructed in their homes. Out of the rubble came old men and women, waving pieces of white cloth attached to sticks. They were followed by children and young adults. Many of the families were carrying luggage of some sort, as if they had been packed for days waiting for this moment, which, for many, was exactly the case.

The job of sorting out the refugees fell mostly to Vietnamese officials. Temporary housing was found at a complex near the MACV compound and at Hue University, where the number of refugees had swollen to 22,000. Most of the refugees were innocent civilians, but some were enemy soldiers or sympathizers—and many were ARVN troops trapped at home on leave for the Tet holidays. All the ARVN soldiers who were fit for duty were put to use helping the marines and MACV advisors with the refugees. Later the ARVN troops would rejoin their outfits currently fighting across the river in the Citadel.

The most difficult assignment was policing up the dead that littered the streets and the destroyed buildings. They were not hard to find. The chilly weather had created a natural mausoleum, and the putrid smell of rotting corpses drifted over the city like a thick fog. The bodies, bloated and vermin infested, attracted rats and stray dogs. So, because of public health concerns, details were formed to bury the bodies as quickly as possible.

Another problem was looting, a practice engaged in by troops on both sides. Early in the battle, marine troops had been guilty of looting any money or booze they found, but they were limited by what they could carry in their packs. The ARVN soldiers were guilty of far greater looting. Assigned mop-up roles behind the marines, some ARVN soldiers could not resist ripping off their own people. They often helped themselves to such things as television sets, cars, and refrigerators, stashing the items in safe hiding until they could return to either sell them or transport them to their own homes.

The actions committed by some of the Vietnamese soldiers against their own people brought only scorn from the marines, who used these examples as yet another reason why they viewed their allies as unworthy.

The Americans took the major role in cleaning up the south side of the city because the Vietnamese were either unwilling or unable to assume that responsibility. As a result, many of the MACV advisors were pressed into duty to enforce a no-looting policy and to oversee the removal of the dead.

I stood watch at several sites where the grim task of pulling bodies from the rubble began on 6 February. The marines in the area also lent a hand in digging through the destruction they had wrought. When a dead NVA soldier was dragged from beneath a pile of blood-soaked rubble, a weathered grunt leaned over and could not resist saying: "Hey zipperhead, how'd you enjoy your visit to Hue City?"

CHAPTER TEN

The Citadel

The 7th of February started with a bang. Enemy sappers and frogmen who had worked throughout the night detonated a huge charge beneath the Nguyen Hoang Bridge, the main bridge across the Perfume River, turning the six-span steel structure into a roller-coaster of bent girders and concrete. The charge, which dropped a 100-meter hunk of the structure into the river, rendered the bridge impassable to vehicular traffic, though later it was repaired sufficiently for foot traffic.

The explosion, which pierced the morning fog and drizzle at 0500, was almost as jarring as the initial rocket barrage that had begun the battle 8 days earlier. It jolted me to an upright position in my guard post 200 meters away at the MACV compound.

In retrospect, the blast turned out to be a parting shot by an enemy that had all but given up in the southern section of Hue. The symbolic Citadel (Map 4) had always been the main prize, and now, with the action on the south side almost over, the NVA and Vietcong had sent a clear signal of their intentions to refocus their energies on the north bank. Their mission was to hang onto the Citadel for as long as possible, squeezing all the international publicity from their prize that they could to achieve their political ends. They would be removed only by force, and any destruction of this historic and revered city would surely be blamed on the Americans.

The destruction of the main bridge between the two sections of Hue was a demonstration of strength and resolve. It was intended as a signal to U.S. and South Vietnamese forces that the battle was far from over. And that is exactly the way it turned out.

The Allies, too, wanted to send a message of strength that day, and did so when a flight of Vietnamese A-1 Skyraiders dropped two dozen 500-pound bombs on the Citadel walls in the largest bombing run of the battle to date. Guided by tiny spotter planes, the slow-moving, propeller-driven bombers chugged in from the east and west, not more than 300 feet off the ground. The explosions resonated off the low clouds, while hunks of brick and mortar flew hundreds of feet in the air. Both sides were flexing their muscles for the coming showdown in the Citadel.

Because of the low cloud cover over Hue the first couple of weeks, the single-engine Skyraiders were much more suitable than the speedier jets. Each aircraft could lift as many as twelve 500-pound bombs or a total load of 6,000 pounds.

On 1 February enemy forces in the Citadel were just as strong as the South Vietnamese, maybe even stronger. The ARVN, which had received limited resupply since the battle began, had just about run out of steam. After pushing out from the 1st Division headquarters about 1,000 meters to recapture Tay Loc Airfield, the ARVN had bogged down. The enemy, which still held 60 percent of the Citadel, had been able to resupply itself with fresh troops and supplies at will from the west since the battle began. Enemy forces were well dug in and, from all appearances, willing to fight it out to the end.

"From a personal standpoint I was very frustrated and disappointed that the Americans couldn't provide us with any food or supplies in the first 10 days," Capt. Jack Chase, the U.S. advisor with the ARVN 3rd Troop, 7th Cavalry, said. "It didn't seem to bother the Vietnamese all that much. They were very resourceful. And the civilians in Hue were very willing to share whatever food they had with us. Thankfully, they had a good stock on hand because of Tet. But there was one time we were reduced to dropping grenades in ponds and eating the fish that floated to the surface. That's how I caught hepatitis."

The resupply of ammunition was another thing entirely. Chase's outfit had had an easier time getting resupplied because it carried carbines: ammunition for that weapon was available through Vietnamese supply channels. The Vietnamese airborne units, which carried M16s, had to get resupplied from U.S. sources. Chase's APCs did run out of .50- and .30-caliber ammunition, however. The solution for most of the ARVN units over the first 10 days was to use weapons and ammunition captured from the enemy. In many cases that was the only option they had.

"The carbine has to be the slowest weapon there is," Chase said. "It is almost useless in house-to-house fighting. I could almost see the bullet leaving the barrel, and I'd have to lead my target by 10 or 20 feet to score a hit."

Also contributing to the stalemate was the lack of heavy weapons and the unavailability of air and artillery support.

"I know the weather was bad but we got hardly any support at all," Chase said.

Captain Chase's outfit did get an unexpected boost, however, when its former commander, Captain Thi, rejoined his old unit on 3 February. Thi, who had been reassigned to the ARVN 7th Cavalry headquarters at An Cuu several weeks earlier, was at home in the Citadel celebrating Tet when the enemy attacked Hue. After hiding in his attic for a couple of days, he saw a chance to break away on 3 February and rejoin his old outfit. He provided a much-needed morale boost to 3/7 over the next 3 weeks.

The three ARVN airborne battalions reported killing over 200 enemy soldiers in the vicinity of the airfield on 2 and 3 February, and the ARVN 1st Battalion, 3rd Regiment captured one of the Citadel gates on the northwest wall on 4 February. To the southeast, the 4th Battalion, 2nd Regiment established a forward line about six blocks from the 1st Division compound, a position that remained stable for more than a week.

Much of the news in the Citadel over the first week was bad, however. The ARVN 7th Airborne commander, Maj. Le Van Ngoc, and the unit's U.S. advisor, Capt. Chuck Jackson, were wounded and medevaced on 2 February.

"It was one of those lucky shots," Jackson said of the mortar round that wounded him and his counterpart and killed his radio operator. "We had just established a battalion CP near the airfield and were looking at a map when a round dropped right between us. It was pure luck, bad luck."

By 4 February, the 3/7 Cavalry was down to three usable APCs and 40 men. The three airborne units were also badly depleted. The 7th and 9th Airborne Battalions, as well as 1/3, had each lost one of its companies in bitter fighting on 31 January before they arrived in the Citadel. The 4/3, which had been flown in from Dong Ha on 1 and 2 February, was having a difficult time covering a wide front to the southeast of the ARVN 1st Division compound. Something had to be done to put more life in the ARVN units holding on in the Citadel.

Also on 4 February, the ARVN 2nd Airborne Battalion, which had arrived in the Citadel at relatively full strength, was planning a surprise night attack on part of the southwest wall beyond the airfield as a means to break the stalemate.

"My counterpart came to me and swore me to secrecy on the night attack. He didn't even tell General Truong," said Captain Cobb, the 2nd Airborne's senior advisor. "He was afraid word would leak out and alert the enemy. The attack was set for midnight. I remember thinking to myself that this is the way to win the battle. I was so proud of them. Then, at 11 p.m., we were told to withdraw to the division compound. I guess they thought there was some kind of threat mounting at the headquarters."

General Truong had decided to rotate the three airborne battalions to the southeast sector to relieve the 4th Battalion, 2nd Regiment, which he then moved to the Tay Loc Airfield. More troop movements were also in the works. Truong had ordered the 2nd Troop, 7th Cavalry Regiment to Hue from Quang Tri on 3 February, but it took the unit 3 days to clean up a heavy engagement with the enemy and proceed south. It finally left Quang Tri on 6 February with a full complement of 15 APCs. Joining the mechanized column was one company from the 2nd Battalion, 1st Infantry.

After stopping off at Camp Evans for the night, a reinforced 2/7 cautiously headed down Route 1. About 12 kilometers northwest of Hue, the column left the highway and cut across country, entering the Citadel at 1700 without meeting any meaningful resistance.

"There was a lot of anxiety and apprehension on the move," said senior advisor Capt. Jim Zimmerman. "Many of the soldiers, including the company commander, Lt. Nguyen Hoa, had family in Hue."

The 2/7 Cavalry immediately relieved 3/7 near the airfield, and the latter unit, down to three APCs and 40 men, was withdrawn to regroup, repair, and provide security for the ARVN 1st Division HQ. The 3/7 was for all intents and purposes no longer an effective combat unit.

The rest of General Truong's 3rd Regiment, the 2nd, 3rd, and 4th Battalions, also arrived on 7 February aboard Vietnamese motorized junks. Each unit had been trying to assault the Citadel from the south after breaking free of enemy pressure at the outset of the battle. The 2nd and 3rd Battalions, which had been bypassed by the enemy invasion a week earlier, had slowly moved eastward along the northern shore of the Perfume River to the base of the Citadel, which they were unable to enter.

The journey of 4/3, which was on an operation a few kilometers southeast of the MACV compound on 31 January, was much more adventuresome. Like its sister unit 1/3, 4/3 had to fight its way out of an encirclement. The initial action was so heavy that the unit's U.S. advisors were extracted by helicopter. By the time 4/3 broke free and made it to the MACV compound on 4 February, it was down to 170 men.

On 8 February all four of 3rd Regiment's battalions

were plugged into positions near the Citadel airstrip, relieving the 4th Battalion, 2nd Regiment, which then assumed new duties as the security force for the river landing dock outside the northern corner of the ARVN 1st Division compound.

I joined many of the other American advisors in the Citadel on 8 February, making the hazardous river crossing in a crowded navy LCU. The flat-bottomed craft, called "whisky boats" by the marines, was packed with ammunition, supplies, ARVN troops returning to their units, and civilian reporters. Enemy gunners on the Citadel walls 600 meters away had a clear view of the navy LCU ramp from across the river, and we were under fire before we even left the shore.

Several small bunkers had been constructed near the ramp site to provide emergency shelter during mortar attacks, but once you were under way and out on the river there was no place to hide.

We crowded aboard the LCU and crouched along its sides as it pulled out into the Perfume River. The distance to the quay outside the Citadel's northern corner was 3 kilometers as the crow flies but twice that because of the winding river. The course ran due north through a deep, narrow channel around an island, then turned sharply west toward the Citadel dock. The entire trip was through enemy territory.

Enemy fire came from both sides of the river, pinging against the metal hulls of the craft and zipping overhead with an ominous whine. We could hear mortar rounds leaving their tubes and then watched in utter helplessness as the shells sent up geysers of water fore and aft. While the LCU gunners raked the banks with .50-caliber ma-

chine gun fire, some passengers leaned over the side to
unload an M16 magazine or two. Most of us just kept
our heads down. Wedged next to me were a couple of
dozen crates of grenades. I tried not to think what damage a mortar round could do to all of us with a direct hit.

The crossing took less than a half-hour but seemed
much longer because everybody was holding his breath.
Once we disembarked at the landing dock, it was only
about 100 meters to the Hau Gate, the only secure entrance to the Citadel. While the ammunition was being
offloaded I double-timed it through the open gate. It felt
good to be on land again.

What a shock it was to see the 1st Division compound
again. It was only 10 days earlier, on a bright sunlit morning, that I had stood in formation on this very parade
ground while the South Vietnamese flag was raised. With
the strains of the Vietnamese national anthem (which
sounded a lot like the French *Marseillaise*) echoing in the
background, General Truong, his staff, and his U.S. advisors, all in freshly starched uniforms, had stood at attention and crisply saluted as the yellow and red colors were
raised to the top of the flagpole.

The scene was much different on my return. General
Truong, a stoic figure in the best of times, looked almost
haggard. Nobody had any starch left in his uniform.
There were shell holes on the parade ground and sandbagged bunkers everywhere. Both of the main buildings
of the headquarters compound were riddled with bullet
holes and damaged by mortar fire. Windows were miss-
ing or partially blown out, wrecked vehicles lay twisted
and burned where they had been hit, and empty shell cas-
ings littered the ground. It was not difficult to imagine

what must have taken place here and how close Truong's forces had come to being overrun.

On paper, General Truong appeared to have more troops than the enemy in the Citadel, which were estimated at three to four battalions. But that was deceiving because of the generous Tet leave policy in effect before the enemy attack and the attrition those units suffered over the course of the first week. The three battalions of the ARVN 1st Airborne Task Force (the 2nd, 7th, and 9th) were actually at less than half their strength. So were the four battalions of the 1st Division's 3rd Regiment, the 4th Battalion of the 2nd Regiment, and the two troops from the division's 7th Cavalry. The Hac Bao and Reconnaissance Companies were also greatly understrength. Injury and death, too often claiming the most experienced personnel, had depleted their ranks and affected morale even further. Many of the furloughed troops were later able to rejoin their units, but others had been taken prisoner or killed.

The ARVN troops were tired, hungry, and discouraged. They were dangerously low on munitions, food, medicine, and clothing. Morale was also at a low ebb. The ARVN had ceased to attack and had gone into a defensive mode. It took all of General Truong's considerable leadership talents to keep his troops in the field while he pleaded for fresh soldiers and more supplies. Truong, himself, looked on the verge of exhaustion.

The three ARVN airborne battalions, which when combined totaled less than one battalion, had found themselves stalemated since moving to the southeast quarter of the Citadel on 5 February. There were shortages of everything.

"Problems of resupply had developed," Maj. Milton Bertrand, the Airborne Task Force advisor, wrote in his after-action report. "All of the ammo at 1st Division had been issued and none had been received from outside sources."

The task force quickly realized that it did not have enough men or the proper supporting weapons to force the enemy from its strongholds. The task force moved into position with the 9th Airborne Battalion on the left flank along the northern edge of Mai Thuc Loan Street just south of the 1st Division compound and the 2nd Airborne Battalion on the right flank. The weakened 7th Airborne Battalion, with Capt. James K. Redding replacing the injured Capt. Chuck Jackson as senior advisor, was used as a floating reserve. The lead units constantly faced heavy fire from the front and flanks, particularly from the northeast wall and the Imperial Palace.

"It became apparent that any further penetration by the [task force] would only result in complete encirclement of the battalions," Bertrand said. "The enemy was strongly entrenched within this area, and it was felt that additional fire support must be made available in order to secure the objectives. The units remained fairly static in their positions during this period, conducting patrol operations, ambushes, and local security for themselves."

Still, the airborne esprit de corps remained high.

"We were all dirty and beat up and our knees were sticking out of our pants," 9th Airborne advisor Sgt. Mike Smith said. "While changing positions [with 3rd Regiment soldiers] our Vietnamese paratroopers made chicken sounds to make fun of the leg infantry, not unlike our U.S. 101st Airborne Division when they were relieving a leg unit at Bastogne in WWII."

Smith also remembered the first big bombing run of Skyraiders on 7 February and the effect the 500-pound bombs had on the NVA bunkers atop the northeast wall.

"We were like only a hundred or so yards away and the earth trembled under our feet," Smith said. "The NVA jumped right back up, shook their heads, and resumed firing. The city was a nightmare. We just couldn't get them out of their holes. Like, where were they going to go anyway?"

During lulls in the firing it was deathly quiet.

"There were times when you couldn't hear a cat meow or a dog bark. I don't think I saw a single civilian while I was in Hue," said Capt. Ty Cobb, the senior advisor of the 2nd Airborne. "They must have been too scared to move."

Cobb's assistant, Capt. Donald Erbes, said the only civilians he saw were dead ones.

"The thing that I remember most about my service in Hue was the civilians we saw when we went into the houses. I saw men, women, and children who were shot to death. There was no doubt they had been executed," Erbes said.

Because the airborne troops were a national reserve force based in Saigon, they were a long way from any supply chain. When they ran out of ammo and food, they were the last to get any resupply.

"There were times when we lived on the food we could find in the houses," Erbes said. "I remember eating a lot of bananas and saltine crackers. We didn't have to worry, though, because the Vietnamese were very resourceful."

General Truong, who had spent the first 12 years of his military career with airborne units, did all he could to share his meager supplies with all the units under his command, but there simply was not enough to go around.

Since I had no counterpart among the Vietnamese units, I became sort of an advisor at large when I arrived in the Citadel. I continued to monitor the civilian press representatives who were starting to pour into the Citadel, and I kept a daily running log of events for briefing purposes. I also stood by in case I was needed elsewhere—and I often was.

My bed was a concrete floor under a tin roof. Next door were a bunker and a latrine. Ammunition was stacked near the bunker. The division headquarters was under sporadic mortar attack, day and night. Much of the shelling came from enemy firing positions within the Imperial Palace complex about 1,500 meters away. Allied forces were prohibited from using anything other than small arms in answering the fire from inside the palace region in order to limit destruction of the historical site.

The weather continued to be lousy: the rain and low clouds limited helicopter resupply and tactical air support. The enemy forces, despite the presence of a weakened battalion from the U.S. 1st Air Cavalry Division 5 kilometers to the west, continued to resupply themselves with fresh troops and ammunition from the west without threat of interdiction. Until the latter problem was alleviated, the stalemate in the Citadel was likely to continue.

Adding to General Truong's troubles was the fact that his superiors in Saigon were demanding the return of the three airborne battalions, which were part of the country's strategic reserve force. They would eventually be replaced, Truong was told, by three battalions of Vietnamese marines, who were part of I Corps reserve. Truong told his superiors that he could not wait much longer for help. He needed it now.

General Truong also reached another conclusion on 9 February. To retake the Citadel he needed heavy weapons, and for that he needed U.S. help.

The original agreement worked out between the Allies was to have ARVN troops clean out the Citadel while U.S. Marines took care of the action in the southern part of the city. The Saigon government and General Truong fully intended to fill their part of the bargain, but the circumstances of the moment dictated a change. It was with great reluctance that the Vietnamese general staff agreed on 10 February to request help from the marines to jump start the campaign in the Citadel.

At first, Lt. Gen. Robert E. Cushman, commander of the III Marine Amphibious Force, was not all that keen on risking any more of his marines to bail out ARVN troops in the Citadel. It took a personal intervention by General Westmoreland to convince him otherwise.

Westmoreland had always seemed to be uncomfortable with the marines' "independent" posture in I Corps, and he had been disappointed in the performance of General Cushman, in particular. In a move to establish more control over actions in I Corps, particularly in the two northernmost provinces of Quang Tri and Thua Thien, Westmoreland had announced on 27 January the formation of a temporary MACV Forward headquarters at Phu Bai to be jointly staffed by U.S. Marine Corps and Army personnel. The new HQ was also needed to maintain control over two new army divisions, the 1st Cavalry and 101st Airborne, that were moving into the region, a decision that was initially questioned by the marines, who considered I Corps their area of operations.

Westmoreland, who was under tremendous pressure from Washington to get the situation in Hue resolved, had not been very happy or confident in General Cushman's handling of the Tet offensive and had flown to Da Nang on 7 February to have a talk with his top Marine Corps commander. Westmoreland later wrote that he thought Cushman and his staff "appeared complacent, seemingly reluctant to use the Army forces I had put at their disposal."

There was a feeling, both in the military and the news media, that the marines seemed to be far less interested in cooperating than in dominating.

Westmoreland had returned from the meeting more determined than ever to make MACV Forward a viable and effective command post no matter the objections from the marines. To do so he put his deputy, U.S. Army Gen. Creighton W. Abrams, in charge. Although this made for an uncomfortable command relationship, it did not result in the total shakeup of the northern command that many marines had feared. Cushman, a heavyset man who wore glasses, weathered the storm in a professional manner. He would later win his fourth star and become commandant of the Marine Corps.

When the call for U.S. help in the Citadel arrived on 10 February, the marines, with prodding from Abrams and Westmoreland, agreed to send the 1st Battalion, 5th Marine Regiment (1/5), which had been bloodied a bit during a combat action south of Phu Bai. Westmoreland cabled Washington about the deployment, saying that "the enemy has approximately three companies in Hue Citadel" and that one battalion should be enough.

At 0930 the following morning, two platoons of Bravo Company arrived by helicopter at the ARVN 1st Division LZ in the Citadel. A third platoon had to turn back to Phu Bai when its helicopter took fire, wounding the pilot. Two hours after landing, the enemy welcomed the marines to the Citadel with a dozen rounds of 122mm rocket fire.

A couple of hours later, 1/5's commanding officer, Maj. Robert Thompson, was en route to Hue in a truck convoy with his three other companies and the remaining platoon from Bravo Company. Major Thompson, a native of Corinth, Mississippi, was a supply officer in the division when he took command of 1/5 on 2 February, which was when the previous commander had been seriously wounded and evacuated. Although junior in grade, he was highly thought of by the Marine Corps brass. Reporting in to Colonel Hughes at the MACV compound, he was told there was little intelligence about what was going on in the Citadel but that it should not take more than a "few days" to clean up the problem.

Thompson's battalion was put under the operational control of Hughes, and Thompson was told in a blunt directive that he was to take orders only from Hughes and not General Truong. Delta Company was to be temporarily detached to Hughes's command on the south side of the river, while Thompson took Alpha and Charlie Companies and the remaining platoon from Bravo with him by LCUs to the Citadel the next morning (12 February).

Also arriving on the scene that day was a young man who would play a key role in the battle plans in the Citadel over the next 2 weeks, Marine Lt. Alexander Wells. Wells, who was due to rotate home within a week, had been volunteered by his commander at Phu Bai to set up a forward fire direction center in the Citadel and had been told that it was a 24-hour mission. Wells flew into the Citadel on 11 February during an enemy mortar attack and took refuge in a Quonset hut that he said was "full of Australians playing cards and drinking scotch."

Lieutenant Wells spent the next 2 weeks on the forward lines of the Citadel calling in supporting fire for both marine and ARVN units from artillery bases near Phu Bai and from naval ships on station east of the city.

Also headed for Hue on 11 February was a marine platoon of five M48 tanks. The platoon, under Lt. Ron Morrison, had left Da Nang aboard LCUs, navigated up the South China Sea, and entered the Perfume River just as it was getting dark. Somebody was needed to meet them at the dock outside the Citadel and guide them through the secure gate into the ARVN 1st Division compound. U.S. Army Colonel Adkisson looked around the room and pointed at me.

Provided with a jeep, I checked my M16 rifle and .45-caliber pistol to make sure they were loaded and told my Vietnamese driver to head out the secure gate toward the landing. He hesitated for a second until I unholstered my .45 and, in the best bluff of my life, jabbed it into his chest. Any language barrier disappeared instantly, and we made it to the landing dock in record time.

The area of the landing dock was secured by the remnants of the ARVN 4th Battalion, 2nd Regiment, which had arrived in Hue back on 1 February. The unit, now badly undermanned, had seen service in the southeast sector before being relieved by airborne units, and then had fought in the vicinity of the Tay Loc Airfield. The 4/2 had been pulled off the line and given this new assignment on 8 February.

While waiting for the marine tanks, I chatted with 4/2's advisor, Capt. David Shepard of Cincinnati, about what his unit had been through the past 10 days. Shepard, a big bear of a man who had served in the Korean War, said he had had no idea what was going on in Hue before he got there.

"We were up at Dong Ha on the DMZ when we got a call to head on down to Hue. We were told it would be a 4-day mission," Shepard said. "Half our battalion was airlifted here on February 1 and the rest arrived the next day. Some of the later arrivals came by junk. We were only about half-strength when we got here because a lot of our troops were away on Tet leave."

After 7 days of action in Hue without any resupply or reinforcements, 4/2 had lost about half its 250-man force.

It was another cool, moonless night as Captain Shepard and I stood there near the dock awaiting the tanks. It was deathly quiet, but soon we heard the engines of the LCUs. The boats came in one at a time, and the tanks rolled off quickly. Captain Shepard notified the 1st Division CP of their arrival, then showed the tank commander, Lieutenant Morrison, a map of the area and where the entrance gate was and told him to follow me.

"Are you sure the gate is wide enough for my tanks?" Morrison asked. I said we would both find out soon enough.

The tanks followed my jeep to the gate and, with minimal adjustments, all five of them squeezed through the narrow portal into the ARVN 1st Division compound with inches to spare. Lieutenant Morrison was greeted like a conquering hero, and then his tanks were immediately dispersed around the compound.

Less than an hour later, Alpha 1/5 left the Hue ramp aboard three LCUs and, utilizing the cover of darkness, proceeded unimpeded to the landing dock outside the Citadel and entered the fortress without incident.

It was only five tanks and a company of marines, but to General Truong it was like an inner tube to a drowning man. I could almost see him exhale with relief. Then I saw just the hint of a smile.

Looking at his situation map, Truong had every reason to think the worst was over. Almost two companies of U.S. Marines (Alpha 1/5 and two platoons of Bravo 1/5) had arrived to relieve the three Vietnamese airborne units on his southern flank, and three Vietnamese marine units were en route to take the pressure off his weary 3rd Regiment in the west. The 2nd Troop, ARVN 7th Cavalry, which had arrived on 7 February with 15 APCs and 87 men, was plugged into duty around the airfield, replacing its sister unit, the 3rd Troop, 7th Cavalry, which was down to 34 men and three APCs.

Ah, yes, things were starting to look and feel a whole lot better.

Though most of the action south of the Perfume River had slowed, the two marine battalions (1/1 and 2/5) in the area were kept busy with mop-up activities and combat patrolling. The two companies of the 1/1 (Alpha and Bravo) had secured the area around the MACV compound and the LCU ramp. The two companies also secured Route 1 to the An Cuu Bridge, which had been blown up on 4 February. An engineer company had been moved into the area to start bridge repair work, which drew intermittent fire from enemy troops in the vicinity.

Meanwhile, the three companies of the 2/5 (Fox, Golf, and Hotel) had moved west along the south bank of the Perfume River to the Phu Cam Canal. On 10 February, the battalion was given orders to turn south and start destroying four bridges over the Phu Cam so that enemy forces could not use them to bring reinforcements into the city from the southwest.

Patrolling and repair work on the two remaining bridges over the Phu Cam continued, but the south bank of the city was officially declared secure on 10 February.

CHAPTER ELEVEN

A Jump Start

Already behind schedule, Maj. Robert Thompson and his 1/5 were still on the wrong side of the river at the beginning of 12 February. One of his companies (Alpha) and two platoons of another (Bravo) were in the Citadel. A third company (Delta) was no longer under his command, having been temporarily attached to 2/5 for assignment on the south side of the Perfume River.

Once again, the marines continued to do things piecemeal.

Thompson's patience, not one of his strong points on good days, was further tested when he, his command group, Charlie Company, and the remaining platoon from Bravo Company were unable to depart from the Hue LCU ramp early that morning because of heavy fire from the Citadel. Major Thompson and his operations officer, Maj. Len Wunderlich, who was also acting as his executive officer, used the delay to pick the brains of marines who had had to deal with the house-to-house fighting in the previous 2 weeks. The information and advice they obtained was to prove valuable in the days to come.

The rest of 1/5 finally left the Hue ramp in late afternoon, but Thompson would have to undergo another trial before he finally joined the other half of his command.

After landing at the secured dock outside the Citadel, Thompson and his command group, acting as the point, marched past the secure entrance and nearly into enemy territory. When he finally got them turned around he was denied access to the Citadel by an ARVN sentinel. The communications problem was quickly alleviated, however, when Thompson threatened to storm the walls with his troops if they were not let in.

Also arriving late on 12 February were two battalions of Vietnamese marines. A third battalion joined the fight 4 days later. The Vietnamese marines, equipped with six 105mm howitzers, had fought in Saigon earlier in the Tet offensive.

It was also moving day for the three ARVN airborne battalions, which were being sent back to their home base of Saigon. The Airborne Task Force HQ and the 9th Airborne were airlifted to Phu Bai at 1650, and the other two battalions left by LCU to the southern bank of the Perfume River and were then trucked to Phu Bai. The entire force then flew to Saigon on 13 February.

The weather continued to be cool and cloudy, which hampered the troop exchanges. But by sundown of 12 February all the airborne troops were at Phu Bai. The Vietnamese marines used the same LCU to come into the Citadel that night.

The Vietnamese paratroopers had suffered 119 killed and 396 wounded during the Hue operation, while killing 910 of the enemy, according to the after-action report written by Maj. Milton Bertrand, the Airborne Task Force senior advisor. The 9th Airborne Battalion reported 55 killed and 125 wounded, most of them during fighting at Quang Tri on 31 January and 1 February. The 7th Airborne had had 47 killed and 156 wounded, most of them coming during an attack through a graveyard outside the Citadel's northwest wall on 31 January, and the 2nd Airborne reported 17 killed and 115 wounded.

The task force was a mere shell of its authorized strength. Bloodied and tired, it took all their energy to execute a successful withdrawal.

"When we boarded the plane to Saigon, we had 169 men, counting the walking wounded," 9th Airborne advisor Captain Blair said.

The plan was for Maj. Thompson's battalion to advance from the ARVN 1st Division HQ compound with three companies in a southeast direction to occupy positions previously held by the Vietnamese Airborne Task Force along the northern edge of Mai Thuc Loan Street, which was now dubbed "Phase Line Green." The newly arrived Vietnamese marines, meanwhile, were to reinforce ARVN units already positioned in the western part of the Citadel.

Thompson was briefed by General Truong and Colonel Adkisson upon his arrival in the Citadel late on 12 February. Truong gave Thompson the ARVN 2nd Battalion, 3rd Regiment as a security force on his right flank and rear. The Vietnamese unit was to also handle any refugee problems and prisoner interrogations.

The sun made a rare appearance on the morning of 13 February, but it did not turn out to be a good omen.

Thompson's force moved out at 0800 and headed for Phase Line Green, the front lines he mistakenly thought were still occupied by the three ARVN airborne units. Just short of his objective, Thompson's lead company

(Alpha) ran into heavy fire, which stopped the entire battalion in its tracks and inflicted heavy casualties.

It is difficult to believe that the marines were unaware of the airborne units' departure, because all the troop withdrawals the day before had taken place from the ARVN 1st Division CP in full view of the newly arrived marines—but Thompson swears he was never told.

"General Truong or one of his officers, I don't remember which, told me the [ARVN] airborne battalions were located to my front," Thompson said many years later. "My plan was to pass through them and take up their positions. They were not there, and consequently my A Company really stepped into it."

The confusion over the airborne units' departure probably resulted because Thompson's battalion was a full day behind schedule. By the time the entire battalion—minus Delta Company—had settled in at the ARVN 1st Division headquarters compound on 12 February, it was getting dark. Thompson had come to the Citadel with virtually no intelligence information, and, because of all the transportation snafus, there was no time to reconnoiter the area. Major Thompson's battalion would have to learn about street fighting in the Citadel the hard way.

At 2015 on 12 February, Thompson radioed Colonel Hughes at MACV about his planned attack the next morning, noting that the two battalions of Vietnamese marines, which were to help protect his extreme right flank, had not yet arrived. Although they had arrived, somehow Major Thompson had not been told. Thompson had said nothing about the Vietnamese airborne in his message to Hughes even though the airborne units had departed the ARVN 1st Division CP that same day.

"If there was any confusion it was a communications problem," Truong said later. "I was in daily contact with the Airborne Task Force commander. He was a good friend of mine. I passed on all the information I had to the Marines."

According to one account of the battle in the Citadel, the marines were extremely critical of the ARVN over this incident, strongly hinting that the lack of intelligence about the airborne withdrawal had resulted in unnecessary marine casualties.

"If I had known the Vietnamese airborne was gone I would have planned differently," Thompson insisted nearly 30 years later.

The U.S. advisors with the airborne units claim that the marines had to have known about the withdrawal because it took place right in front of them.

"Normally you would have a relief in place, but we were under orders to pull back and get on those LCUs," said Captain Cobb, the U.S. advisor with the ARVN 2nd Airborne Battalion. "It really bothers me that the marines thought we pulled out early and left them high and dry. We pulled back because we were told to. My guys never ran from anybody or anything."

Captain Blair, the 9th Airborne Battalion advisor, remembered meeting with one of the marine company commanders early on 12 February to brief him on the 9th's departure.

"We were all set to leave on some choppers that morning and had assembled at the 1st Division compound, but the choppers never showed up," Blair said. "I talked to this marine captain and then we went back to our positions. Later that day, we returned to the heliport at the division HQ and flew out to Phu Bai."

Whatever the circumstances, the marines were caught by surprise when they moved out on the morning of 13 February. In the first hour of the attack Thompson's lead element, Alpha Company, suffered two killed and 33 wounded. The wounded included the company commander, Capt. J. J. Bowe, and his executive officer. Already understrength, Alpha Company was withdrawn to reorganize and was never again an effective force in Hue. By noon, Major Thompson was forced to request the return of Delta Company, which had been temporarily reassigned to duty south of the Perfume River.

The marines did run into some friendly forces on their initial move and they assumed it was a rear-guard element of the airborne. In fact, it may have been some troops from the ARVN 1st Division's 3rd Regiment who were temporarily assigned to replace a section of the airborne line.

Thompson was forced to call up Charlie Company to replace Alpha Company on the point. Charlie Company immediately ran into withering fire from high atop the wall and from rooftops and second-story windows. The marines, inexperienced in street fighting, were confused and hesitated to move forward. It would take them another day or two to get the hang of street fighting, just as it had earlier for their sister battalions, 1/1 and 2/5, in the southern part of Hue.

Many years later, an embittered platoon leader of Charlie Company, 2nd Lt. Nicholas Warr, wrote that the marines were victims of political expediency in the disaster that took place in Hue Citadel on 13 February 1968. In his book *Phase Line Green, the Battle for Hue, 1968,* Warr said he was never told that his unit was replacing any ARVN airborne troops. He was instructed by his company commander, Lt. Scott Nelson, to proceed to the northern edge of Mai Thuc Loan Street (Phase Line Green) and wait for a coordinated frontal assault across the thoroughfare.

He was also told that there would be no preparation fire so as to limit damage to the Citadel, which the Vietnamese considered a national shrine. It was purely a political decision, one that even Major Thompson could not do a thing about. It was a trade-off, marines for buildings.

Warr wrote in disgust:

This insanity, these damnable rules of engagement that prevented American fighting men from using the only tactical assets that gave us an advantage during firefights—that of our vastly superior firepower represented by air strikes, artillery and naval gunfire—these orders continued to remain in force and hinder, wound and kill 1/5 Marines until the fourth day of fighting inside the Citadel of Hue.

In fact, after the initial rules of engagement were rescinded and 1/5's frantic requests for heavy support were finally approved it took another three days of heavy fighting, including many artillery missions; round after round of 90-mm cannon fire from the tanks and 106-mm recoilless rifles from the Ontos; many sorties of napalm, 250-pound and 500-pound high explosive bombs from F-4s; and even some naval gunfire, combined with the small arms and M-79 grenades of two Marine rifle companies (Alpha and Bravo) before the first block directly across Phase Line Green on that first day was finally secured. In the process, all the two-story buildings lining the southern enemy side of Phase

Line Green were flattened. So much for trying to protect this valuable real estate.

Warr, a farm boy from southwestern Oregon, had every reason to be bitter. His 51-man 1st Platoon of Charlie Company suffered seven killed and 20 wounded that first day. The survivors were reassigned to other platoons for the rest of the campaign as the first platoon was dissolved. When the battle for the Citadel finally ended, there were only 13 members of Warr's original platoon left.

It took 7 hours for 1/5 to finally reach Phase Line Green that first day. At 1500 the unit was ordered to cease for the day, consolidate its positions, and get ready for the next day.

That first day of combat for 1/5 was a busy one back at the ARVN 1st Division HQ as well. A steady stream of wounded marines had made its way back to the LZ for evacuation. Because of the weather and deadly enemy fire, helicopters had only a brief period to get in and out of the Citadel. Because fire came from three sides, strict air corridors were established: pilots who varied their flight paths risked getting shot down. Before the battle in the Citadel was finally over, some 60 helicopters were either shot down or took damaging hits over the city.

The first batch of wounded marines looked dazed. Many of them had experience fighting in the rice paddies, but this house-to-house combat was new to them. Jeeps and flatbed vehicles called "mules" raced in and out of the division compound all day carrying dead and wounded marines. Some of the wounds were gruesome, and some proved fatal.

All of us pitched in to help get the wounded medical attention. Others hung out by the stretchers as moral support, offering cigarettes or a sympathetic ear. The dead were covered with ponchos and put in an area by the heliport for evacuation. The living had first priority, however.

It was déjà vu for me, having gone through the same scene south of the river. These marines in the Citadel looked just as young as their brothers had earlier in the battle. They were also just as stoic, clenching their teeth to bear the pain rather than crying out. The blood was just as red. The dead were just as dead.

All five of Lieutenant Morrison's tanks were hit during the first day, and one was temporarily disabled. The narrow streets and courtyard walls left the tanks with little room to maneuver, and the lumbering 50-ton vehicles, which were forbidden to use their 90mm cannons, became easy targets. Some crewmen complained of headaches from the B-40 rockets that banged into the tanks' hulls, and others suffered concussions and had to be medevaced. All five tanks returned to the division CP for repairs that first day and did so each day they were in action.

Morrison walked around one of his tanks, looked at the dents and burn marks, and shook his head.

"Hey Lieutenant, take a look at this," one of his crewmen called out. A large burn mark just to the left of the driver's eye opening was still hot to the touch. "A little bit to the right and I would be history. Ain't war a bitch."

The crewman's hands shook as he tried to light a cigarette. He spoke in a loud voice as if his hearing was impaired. It probably was. Later that night, he got one of his buddies to open his C ration box and the cans inside because he was still shaking so badly that he could barely get the food to his mouth.

A couple of reporters wandered over to one of the tanks and struck up a conversation with the crewmen. Just kids, the crewmen enjoyed their moment in the limelight, bragging of their exploits that day and embellishing each story with false bravado and a heavy dose of machismo.

"There was one dink we blasted off the top of a building who turned a complete somersault before he hit the pavement like a turd from a tall cow's ass," gushed one tanker as his crew laughed behind him.

My friend Mike Morrow, who had been out with one of the ARVN battalions before Tet, dropped in to say hello. Morrow was in the field with the ARVN 4th Battalion, 3rd Regiment, which had been surrounded and nearly wiped out at the outset of the battle. He was still jumpy from the experience. We spent the night swapping war stories and offering opinions on the war itself. We talked right through a mortar attack. I can still hear the clang and rattle of shrapnel on my tin roof. Morrow referred to mortar rounds as "random agents of doom."

Like many of his colleagues in the civilian press, Morrow was thoroughly against the war in Vietnam. It was not that he was against the military or his country; he just did not believe that the United States had any of its national interests at stake in Vietnam. He believed that his country was throwing away its youth in a venture that was not only ill advised but impossible to win. The cost in lives, which he had seen firsthand too many times, was particularly troubling to him, as it was to everyone. The military had the politicians hoodwinked, he argued, and the politicians were conning the public.

We had a lot of good-natured arguments, but mostly we talked just to make us feel better.

"The trouble with you, Morrow, is that you don't have any experience in wearing a uniform," I said, more to get him mad than anything else. "Do you think if the U.S. military packed up its weapons and went home, all the killing would stop? There are a lot of people who think if we leave it will only get worse. Once South Vietnam falls into the hands of the Communists, who's next?"

"It's all none of our goddam business," Morrow shot back.

We dug into a couple of boxes of C rations, swapping stuff we did not like. There was nothing to drink; the water system was out at the compound, just as it was throughout the city. Without any purification tablets, nobody touched the water that was available.

The latrines were foul, too. Nobody had time to clean them. Everyone was too busy trying to stay alive. As a result, many staked out their own latrines: this had become quite a problem early in the battle.

"If we don't stand up to aggression here, it will just encourage it elsewhere. Where does it stop?" I asked Morrow as I devoured a can of peaches.

"The domino theory is full of crap," Morrow shot back as he brushed some crumbs from his beard. "Is it worth all this destruction, all this killing? I think not."

The next day we went out and saw for ourselves what the Allies were up against in the Citadel. You did not have far to travel to get to the front lines. In November

1970, Morrow, still an independent stringer, was disaccredited by the South Vietnamese government for addressing a meeting of anti–President Thieu demonstrators.

The clearance of the Citadel was not moving fast enough for General Westmoreland. With every other enemy action of the Tet offensive in South Vietnam under control, Westmoreland was under mounting pressure from Washington to get Hue off the front pages so that the Allies could get on with winning the war. Westmoreland even sent his deputy, Gen. Creighton Abrams, to MACV forward headquarters at Phu Bai on 13 February to keep him (Westmoreland) personally informed on the progress in Hue.

It was clear as 14 February began that little progress could be made until 1/5's left flank, the northeast wall, could be neutralized. The wall, which varied in thickness from 20 to 40 feet, was dominated by a two-story tower above the Dong Ba Gate. The Dong Ba Tower, which the marines called the Dong Ba Porch, overlooked the entire area. The marines tried to work their way up onto the wall but were turned back again and again by heavy fire and a hail of grenades.

Tanks were unable to render effective fire because of the dense concentration of buildings. Barely able to squeeze through the narrow streets, the tanks had no room to maneuver. The same was true later for the Ontos vehicles with their 106mm recoilless rifles. The narrow passageways also produced echoes, which made it difficult to determine where fire was coming from. Ricochets could strike from any direction, and many of the injuries were caused by flying masonry chips and concussions. A few strategically placed machine guns in well-fortified positions could hold up an entire company, but in this case they were holding up an entire battalion.

The marines could not get across Mai Thuc Loan Street. The enemy sniper fire was simply too intense. As long as the enemy held the high ground and could watch every move the marines made, it was suicidal to try anything sudden in the open.

The Citadel was proving to be a much tougher nut to crack than the more wide-open terrain of the southern part of the city, especially in the absence of any heavy supporting fire. For one thing, the buildings in the Citadel seemed to be constructed of a much sturdier mix of stone and masonry. The narrower streets made it much easier for the enemy to throw up roadblocks of overturned vehicles or household furniture. Each structure seemed to have its own surrounding high wall or hedgerow. Pieces of broken glass or other sharp objects were embedded in the tops of the walls, and the hedgerows were laced with barbed wire. With all the rubble on the sidewalks and in the street, the marines had to watch their step to avoid tripping. Watching one's feet made it tough to spot snipers.

The NVA forces had had a couple of weeks to prepare their defensive positions in the Citadel. Firing positions were cleverly concealed not only in buildings and on rooftops but in spider holes at street level. The thick shrubbery between houses gave the enemy an almost invisible fighting position. It was also very easy for the marine riflemen to be distracted by the enormity of the architecture. Further, many of the houses had their own bunkers or foxholes, which made every building a separate defensive position.

Slow and easy was the only way to go. The marines had to make sure that they did not accidentally walk past any hidden enemies who could pop up and attack them from the rear.

"There was virtually no visibility at all. If you could find 20 meters of open space you were lucky," Major Thompson said. "Fighting in the Citadel was unlike anything I had ever experienced. We were in such close quarters with the enemy, often just meters away. We had no room to fire and maneuver. In essence, the fighting was an exercise of reducing fortified positions."

The same situation faced the ARVN troops in the western section of the Citadel, except that the ARVN did not have any tanks or 106mm recoilless rifles. Also, the ARVN troops were at the bottom of the priority list for supporting fire and resupply.

The situation in the western half of the Citadel was just as chaotic, a condition made even worse by an obvious lack of leadership. The two battalions of Vietnamese marines were supposed to launch a coordinated attack in a southeasterly direction on the other side of the Imperial Palace compound but were delayed. Enemy troops were still in their rear. In fact, elements of General Truong's 3rd Regiment were cut off and surrounded on 13 February. It took 2 days of fighting and another heroic effort by the Hac Bao Company to break the encirclement.

While action was underway in their rear, the Vietnamese marines could not—or would not—begin their push. So they sat and they waited.

Meanwhile Major Thompson, after his troops were unable to budge from Phase Line Green for a second day and casualties continued to escalate, finally got the approval to use heavy weapons. No half-measures were to be taken from now on. The full package was laid on, 105mm howitzers and 8-inch guns from Phu Bai, as well as an air and sea bombardment. After 1/5 pulled back a couple of hundred yards to get clear of the barrage, the coordinated onslaught began late in the afternoon of 14 February and continued throughout the night.

The symphony of sound and fury that afternoon and through the night was awesome, particularly the naval gunfire. Stationed more than 2 miles offshore in the South China Sea, the destroyer USS *Manley* lobbed 50 rounds from its 5-inch guns, and the cruiser USS *Providence* fired 150 rounds from its 6-inch guns into the vicinity of the Dong Ba Gate. Most of the rounds were fuse-delayed high-explosive charges to ensure the greatest penetration before exploding.

One of the best places to watch the bombardment, other than in a spotter plane, was from the roof of the ARVN 1st Division headquarters. The view was spectacular and a little dangerous. I could watch the relatively slow-moving Skyraiders gliding in from the east and west, but I risked showing myself to an enemy sniper. For the most part, however, enemy sharpshooters hunkered down during the barrage. The rooftop was used by liaison officers and forward observers to adjust and coordinate a multitude of missions. But there were some staff officers and media people on the roof, as well.

The air attack also included a few jets when the weather permitted, including the single-seat F-100s and A-37 trainers and the twin-seat F-4 Phantom. The jets flew out of Da Nang, Tuy Hoa, and Pleiku. The bulk of the ordnance, however, was delivered by the workhorse propeller-driven Skyraiders, flown by both Vietnamese and U.S. pilots.

It was almost like watching a thunderstorm. I could see the explosions a split second before I heard the rumble. Chunks of mortar flew a hundred feet in the air after the delay fuses exploded and then fell to earth in all directions. Training my binoculars to the east I could see the lightning-like flashes of the naval guns of the U.S. Seventh Fleet.

The naval shells sounded like freight trains roaring past a crossing on some Midwestern plain. I had first heard the guns on 3 February when I was on the south side of the river. It was later reported that the U.S. Navy had fired over 4,700 shells into Hue and surrounding areas during the battle. That seemed high, but many of the fire missions were called in by friendly troops to the west of Hue, which meant the shells traveled right over the Citadel on their way to the target.

When the naval guns were not firing, the heavily loaded Skyraiders and jets roared in with high-explosive bombs, napalm, and tear gas. It was hard to imagine anyone surviving this continuous bombardment—but the enemy soldiers did. In fact, some of them popped out of their holes to fire rounds at the departing planes in a show of defiance. It was a glowing testament not only to the enemy's fortitude and resilience but to the builders of this 19th-century fortress as well.

The artillery bombardments in the Citadel were especially dangerous because the marine guns to the south at Phu Bai had to fire into the faces of the infantry they were supporting. As a result, artillery fire in the Citadel was limited. To compensate, the marines relied heavily on their 4.2-inch mortar capability from firing positions near Doc Lao Park on the south bank of the Perfume River.

The coordination of fire support was a complex endeavor, and much of the credit for its successful implementation belonged to the senior advisor, Colonel Adkisson. One of the first things he did when he had arrived in the Citadel 10 days before was to establish a central agency at the ARVN 1st Division HQ to coordinate and control artillery, air, and naval fire. Manned by U.S. advisors, the agency was put to a severe test on 14–15 February. At times air and artillery missions were carried out simultaneously, often in two languages.

The fire control center at the 1st Division compound was one wild and crazy scene with dozens of personnel running around in a near frenzy. Each mission was plotted with as much care as possible. Adjustments, confirmation, and requests for more fire in different locations kept the fire support staff hopping like frogs on a hot stove.

Coordinating air strikes in such a compact area was the trickiest part. Normal clearance requirements for skyspots, as they were called, were 2,000 meters from friendly troops, but in the Citadel it was reduced to 500 meters and, in some cases, even less. All air strikes were planned to cross the Citadel walls at low angles (30 degrees or less) and in a direction that would not overfly friendly troops. To prevent casualties from "long" bombs, sometimes caused by hang-ups in releasing the bombs, all strikes approached the walls from inside the Citadel and crossed to the outside. To make matters a little more dangerous, only 750-pound bombs were available instead of the requested 250-pounders.

Napalm was the bomb of choice as the battle raged on and on.

"Normal bombing just creates more rubble that the enemy can dig back down into," one of the U.S. Air Force forward observers said. "With napalm, if it doesn't set them on fire, it sucks out the oxygen from the bunkers. Napalm is the best thing you can use against bunker complexes, no question about it."

Delta Company, which had been released back to Major Thompson's control, was trying to reach the Citadel while the bombardment was underway. The company commander, Capt. Myron Harrington, his command group, and one rifle squad managed to hitch a ride on a resupply LCU on the afternoon of 14 February, but the LCU commander refused to return and get the rest of the company because of the heavy shelling.

Looking back on all the LCU and Vietnamese junk runs made through the narrow waterways to the back door of the Citadel, it seems incredible that more vessels were not sunk and more casualties taken. The channel from the loading dock on the south side of the river all the way to the Citadel was through completely hostile territory.

Captain Harrington spent the next several hours on the radio, pleading with anyone who would listen to help him find transportation to the Citadel for the rest of his company. The South Vietnamese Navy finally answered his call, providing three motorized patrol junks. Just before dark, as the crowded junks approached the dock outside the Citadel, a U.S. Marine F-4B Phantom jet streaked overhead and dropped several tear gas canisters on the wall. The wind shifted and carried the gas over the junks, forcing many of the 100 marines, who were not equipped with gas masks, to jump overboard. There were no injuries, however.

Late the next morning after the bombardment had been lifted, Major Thompson assigned Harrington's Delta Company to the area's hot spot, the left flank along the northeastern wall. The company had left one of its platoons on the other side of the river for convoy security duty on Route 1. Once again, the marines went into battle in piecemeal fashion.

Harrington's understrength company immediately ran into stiff resistance from the Dong Ba Tower area. A squad from the 1st Platoon climbed up on the wall about 150 meters from the tower and slowly began inching forward under covering fire. When the squad reached the base of the tower it was reinforced by another squad, and by nightfall of 15 February the objective was taken. It had cost Delta Company 6 killed and 50 wounded. Forced out briefly during the night, the 1st Platoon counterattacked and retook the tower.

Delta Company spent the next day consolidating its gains made the previous day and edging ever slightly forward. By nightfall after 2 days in the Citadel, Delta Company's casualty figures had reached 13 killed and 80 wounded, with another 15 soldiers patched up and returned to duty.

General Truong used the lull on 16 February to fly down to Phu Bai and brief Vice-President Nguyen Cao Ky. Truong told Ky that the Allies were beginning to turn up the pressure and the enemy was starting to crack. Ky promised Truong additional support and expressed his confidence in a total victory. Ky also said he would accept the responsibility for any damage or destruction of schools, hospitals, and cultural structures if it was necessary to drive the enemy from the city. Ky, too, was under pressure to get the embarrassing struggle in Hue over with.

Later that day, a third battalion of Vietnamese marines finally arrived in the Citadel. The fresh 700-man unit was sent into action the next day with its sister units near the western corner of the wall.

Briefing the new ARVN soldiers on the terrain was Lieutenant Hue. Hue's Hac Bao Company guided the Vietnamese marines into position and then participated in a push along the northwestern wall. The fresh unit also helped relieve pressure on the 1st Battalion, 3rd Regiment, which had fought off an encirclement the day before.

The Hac Bao Company was now up to about 150 men, as many of its soldiers who were on duty on the south side before the battle or trapped inside the Citadel began making their way back to the company. One of the returning troops told Lieutenant Hue that he had been captured across the river and, with about 50 others, made to dig what they were told was a trench to protect them from artillery fire. In fact it was a burial trench. The NVA had lined up the 50 men along the edge of the trench and started shooting them in the back of the head. When the executioner reached the Hac Bao soldier, the latter reached up and plunged a knife into the enemy soldier's stomach and made his escape.

Lieutenant Hue also captured several prisoners who told him morale was low and that many troops were suffering from shell shock. One unit of Vietnamese marines reported overrunning a building and finding three enemy soldiers chained to their machine guns. Other prisoners said that although they had orders to stay and fight, many of their officers had already withdrawn from the Citadel. One dead soldier killed by the Hac Bao had a tattoo etched on the upper part of his right arm that, when translated, read: "Born in North Vietnam, to Die in South Vietnam."

The enemy suffered a huge blow on the night of 16 February when an Allied fire mission nearly wiped out a battalion-sized force trying to infiltrate through a gate on the southwest wall. According to U.S. Marine Lt. Alexander Wells, a forward observer with the Vietnamese marines, ARVN troops had intercepted a radio message ordering a group of enemy reinforcements to cross into the Citadel through a specific gate at a certain time. Lieutenant Wells then scheduled an artillery mission to commence at the exact time of the enemy movement.

"There was screaming on the enemy radio. They had received a direct hit on the moat bridge, killing their general," Wells later reported. The general apparently was a regimental commander of the enemy forces within the Citadel. About midnight, his successor radioed his superiors the news of the general's death and requested permission to withdraw his forces from the city. Higher headquarters denied this request and told the new commanding officer to remain in position and fight.

Despite the orders to stay and fight, it was becoming clear that even though the NVA forces were not quite ready to leave the Citadel, they were adjusting their strategy from a defense in place to a rear-guard action.

More U.S. Army troops were also committed to sealing off the enemy's escape routes to the west. The 1st Cavalry

Division, which had committed its 2nd Battalion, 12th Cavalry Regiment back on 2 February and then reinforced that unit with the 5th Battalion, 7th Cavalry Regiment three days later, upped the ante on 18 February with the 1st Battalion, 7th Cav. Also joining the fight that day was the 2nd Battalion (Airborne), 501st Infantry of the 101st Airborne Division, which had moved into the area in late January.

The main target of the army troops continued to be a wooded NVA regimental headquarters area near the village of La Chu about 5 kilometers northwest of Hue and west of Route 1. The area was believed to be the enemy's main staging and resupply base for those troops fighting in Hue. The cav units had been dealing with this formidable pocket of resistance for over 2 weeks with little result. The fighting at La Chu was the cav's baptism of fire since moving from central II Corps to I Corps the previous month. The Americans had gained a healthy respect for their NVA adversaries, who were proving far more dogged and resilient than the Vietcong forces they had faced previously.

The initial cav unit to attempt to engage the enemy headquarters complex at La Chu, Lt. Col. Dick Sweet's 2/12 Cav, was outnumbered and badly mauled on 4–5 February. The unit managed to escape heavy casualties by executing a difficult night withdrawal to a secure hilltop location, where they remained for nearly a week.

The next cavalry unit sent into the wooded enemy enclave was Lt. Col. Jim Vaught's 5/7. Vaught, who had just been given command of 5/7 a few days earlier, moved his unit south from Camp Evans to PK 17 on 4 February. The next day, the same day that Sweet's unit had completed its withdrawal, Vaught led his battalion toward the enemy stronghold.

Like Sweet, Vaught went into combat on foot because of a shortage of troop-carrying helicopters. The weather was cold, rainy, and overcast. The troopers met light resistance the first couple of days until they entered the wooded area around La Chu on 8 February. The lead platoon was ambushed from three sides, and every man in the point squad was either killed or wounded.

The wounded could not be medevaced until after dark because the NVA had most of the clearings staked out with machine gun fire. When the choppers finally arrived the weather was so bad the crews could not locate the strobe lights that marked the LZ. The pilots were forced to turn on their landing lights and hope that the ground personnel could guide them down safely.

Over the course of the next few days, cav troopers came to call the enemy strongpoint "T-T Woods." The "T-T" stood for tough titty.

On 9 February, Lieutenant Colonel Sweet's 2/12 Cav got back in the fight, leaving its hilltop position 5 kilometers west of Hue and attacking a hamlet 2 kilometers south of La Chu. On 12 February, both battalions were supposed to jump off on a coordinated assault of La Chu, but 2/12 could not get going because of strong local resistance. Lieutenant Colonel Vaught's force was delayed because supporting artillery fire was not available until the afternoon.

Vaught's attack soon bogged down because of heavy enemy fire. Four separate jet strikes were conducted against the stronghold despite the poor weather. None of them did any significant damage, however.

As they had done more than a week earlier, the enemy

let the cav troopers enter the tree line and get past carefully camouflaged positions before opening fire from two different directions. Caught in the middle, the three assaulting companies were immediately pinned down. Fifteen minutes after the attack began it was called off at a cost of nine killed and 35 wounded.

T-T Woods had more than lived up to its nickname.

Disappointed but not discouraged, the cavalry's division commander, Maj. Gen. Jack Tolson, flew out to see Lieutenant Colonel Vaught on 13 February. Tolson told Vaught that he hoped to mount a three-battalion attack on the enemy stronghold as soon as he could assemble enough troops. Tolson hoped that the impending arrival of the cav 2nd Brigade from central II Corps would allow the use of the 1/7 Cav, which was now serving as the palace guard at Camp Evans. Also arriving in the area were elements of the U.S. 101st Airborne Division, which were now guarding the ARVN base at PK 17. Tolson was even optimistic about getting some armored help for the assault.

On 15 February, Lieutenant Colonel Sweet's 2/12 Cav and Company D, 2/501 Airborne were committed to a new attack on the La Chu area. The latter unit was attached to Lieutenant Colonel Vaught's 5/7 Cav for operational control. The next day the rest of 2/501 came aboard.

A huge package of supporting arms fire was laid on the La Chu area on 16 February in preparation for an all-out push to overrun the regimental headquarters complex. The package included 1,000 high-explosive rounds from land-based artillery and 4,000 high-explosive rounds from U.S. Navy ships in the South China Sea. The barrage also included 35 tons of assorted high-explosive and napalm bombs from U.S. and Vietnamese aircraft.

On 17 February Vaught's operations officer, Maj. Charles R. Baker, flew over T-T Woods in an O-1 spotter plane but had a difficult time locating the NVA defensive positions. The pilot went in for a closer look, diving down to 100 feet. The fourth such dive not only drew fire from enemy positions but caused Baker to lose his lunch.

All four army battalions engaged in aggressive patrolling over the next few days, slowly moving in a southeasterly direction west of Route 1 toward La Chu Woods. With their area of operations extended south to the Perfume River, the plan was for the four battalions to get themselves in position to jump off on a coordinated attack on 21 February and finally eliminate the enemy's main supply and control point.

The enemy had also been engaging in aggressive patrolling in the past few days, testing the patience and nerves of the cav and airborne troopers who were unaccustomed to facing front-line NVA troops. At night, the NVA units sometimes sounded bugles or blew whistles, keeping the green U.S. troops awake and tense.

D-Day was 21 February. The 5/7 Cav would attack from the north, the 2/12 Cav from the south, and the 2/501 Airborne from the west. The 1/7 Cav would support the 5/7 Cav from the north. Two companies of the 2/12 Cav would be withheld as a reserve force. There were no tanks available, but General Tolson did manage to secure the services of one U.S. Army M-42 Duster with its dual 40mm cannons.

The attack plan was complex and not easily understood by some of the troopers of the 5/7 Cav. Some, apparently unnerved by the NVA's nightly mind games of the past few days, were threatening to not participate in the attack. The plan called for two companies to seize their first objectives in the dark, then, after a brief but intense artillery and naval gunfire barrage around dawn, link up with the rest of the battalion for a coordinated attack south through T-T Woods, hopefully all the way through La Chu to the NVA headquarters bunker. The bunker, which had been designed and built with U.S. finances, was constructed of ferroconcrete. It was three stories high and two stories deep.

Initially all went well. The night objectives were seized without opposition, and discipline was excellent. Then, shortly after the lead elements of 5/7's B Company entered a bamboo thicket, its commander, Capt. Howard Prince, was seriously wounded by a mortar round, leaving only one officer in the company. When Lieutenant Colonel Vaught heard on the radio that Captain Prince was down he immediately ordered his operations officer, Major Baker, to hustle up to the front and take command of B Company.

When Baker reached the bamboo thicket Prince was unconscious. The stunned troopers had hunkered down behind whatever cover they could find and were waiting for someone to tell them what to do. Behind them was Company D, also hunkered down waiting for Company B to get its act together. The scene had all the makings of a disaster.

Company B, it was later learned, had walked straight into heavy fire from a newly constructed bunker guarding the NVA's outer defenses. This had to be neutralized before any advance could continue. Major Baker asked for volunteers to take out the bunker. With 40mm covering fire from the battalion's lone Duster, Pfc. Albert Rocha of D Company crawled forward with a specially rigged pole charge. A rifle shot from within the bunker hit the handguard of his M16 but Rocha pushed on. Racing up to assist was 1st Lt. Frederick Krupa of D Company. Then, while Rocha provided covering fire, Krupa shoved the 10-pound pole charge through an opening and held on while the NVA tried to push it out. Rocha picked off one NVA soldier exiting the rear of the bunker just before the charge exploded.

The destruction of the bunker seemed to energize the cav troopers and marked the beginning of the end for the enemy force at T-T Woods. When Allied forces finally reached the enemy's three-story headquarters bunker later that day, it was abandoned. A 2/12 Cav trooper attached to the 5/7 Cav led a graves registration team to the former mortar pit in which 11 of his comrades had been temporarily buried on the night of 4 February.

The 2/501st Airborne also had an especially bloody engagement with the enemy that day. Two squad leaders with the 2/501's point element, Delta Company, S. Sgt. Joe R. Hooper and Sgt. Clifford C. Sims, were each awarded the Congressional Medal of Honor, the latter posthumously, for action at La Chu Woods.

Hooper led his eight-man squad across the same stream the 2/12 Cav had crossed 2 weeks earlier on its night withdrawal, and set up a machine gun position just inside the nearby woods. No sooner had they set up the position when two grenades exploded, wounding Hooper in the leg and groin. The injuries did not stop him from recrossing the river and leading more men into the woods.

Once in the woods, Staff Sergeant Hooper helped

destroy five enemy positions in hand-to-hand combat, even bayoneting an NVA officer. Though severely wounded, Hooper continued to lead the assault into the woods.

Despite an unwritten rule prohibiting Medal of Honor recipients from serving again in combat, Hooper returned to Vietnam 2 years later to serve once more with the 101st Airborne. He died after a sudden illness on 6 May 1979.

Staff Sergeant Sims led his squad against an enemy force that had pinned down another platoon from Delta Company. Moving forward, Sims's squad came upon a burning ammunition shack: exploding ordnance injured two men almost immediately, and Sims moved the rest of the men back.

On the move again, Sims and his men were advancing through the woods when they suddenly heard a distinctive click—the sound of a trip wire activating a booby trap. Shouting a warning to his men, Sims threw himself on the charge and was killed instantly by the blast. Saved by their squad leader, the men pressed on through the woods.

When the battle was over later that day, all but eight of the 190 members of Delta Company had been killed or wounded.

By the end of 21 February, all four of the battalions had reached their objectives and closed to within 5 kilometers of Hue Citadel. The distance was closed to two and a half kilometers the next day, hastening the enemy's withdrawal plans from the Citadel.

Thanks to the intense preparation fires and a well-coordinated Allied assault, the enemy chose to slip away from La Chu rather than risk capture or annihilation. When the NVA forces were compelled to give up their headquarters complex on the outskirts of Hue it sealed the fate of their comrades remaining behind in the Citadel.

When that happened the strategic battle for Hue was over.

CHAPTER TWELVE

The Beginning of the End

The enemy was beginning to show the effects of constant pressure, but it was equally apparent that friendly forces, particularly Major Thompson's marine battalion, were running out of gas, not to mention troops, bullets, and food.

The overcast weather and accurate sniper fire had greatly limited helicopter resupply missions and the evacuation of wounded. The LZ at the ARVN 1st Division headquarters was crowded with wounded troops, prisoners, and vehicles waiting to carry supplies to the front lines. Medevacs for the seriously wounded had top priority, so the slightly wounded and the dead, who were loosely wrapped in ponchos, stayed where they were along the fringe of the LZ. It was a gruesome sight to see the faces of the dead suddenly uncovered by the wash of a helicopter as it landed or took off at the LZ.

The ARVN 1st Division HQ was also swamped with refugees and prisoners, all of whom went through some kind of interrogation process. The refugees were herded into a couple of nearby school buildings, where they more or less camped out on their own. The prisoners, blindfolded and tied together with rope, sat on their haunches waiting for a flight out to some higher headquarters. Occasionally, ARVN soldiers walked by and spit on the prisoners. Some poked them with their rifles or delivered a slap to the head. The prisoners rarely cried out. They stood up to the verbal and physical abuse without a whimper, showing a hardness that was disarming to the ARVN soldiers and Americans alike.

Some of the prisoners had burlap bags over their heads. They were dressed in ragged T-shirts and shorts and either wore sandals or were barefoot. None that I saw wore uniforms, boots, or helmets. They looked like a bunch of dirty hobos and not at all what I thought a regular NVA soldier should look like.

Interrogations were sometimes conducted in a building on the other side of the compound. I heard some stories of what went on in that building and occasionally I could hear some yelling and screaming, but I never witnessed anything.

By 17 February General Westmoreland had seen and heard enough about Hue. He flew to Phu Bai that day for a council of war with his marine commander, General Cushman. Cushman, who had won the Navy Cross at Guam in World War II, had direct command of over 100,000 marines, sailors, and soldiers in I Corps, and yet the struggle in Hue went on and on. The ramrod Westmoreland kept asking the pudgy, bespectacled Cushman why sufficient force was not being used to end this embarrassment, for that was what Hue had become.

Westmoreland, a by-the-book army man from his days at West Point to the present, did not appear to fully understand nor appreciate the mentality of the Marine Corps. The marines, tempered by an almost fanatical pride, had fought hard to maintain an independence from the other branches of the service. What anyone else could do, they could do better—without any outside help. That was why some of the hardcore marines objected to the movement of two army divisions into their area and the establishment of MACV Forward. To emphasize their independence, the marines even insisted that their troops serve a 13-month tour in Vietnam, 1 more month than other branches of the service.

The marines believe deeply that what they start they finish. Nobody will ever say that a marine force could not or would not complete a task it had begun. To do otherwise would be to admit failure, and that was not a word in the marine vocabulary. It was this type of mentality that caused Westmoreland and other high-ranking army officials to shake their heads in wonderment.

Westmoreland immediately committed a third battalion (1/7) from the 1st Cavalry Division and a battalion (2/501) of the 101st Airborne Division to help in closing the back door to Hue. But it would be 4 more days before the marines could come up with the necessary troops to reinforce Major Thompson's battered command in the Citadel.

Abrams was not shy about voicing his opinion. On 20 February he radioed Cushman to say he considered "the measures so far taken [in the Citadel] to be inadequate." He also voiced his displeasure with the performance of the Vietnamese marines in the Citadel. Almost 2,000 men strong, the Vietnamese marines proved generally disappointing, leading Abrams to recommend to the ARVN Joint General Staff that they be replaced with an ARVN force that would fight, not delay.

Meanwhile, Thompson's marines plodded on in the Citadel. With Delta Company on the left, Bravo in the center, and Charlie on the right, 1/5 had maneuvered half-way down the Imperial Palace's northeast wall and were within three blocks of its main objective. Ironically, the closer 1/5 got to sweeping the NVA forces from its sector, the less it could call on supporting fire for fear of hitting its own troops. The enemy was clearly pulling back, using delaying and rear-guard tactics, but showed no intention of surrendering. Thompson's force was nearing exhaustion. By 17 February the marines were out of tank ammunition and shells for their 106mm recoilless rifles. They were also down to a 1-day supply of C rations.

On 18 February Gen. Truong, recognizing 1/5's deteriorating state, sent Lieutenant Hue and his Hac Bao Company to help Major Thompson secure his right flank along the wall of the Imperial Palace compound. Hue had been given permission from Truong to assault the palace itself if the opportunity arose.

"I asked Major Thompson to blow a hole in the wall, and my troops would rush in and kill everybody inside," Hue said. Thompson, after checking with Colonel Hughes, did not think it was a good idea and declined to accept Hue's offer.

"I told Major Thompson that we were ready to go and that I would take care of everything if he would just blow a hole in the wall," Hue said many years later. "He said no. His troops looked very tired so I offered to have my troops take over the point for awhile. I wanted the marines to relax a little bit, and Major Thompson agreed."

Thompson was under orders to maintain complete control over his area of operations. And that meant not letting any other unit, whether it be Vietnamese or U.S., steal any of the glory from the marines, particularly when there were so many correspondents following his battalion.

The marines also turned over a 16-year-old prisoner they had captured for Lieutenant Hue to interrogate. The prisoner told Hue that he had been captured by the Vietcong at the beginning of the battle and given an AK-47 rifle. On 13 February he was sent out to gather some food but instead surrendered to a marine.

When the Hac Bao Company was diverted to the northwest wall to help the ARVN 3rd Regiment, Hue took the prisoner along with him. The kid asked one of Hue's platoon sergeants to give him two grenades so that he could assault an enemy position alone, proving that he was not a VC soldier. Before he went on the mission, he told the sergeant that if he was killed to please have Lieutenant Hue deliver his body to his family as proof he was not VC. He survived without a scratch, but Hue still was not ready to give him a rifle, using him instead to run errands. A few days later, however, Hue finally gave him an M16, and the kid turned out to be a pretty good soldier.

Sgt. Steve Berntson was a writer, not a fighter. A marine correspondent, Berntson had been in Hue from the beginning. He and his partner, Sgt. Dale Dye, had roamed the mean streets south of the Perfume River for a week and a half with the marine grunts of 1/1 and 2/5 before moving over to the Citadel.

Trained as marines, Berntson and Dye did not hesitate to put down their pens and cameras and jump right into the action. They, as well as some civilian correspondents, helped evacuate the wounded and ferried supplies and ammo to the front lines. Time and again, they exposed themselves to heavy fire. On 19 February Berntson barely survived his closest brush with death.

After helping pull a badly wounded marine out of the line of fire, Berntson was knocked unconscious by a B-40 rocket. When he came to he could taste the blood oozing down from his forehead. He could see but he could not move. He recognized the faces of several civilian correspondents in the area, particularly UPI's Al Webb, David Greenway of *Time*, and Charles Mohr of the *New York Times*. All three had pitched in to help evacuate wounded marines. Webb had taken shrapnel in an ankle and leg, and Berntson had shrapnel in his chest and legs.

Berntson got through the ride back to the aid station at the ARVN 1st Division HQ and then passed out again. He woke up as the medics were carrying him to the LZ. Too weak to move, he panicked when the wash from the marine Sea Knight helicopter blew a poncho over his face: he was afraid that he might be considered dead. After passing out a third time, he awoke at the Phu Bai aid station.

Twelve years later, Webb, Greenway, and Mohr were all awarded Bronze Stars by the commandant of the Marine Corps, the only civilians so honored by the Corps during the Vietnam War. Berntson and Dye also received Bronze Stars.

By the end of 20 February, after 6 days of fighting, 1/5 had suffered 47 killed and 240 wounded (60 more wounded were patched up and returned to duty). Each of its four companies had fewer than a hundred men. Captain Harrington was the only officer left in Delta Company; three of Bravo Company's platoons were led by corporals. The troops had not been adequately fed in 4 days, and morale was lower than a GI's bootlaces.

"Part of the problem we had was that because of all

the replacements coming and going we never really got to know each other or the battalion very well," Major Thompson said.

There was nobody the marines could complain to. Even the chaplain had been killed. Army Maj. Aloysius P. McGonigal, who was the Catholic chaplain at the MACV compound, had volunteered to join Thompson's battalion when it shipped over to the Citadel back on 12 February. He disappeared on 17 February, and his body was found the next day in a building near the front lines. He had been killed by a shrapnel wound to the back of his head. In his short time with the marines Father McGonigal had made many friends, and his loss was deeply felt.

There were at least two dozen members of the news media trailing 1/5 during this period, camping out with the marines on the front lines and listening to all sorts of horror stories. The grunts were only too willing to air their grievances, and the correspondents kept their pens and cameras moving. Surprisingly, the death and destruction all around them was not foremost on the marines' gripe list. Crouching in the background looking for stories myself, I filled up a couple of notebooks on one visit to the front. One dust-covered grunt told a reporter,

> I can take the snipers and the mortars. What I'd really like is a minute or two of calm so I can take a shit. And, while I'm at it, how about some decent chow? All we get are C rations, cold C rations. We don't have the time to heat them up. Fires are frowned on. You like cold lima beans? Here, I'll trade you. I tell you when I get out of this chickenshit scene I'm gonna have a hot

bath, an even hotter woman and a thick, juicy steak, though not necessarily in that order.

Others took a more philosophical approach to their predicament.

"You know what else is fucked up about this war?" a marine private said to a couple of interested correspondents.

We don't really get a chance to waste a target, you know, like in basic training. The gooks hit and run or they hide. Sure, the artillery is getting some kills but we're not getting our share. Once in a while we flush out some gooks and get off a few rounds at them. But mostly we just shoot at buildings or windows. We never know if we get any kills. You understand how that feels to us? We're trained to kill gooks and we hardly ever get a chance to get one in our sights. That's why we're here, isn't it? I envy the snipers. A sniper I know in another outfit got credit for five kills. All of them were clean shots to the head. Man that must have felt good.

"And you know what else is the pits?" piped in another marine. "You don't get any sleep, any real sleep that is. At night we get together and a couple of us stay awake while the rest of us lie down on the ground for a nap. But whatever sleep you get is brief. You never forget where you are and you know that at any time the dinks could drop a mortar round in your lap."

Almost on cue, we could hear a mortar round leave a tube inside the palace compound. We scattered to find the best cover. It was just one round. We guessed the enemy was low on ammo, too.

The towers and thick walls of the Citadel reminded many of the grunts of a haunted medieval castle, a hunk of hard, cold stone against a gray, misty sky. Some of the marines, with their sunken eyes, looked like ghosts. They were unshaven, grimy, and covered with dust from the shattered brick and stone buildings. Sweat and blood-stains covered their fatigues. Elbows and knees stuck out of holes in their uniforms, the same ones they had worn for two weeks.

The situation was no ghost story, however. It was deadly real.

The marines, who were trained to be a mobile, am-phibious reaction force, had become moles. They had be-come a static, immobile collection of rats, hunkered down in a junk pile of crumbled houses, surrounded by shell-pocked courtyard walls, burned-out automobiles, and downed trees and power lines. Death was waiting to tap them on the shoulder at any time, and many would never know where it came from. It was getting to the point where some of them did not seem to care.

The correspondents and TV crews, in groups of two and three, scurried from one fighting position to another looking for stories. And they found plenty of them. In a way, the reporters' presence was good for the marines: it took their minds off what had become almost an unbear-able nightmare. The correspondents also helped bring out some of the humor of the situation, which helped re-lieve some of the tension.

"What's the worst thing I've seen? I saw this gook with his head blown clean off," said one marine in re-sponse to a reporter's question.

We looked around for it but couldn't find it. How can you lose a head? I also saw one of our guys get blown 20 feet in the air by a mortar. When they carried him off to a medevac chopper his foot was dangling from his leg by a thin piece of flesh. The corpsman reached over and snipped the piece of flesh with a pair of scissors and put the foot in the guy's lap. The guy didn't make a sound. I guess he was passed out.

Body odor was a big problem with the marines. None of them had showered or shaved since arriving in the Citadel, and very few even had a spare pair of socks. The flak vests kept their shirts stuck to their bodies, trapping much of the odor.

"As bad as we smell, nobody goes anywhere without the vest, not in this place," a grunt told a reporter. "A friend of mine took a piece of shrapnel right in the chest. It blew him back 10 feet and gave him a nasty bruise. Without the vest, he wouldn't have a chest."

Many of the grunts had names or slogans written on their helmets. Some had peace buttons or other trinkets pinned to their shirts or vests. The inside of the helmet was a favorite place to keep letters and a short-timer's calendar with a stubby pencil to mark off the days remaining until they rotated home. It was checked every day, sometimes two and three times.

Among the popular helmet slogans were the macho types, like "Pray for War," "Born to Kill," "High on War," and "Swinging Dick." Others had a more philosophical view, like "Born to Die," "Why Me?" or "Time Is on My Side." Still others made statements with their graffiti, like "Hell Sucks."

Some of the troops had that "1,000-yard stare" and

appeared to have given up any hope of getting out of Hue alive.

"Man, the only way we're going to get out of here is on a stretcher or in one of those rubber suits," a grunt said to his buddy. "Hey, that may not be such a bad idea—on a stretcher, I mean."

Some of the troops were so weary and fed up that they talked about the best places to get a self-inflicted wound. A wound, not too serious, mind you, was a guaranteed ticket off the line. But it had to be bad enough to get medevaced. Any minor injury would be patched up and you would be right back on the line.

"The leg is the best place, not the foot but maybe in the calf," one grunt offered.

A couple of correspondents who had been listening in the background joined in on the conversation.

"I don't think shooting yourself is such a good idea," one of the press types said.

I knew a marine up at Khe Sanh who tried to do the same thing. He shot himself in the foot, and when the corpsman told his company commander what happened the old man was so pissed off he told the corpsman to give him an aspirin. By the time the wound was taken care of the guy had developed gangrene. It spread to his knee. They had to cut the leg off at the thigh. Now he's back home in a rocking chair cursing the day he ever joined the Corps.

The grunts, many of them teenagers, listened to the story with their mouths open, not knowing whether to believe it or not. None of them said a word as the correspondents shuffled off to another area.

Rarely was there a discouraging word said about the Marine Corps, however.

"You know why I'm not afraid of getting hit? Because the corpsmen here are the greatest," said a grunt. "They will do anything to see to it you have the best chance of survival. Marines don't abandon their own, either. As my DI told us in boot camp, it's against regulations for a marine to die."

Some of the grunts even found something positive about street fighting.

"It's much drier than a rice paddy," a sergeant said. "All these buildings offer plenty of cover and if you want to take a nap you can go into a building instead of digging a foxhole."

Major Thompson, who had barely slept in a week, was at the breaking point, both physically and mentally. He and his battalion had hit the wall and there were rumors he was about to be relieved. He did not care.

His relief was actually announced to reporters on 20 February by General Cushman. Cushman had ordered Colonel Hughes to fire Thompson, but Hughes said that he would resign first. Cushman then had to eat his words. The first Thompson heard of his near dismissal was in a letter from his wife, who read about his relief in her local newspaper.

Hughes, who had promised Thompson he would handle all interference from higher headquarters, had kept his word.

"The great thing about Colonel Hughes was that he took the pressure off me. He was very concerned about every Marine, and that wasn't always true with other officers in the Corps," Thompson said.

Finally, the marines found some fresh troops for Thompson. It would be Lima Company of the 3rd Battalion, 5th Regiment. The marines were determined that history would show that Hue Citadel was liberated by elements of the 5th Regiment and nobody else. Bravo 1/5, which had been reduced to 61 men, was pulled out of the Citadel for a much-needed rest after the arrival of Lima 3/5. Thompson was given these additional troops with the clear understanding that the rest of 1/5 would stay on the job until the end, even if it took every man he had. It very nearly did.

Spurred on by a last jolt of esprit de corps, Thompson ordered a night raid on 20 February that quickly occupied several multistory buildings on either side of the Thuong Tu Gate, just a hundred or so meters from the Citadel's main flagpole area.

Bolstered by the advance guard of Lima 3/5, Thompson began a big push on 21 February, wheeling his battalion to the right toward the Imperial Palace. At the same time west of the city, three battalions of the U.S. 1st Cavalry Regiment and a battalion of the 101st Airborne Division swept through the NVA's regimental command and resupply headquarters, slowly choking off the enemy's escape routes. Two days later the enemy commander in Hue was finally given permission to withdraw from the city.

Also joining the attack on 21 February were two battalions of Vietnamese rangers, who were given the assignment of clearing the enemy from the heretofore untouched Gia Hoi region east of the Citadel. That action finally silenced enemy fire that had harassed all the river traffic between the LCU dock on the south side of the Perfume River and the loading quay at the back door of the Citadel.

Enemy forces were on the run.

Strategically the battle for Hue was over, but the enemy was not about to leave without inflicting as much destruction, pain, and death as it could. Vietcong security units intensified their efforts to flush out South Vietnamese personnel who had remained hidden in the city during the battle. Hundreds of citizens of all ages were taken away for "meetings" and never returned. Others were executed on the spot.

Resistance continued to be fierce on 22 February as remnants of the enemy force, which had slowly withdrawn in and around the Imperial Palace compound, prepared for a last-ditch stand. The Allies had conscientiously avoided using any heavy firepower on the palace compound, but when three marine tanks were temporarily knocked out by B-40 rocket fire from inside the palace, the rules of the game changed.

For tank gunner Ed Scott, 22 February was the longest day of the war. Scott, of New Milford, Connecticut, had begun his second tour in Vietnam at Da Nang on 31 January. On 11 February he was part of a five-tank convoy that was rushed to Hue Citadel by LCU. All five tanks had been in continuous action for almost 2 weeks. Like most of the marines in Hue, Scott worried more about his creature comforts than the enemy.

"They always brought up ammunition but never any food. I went without eating for days during the fighting," Scott said later. Then, on 22 February, Scott's tank, which was maneuvering near the Imperial Palace wall, took a crippling hit that landed him in the hospital.

"All of a sudden, we got hit. To this day I don't know what they threw at us," Scott said.

It wasn't hand-held, that's for sure. The round penetrated 10 inches of steel. The round hit the turret and entered on the loader's side. He got killed along with the tank commander. I was wounded also. Pieces of shrapnel were flying inside and destroyed all the radios and started a flash fire. There was so much smoke you couldn't see anything. The driver was untouched because he sat in a separate compartment in the hull. He got us out of there and drove to an aid station. I hadn't been able to free myself. I had bodies on top of me trapping me inside. There isn't much room inside a tank.

Then, for the first time in the battle, an air strike was called on the Imperial Palace compound. One Skyraider was shot down during the run, but the pilot was rescued.

The fresh troops of Lima 3/5, after 1 day of on-the-job training in street fighting, spearheaded an attack that brought the marines to within a block of the palace. In the western section of the Citadel, the Vietnamese marines had pushed to within a block of the Huu Gate, the main access and egress point used by the enemy since the battle began.

With victory in sight on 23 February, Major Thompson and his exec, Major Wunderlich, almost did not live to see it. A marine M48 tank, which had become disoriented, accidentally fired a round into the battalion CP, showering both men with rubble. Luckily, both escaped without a scratch.

It was not the first time the marines were shelled by

their own troops. An Ontos vehicle had leveled two houses manned by marines earlier in the Citadel fighting, but no one was killed.

The last bit of resistance by the enemy occurred on the night of 23 February, when NVA troops launched a rocket and mortar attack against the ARVN 3rd Regiment near the northwest wall. The regimental CP took a direct mortar hit but suffered no casualties. The attack proved to be a parting gesture on the enemy forces' part and a cover for their own withdrawal.

Word spread quickly that plans were being made to assault the main flagpole area and the Imperial Palace compound the next day. It had been decided earlier that ARVN forces would be given the assignment of retaking these two historic sites. General Truong invited me to go along on the predawn raid at the flagpole, but for some reason I did not go, and I have regretted it ever since.

ARVN troops of the 2nd Battalion, 3rd Regiment, who had earned Major Thompson's scorn for nearly 2 weeks, were given the opportunity to seize the undefended flagpole area at 0500 on 24 February. The huge National Liberation Front flag that had flown for 25 days was hauled down, and the yellow and red flag of South Vietnam raised in its place. The troops stood at the base of the flagpole and cheered like conquering heroes.

The assignment of sweeping through the Imperial Palace was given to the newly promoted Captain Hue and his Hac Bao Company. After a brief artillery prep, the Black Panthers overcame light resistance and charged into the compound. The Hac Bao Company found the bodies of 64 enemy soldiers who appeared to have been killed by artillery. The enemy had left behind a cache of rifles and ammunition, along with the carcasses of a horse and a dog that they had slaughtered for food.

By 1800 effective resistance in the Citadel had ceased.

Outside the walls of the Citadel to the west, elements of the U.S. 1st Cavalry's 3rd Brigade continued its destruction of the enemy's regimental headquarters at La Chu. While 1/7 Cav remained in the La Chu area to police the battlefield and eliminate small pockets of resistance, the other three battalions—5/7 Cav, 2/12 Cav, and the 2/501 Airborne—continued to move east toward Hue and south to the Perfume River, meeting heavy resistance from enemy troops fleeing the battle area.

As the 1st Cav advanced toward Hue from the west and action continued in the Citadel, fire support coordination became a major concern. On 21 February, Brig. Gen. Oscar E. Davis, one of two assistant commanders of the 1st Cav, flew into the Citadel to become the area's fire support coordinator.

Davis was also sent to the Citadel to take overall command of the situation, a decision that was long overdue. Until Davis arrived the various Allied forces had acted in isolation from each other. The marines took their orders from Task Force X-Ray, the ARVN obeyed the commands of General Truong, and the U.S. Army troops to the west, ignorant of what the marines and ARVN forces were doing, operated on their own.

The lack of a hands-on overall commander meant that there was no general battle plan for retaking Hue, no one to set priorities, and no one person to accept the responsibility if things went wrong. Also, there was no overall system to ensure an equitable distribution of resupply. The marines and army scrambled to take care of their own, and the ARVN got next to nothing. It was a command blunder of the first order.

Unfortunately, by the time General Davis had arrived in Hue there was not much left to coordinate.

On 22 February the ARVN 21st and 39th Ranger Battalions, two-thirds of an I Corps reaction force, arrived in Hue and were deployed in the Gia Hoi section just to the east of the city. The rangers conducted a 3-day sweep of the area, meeting light resistance.

There was still plenty of heavy fighting west of the city, however. Company B of the 5/7 Cav, augmented by an armored cavalry platoon, swept the area just north of Hue on 23 February and reached the Citadel walls the following day. The other Cav units and the 2/501 Airborne pushed south and then east. The latter unit captured a key bridge over the Song Sau River 3 kilometers west of the city on 23 February, and the 2/12 Cav uncovered what appeared to have been a major medical facility near the bridge.

The 1st Brigade of the 101st Airborne was committed in the final few days to help seal off enemy escape routes from the city to the south. The airborne troops worked with the remaining marine forces south of the city in mop-up operations for the next 2 weeks. By then, all but a few of the enemy's front-line troops who had terrorized the city for nearly a month were long gone.

Operation Hue City was officially terminated at midnight on 2 March.

CHAPTER THIRTEEN

Credit the ARVN

Most contemporary historians seem all too willing to give the U.S. Marine Corps full credit for the retaking of Hue Citadel, while giving scant recognition to the contributions of the 1st Cavalry and 101st Airborne troops and, in particular, the South Vietnamese forces. The facts strongly suggest that that view is not only simplistic, it is flat wrong.

Certainly, the 1st Battalion of the 5th Marines, with its complement of heavy weapons, did jump start a campaign that had reached stalemate conditions when it arrived in the Citadel on 11 February. But, in the overall scheme of the 26-day battle, the success of the marines would not have been possible without the efforts of the Cav, the 101st, and ARVN forces. The first two units took some of the pressure off the marines, though not nearly enough, and the latter units did most of the killing and most of the dying in some of the toughest sectors of the Citadel.

According to Marine Capt. Jim Coolican, who served as an advisor to the elite Hac Bao Company, the ARVN contributions were almost entirely overlooked by an international media that almost solely concentrated on the efforts of the U.S. Marine Corps.

"The stories and books about the battle have really exaggerated the role of the U.S. Marines while understating the role of the ARVN," said Coolican, who won a Navy Cross during the battle.

Until the marines had arrived, there were few correspondents who bothered to cross the Perfume River to see what was going on in the Citadel. Those who did went over to snap a few pictures and get out as quickly as possible. There was virtually no effort by the media to follow any Vietnamese units or interview their U.S. advisors. The only after-action reports cited by authors who did follow-up stories or books about the action are those compiled by the U.S. Marine Corps.

"In the first week we were [in the Citadel] the only time I saw somebody from the media was when we had just taken back the airfield," said Capt. Jack Chase, an advisor with the ARVN 3rd Troop, 7th Cavalry. "A truck came up to cart off the bodies of some of our dead and I believe there was a photographer from the Associated Press who was on the back of the truck. He snapped a couple of pictures but never got off the truck. No wonder Americans think the marines did all the fighting."

To be truthful, ARVN soldiers, when properly led, were probably better suited than the marines to conduct the house-to-house fighting that went on in the Citadel. Being smaller in build, they presented less of a target, and their size enabled them to make better use of cover provided by the rubble. The ARVN soldiers moved quicker because they carried much less equipment. And they were more motivated because for many of the soldiers, Hue was home.

ARVN soldiers also knew the terrain and enemy better. With good leadership, they were often prepared to stand and die for something they valued so highly. The experience factor also favored the ARVN troops, who had been in continuous combat for many years. While the marines often counted the days until they rotated home, the ARVN soldiers knew they were in for the duration.

"The company commander of my outfit could have taken over an American company and done just as well. That's how good he was and that's how good his soldiers were," said Capt. Ty Cobb, the advisor to the ARVN 2nd Airborne Battalion.

Capt. James Zimmerman, the advisor to the ARVN 2nd Troop, 7th Cavalry, said his unit was so professional that it could have held its own against any unit in any country. Formed in January of 1965, 2/7 had earned six Vietnamese unit citations for gallantry in 3 years, making it one of the most highly decorated units in the country.

"Our unit wasn't on alert before Tet but we didn't need any alert," Zimmerman said. "We were always ready to roll at a second's notice."

Still, South Vietnamese troops, particularly the officer corps, were maligned throughout the war by U.S. troops and correspondents alike. Army Col. David Hackworth, one of our most decorated soldiers and the author of the acclaimed book *About Face*, spoke for many of his peers in a letter he wrote to a friend in 1970. Hackworth, who served two tours in Vietnam, was convinced that the ARVN soldiers would never be able to defend their country against the North Vietnamese.

"The individual soldier has the potential to be great. But to be great he needs leadership and that is the rub," Hackworth wrote.

The Vietnamese just don't produce leaders. It is something in their sociological makeup. As a young officer they are afraid to make a decision; as they grow older and develop and gain rank, they acquire the minimum creature comforts—neat apartment, Rolex, several wives, the little leaguers a Honda and big boys a Toyota. To have these goodies they must wheel, and wheel they do. Virtually everybody has a gimmick going for him . . . designed to produce loot. Now producing loot leaves little time for fighting a war. And after a fellow has his fair share of goodies who really wants to fight?

Hackworth was not in Hue during the Tet offensive, nor had he ever had any experience with the ARVN 1st Division. Although Hackworth's comments may have accurately described other ARVN outfits, they did not apply to many of the ARVN forces who fought in Hue.

Unfortunately, the marines who fought in Hue continued to stereotype all ARVN forces, lumping the 1st Division with all the rest. One of the basest indictments came from 1/5 commander Maj. Robert Thompson, who may have been suffering from battle fatigue when he made the following comment to a reporter soon after the battle had ended.

"The MACV records will reflect that the ARVN, assisted by the 1/5, took the Citadel," Thompson said at his first and only press conference the day the battle ended. "That was strictly public relations hogwash, like so much that MACV put out during the war. The 1st Battalion, 5th Marines took the Citadel. The ARVN were spectators."

Many U.S. advisors with Vietnamese units in Hue

strongly disagree with Major Thompson's blanket assessment and generally decry the lack of credit given the ARVN in many areas of the country. The Americans, for example, loved to say that if you saw any ARVN troops you knew you were safe from the Vietcong because everybody knew the ARVN ran away from the VC.

"I can't speak for any other unit but I never saw a Vietnamese soldier or unit turn and run from a battle unless their American advisor did," Captain Chase said. "I want to tell you that I learned far more from them on how to fight a war than they learned from me."

That latter assessment by Captain Chase was echoed by many of the U.S. advisors I came in contact with. Most of the Americans with the ARVN 1st Division were advisors in name only.

"We were fire support coordinators and liaison officers to adjacent or supporting American units," said Capt. Chuck Jackson, senior advisor to the ARVN 7th Airborne. The advisors also took care of "unofficial" logistical matters that the Vietnamese were unable to accomplish through their own supply chain. And, in many but not all cases, the U.S. advisors were partners in tactical matters.

"If you earned the respect of your counterpart, you were a full partner, adding value where you could and being consulted on a routine basis," Jackson said. "If you lost that respect, or could not earn it to start with, you were a radio telephone operator or a fire support center."

Having witnessed the fighting on both sides of the Perfume River, I believe that the enemy resistance was strongest in the Citadel, particularly in the west and southwest sectors where ARVN troops were deployed. That area of operations was the closest point to the enemy's command and resupply headquarters. The ARVN units, lacking the marines' heavy weapons capability, particularly tanks and 106mm recoilless rifles, faced fresh troops almost daily for 3 weeks.

All four of the enemy reinforcement battalions brought down from Khe Sanh and the DMZ in the latter stages of the battle were deployed in the western part of the Citadel, either as replacements or as a moving reserve. A fifth enemy reserve battalion was used to replenish forces operating in the Imperial Palace.

While there may have been ARVN units, particularly the Vietnamese marines, that did not measure up to U.S. standards, it cannot in any way be inferred, as Major Thompson so recklessly stated, that the ARVN soldiers were mere spectators in the battle for Hue. Quite the opposite was true.

In an interview 29 years later, Thompson stood by his original statement about the ARVN troops being "spectators" in the retaking of the Citadel—with a few exceptions.

"First, I'd like to say that General Truong was an excellent commander. He did everything I asked him to do," Thompson said. "He was a good man and I respected him greatly. But I think he had a very difficult time getting his battalion commanders to fight."

Thompson never saw the Vietnamese airborne units in action because they had left the Citadel when the marines arrived.

Of the ARVN troops he had direct contact with, he praised Captain Hue's Hac Bao Company and Lieutenant Tan's Reconnaissance Company but had nothing good to say about any other unit.

"Captain Hue was a very good man and so was his American advisor, Captain Coolican. They were both terrific," Thompson said.

Thompson's assessment of the Vietnamese marines and the ARVN 2nd Battalion, 3rd Regiment, which was assigned to provide rear and flank security for his unit, was blunt and harsh.

"The Vietnamese marines didn't do anything and 2/3 was worthless. The latter's commanding officer was a wimp," Thompson said.

There were some truly spectacular performances turned in by ARVN units, none more so than the 1st Division's reaction force, the Hac Bao (Black Panther) Company, which was garrisoned in the Citadel. Its leader, Capt. Tran Ngoc Hue, was a legendary figure who became one of the most highly decorated soldiers in Vietnamese history. If there was one man who deserved credit for preventing the enemy from overrunning the Citadel the first day, it was the dynamic and fearless 26-year-old Hue.

Hue was named by his parents after the city of his birth. (According to Vietnamese custom, surnames appear first and given names are last). He was commissioned a 2nd Lieutenant upon graduation from the South Vietnamese Military Academy at Dalat in 1963 and was assigned to the 1st Division's 2nd Battalion, 3rd Regiment. In 1967 he took command of the prestigious 250-man Hac Bao Company.

Taller and heavier than most Vietnamese, Hue had a round face that accented his broad smile. Behind that baby-faced smile, however, was a born military leader. Called "Harry" by his U.S. advisors, Hue was a popular figure with the marines along the DMZ and at Phu Bai. A shrewd trader, he had an exuberance and a sense of humor that charmed the leathernecks.

Shortly before Tet, dressed in his tiger fatigues and black beret, Hue drove down to Phu Bai to stock up on LAAWs, flak jackets, and Claymore mines. His favorite trading tool was the new 7.62mm SKS rifle the enemy was using.

"The marines didn't want the AK-47 rifle because they couldn't take it home with them," Hue said.

Hue's company had just received the M16 rifle a couple of months before Tet, but he needed a weapon that would counter the RPG launcher the NVA had. The LAAW was just what he needed, and he knew that the marines were always in the market for captured weapons and other NVA paraphernalia.

The Hac Bao had their own patch, a snarling panther, which they wore on the left pocket of their tiger fatigues and on their black berets. They were experts at airmobile operations and were trained for instant deployment. Their leader, Hue, was a young man of dash and high energy. He took no pity on the enemy and was relentless to a fault. There was nothing his men would not do for him.

"I wanted to be a part of that unit the first time I saw them," said Coolican, who retired from the marines as a full colonel. "I sought that job hard because I wanted to be where the action was. While I was an advisor with them I always felt I was with the best. Harry and I did everything together. Looking back on my career I don't think I ever felt more a part of a unit than when I was with the Hac Bao."

Sometimes Hue's boundless energy got him in trouble with U.S. advisors who did not share the same qualities.

"When I got to MACV in Hue, everyone warned me

what a problem Harry was—his big head, how he hated advisors, if not all Americans, and how he expected advisors to go everywhere with him," said Marine Maj. David L. Wiseman, who became Hue's advisor in 1970.

Those of us who were any help to Harry found him fiercely protective of us (and our secure radio), particularly when he realized that we weren't going to sneak into Dong Ha every chance we got for American chow and hookers. Harry was a warrior and a devout family man—those of us who also were, well, we got along fine. I can't remember such a quick bonding and immediate rapport ever in my life, before or since then.

Hue's reputation on the battlefield was nonpareil. "He was bigger than life in the field," Captain Coolican said. Other U.S. advisors called him "absolutely fearless" in battle. He would walk through a mortar attack and never once flinch or dive for cover. He seemed to like the smell and taste of war. No one had ever seen him lose his cool under fire.

The Hac Bao Company, which had scattered its forces throughout the city on the first day of Tet, had barely 50 men to counter an assault by two enemy battalions at the Citadel's airfield on the morning of 31 January. Somehow, Hue managed to position his small force to divert the enemy just enough to prevent them from sweeping over the entire Citadel the first day. In counterattacking the initial wave of enemy troops at the Tay Loc Airfield, Hue's Black Panthers killed over 50 NVA soldiers and rescued two U.S. Marines in the process. A few months later Gen. Creighton Abrams pinned the Silver Star and

Bronze Star medals on Hue's fatigues. The Silver Star is the highest medal for valor the United States can bestow on an Allied soldier. Later in his career Hue was cited for a Silver Star in an action with the 101st Airborne, but has yet to receive the award.

"I am very rich in decorations," Hue said when asked how many medals he has earned. He has been awarded his nation's highest medal, the National Order, and has about 50 Crosses of Gallantry.

Hue and the Black Panthers became General Truong's security force at the ARVN 1st Division HQ compound early in the battle, an assignment he accepted only reluctantly. Although only a first lieutenant at the time, Hue took command of the defenses at the division compound and fought off every attempt to overrun it.

Later, Truong sent the Black Panthers to every hot spot in the Citadel, putting out fires and lifting the morale of all the troops in the area. Just having Hue and his battle-hardened Panthers around was worth a battalion of infantry. Truong had to keep the reins on the energetic Hue sometimes, but the two men were a formidable team.

"I kept telling General Truong that I wanted to get into the battle. I didn't want to sit. I wanted to run," Hue said. "I always respected him and he respected me too. A lot of his officers were scared of him—but not Harry."

On 1 February, it was a platoon of Black Panthers that guided the first ARVN relief forces into the Citadel and then helped them take up defensive positions at the 1st Division compound. Later the next day Hue's experienced troops led the reinforcements into position to retake the airfield. Over the next few days, the Panthers were called upon to counterattack enemy moves and plug holes in the defensive perimeter. Most important,

Hue became Truong's most valued advisor and commander because of his knowledge of the city.

Hue's familiarity with the streets and alleys of the city of his birth proved doubly rewarding as he was able to rally ARVN forces who were forced into hiding by the NVA assault. He knew where the likely hiding places were and was able to locate and rescue hundreds of soldiers who then rejoined their units and helped push the enemy out of the city.

On 14 February, the Black Panthers were rushed to the northwest wall and helped rescue the 1st Battalion of the 3rd Regiment, which had become surrounded. Later on the same mission Hue retook his own home, which had been occupied by the NVA since the first day, and rescued his parents, wife, and baby daughter.

Four days later, the Black Panthers provided Major Thompson's weary 1/5 marines with a much-needed breather by securing that unit's right flank along the Imperial Palace compound.

On 22 February, the Hac Bao was shuttled back to the northwest wall in time to help turn back an attack by a new enemy unit that had come down from the Khe Sanh area. The Panthers nearly wiped out a company-sized force that obviously was sent to Hue to participate in the final push to take the city.

"They were wearing what looked like brand-new uniforms with red stars on their collars. They told me they came to Hue to march in a victory parade," Hue said. "We killed hundreds of them and captured a lot of AK-54 and AK-58 pistols. Later, they turned out to be great trading weapons with the marines."

General Truong showed up later that day and promoted

Hue to captain on the spot. When Hue received his new insignia from General Truong, he was already wearing the epaulets of a recently killed North Vietnamese officer on his flak jacket, along with Marine Corps captain's bars provided by his advisor, Captain Coolican.

On the next day, Hue and his unit were alerted to prepare for an assault on the Imperial Palace. Troops of the 2nd Battalion, 3rd Regiment were given the assignment of taking down the enemy flag flying from the Citadel's main flagpole because they were in the vicinity, but the Hac Bao Company was given the honor of retaking the palace compound.

"It was an emotional moment," Hue remembered. "There were a lot of enemy bodies lying around and there was a lot of damage from artillery. But there were no enemy soldiers."

The first chance I had to talk to Hue was about a week after the battle, when I brought an American correspondent to see him at his headquarters near the airfield. Hue was relaxing in a hammock on the front porch of his house.

"Captain Smith," he said, calling me aside. "You should have called me first to let me know you were coming. This doesn't look very good. At least give me time to put on a clean uniform."

He was right and I apologized. Then, after putting on his best uniform, Hue showed the young reporter around his compound and gave him a terrific interview that later appeared in *Stars and Stripes*. The story's headline read: "Hue's Panthers Fight Like Tigers." A few months later, the now famous Hue was invited to attend a ceremony aboard a ship of the U.S. 7th Fleet in the South China Sea.

"They sent a slick [helicopter] for me and flew me to the ship. I had never been on a warship before," Hue said, smiling broadly as he retold the story. "The only trouble was I forgot to tell General Truong I was going. When he came to my headquarters looking for me, one of my men told him I had flown out to a U.S. ship and would be back later that afternoon. Later, we both laughed over it."

In 1969, Hue was promoted to major and given command of the ARVN 1st Division's 2nd Battalion, 2nd Regiment (the Black Wolf Regiment), the same unit his father had commanded in the 1950s. Two years later, Hue, now a newly promoted lieutenant colonel, was captured by enemy troops on a mission in Laos.

U.S. advisors were prohibited from accompanying their units on Hue's last mission into Laos in March of 1971. It had been planned as an all-Vietnamese show, and U.S. advisors were told they could be court-martialed if they went along. After successfully completing the mission, Hue's battalion was to protect the withdrawal of the ARVN forces by helicopter. Hue's unit was ambushed, and, after several hours of hand-to-hand combat, Hue was wounded and captured. He lost most of four fingers on his left hand in the fighting. It was his fifth combat wound.

Following his capture, the NVA allowed all the officers to say a few words on a radio broadcast from just north of the DMZ. Hue told his wife, Cam, that he was okay and asked her to take care of his three young daughters.

He spent almost 13 years in North Vietnamese prison camps, resisting all efforts made on him to defect. The

first 4 years were spent in solitary confinement at the in-
famous Hanoi Hilton, and the last 8-plus years were in
reeducation camps, where he became a Christian. When
things were toughest, he called on his belief in a divine
spirit and thoughts of his wife and three young daughters
to see him through.

Hue's reputation as a combat soldier and leader of
men was well known to the Communists. His abilities
were precisely the characteristics they were looking for
in their own army, which had been depleted by many
years of heavy fighting. His captors argued that he would
be on the winning side if he defected.

"They promised to make me a general if I defected. I
kept saying no," Hue said.

Ironically, one of his interrogators was a former colleague of his with the 1st ARVN Division, Pham Van
Dinh. Dinh's company had been given the honor of taking down the NLF banner from the Citadel flagpole in
the final days of the Hue battle in 1968.

In April of 1972, Dinh, then a lieutenant colonel,
stunned his U.S. advisors by surrendering his command
at Camp Carroll near the DMZ and defecting to the
NVA. The next day, Dinh made a broadcast over Radio
Hanoi saying that he had been well treated and urging all
ARVN soldiers to refuse to fight. Today, Dinh is a high-
ranking official of the communist government in Hue.

During the so-called false truce of 1973, Hue's wife
traveled to a rumored prisoner-of-war exchange point in
northern I Corps that proved to be a false alarm.

Finally released in 1984, Hue settled into an anony-
mous life in Saigon because he feared that he would be
killed if he returned to his home in Hue. It took him more
than a year to have his wife and three daughters join him

in Saigon, where he was under virtual house arrest. He had been given a job of extracting gold and other precious metals from old U.S. radios and was paid barely enough to keep his family alive. Still, it was better than rotting away in a prison.

In the meanwhile, one of Hue's former advisors, Marine Maj. David Wiseman, had begun a search for his former comrade. "I was told by an ARVN general in 1976 that Harry had died in prison. But it just didn't add up," Wiseman said. "They would have had to kill him . . . he wouldn't just die."

Wiseman began circulating photos he had taken of Hue among the large Vietnamese community in Northern Virginia in the hopes someone would recognize him and confirm whether he was dead or alive. Finally in 1990, Wiseman, then a lieutenant colonel, found a recent immigrant from South Vietnam who recognized the photo and said that she had seen him in Saigon. Wiseman immediately wrote to Hue and began sending him $100 a month to help support his family. Wiseman then petitioned the U.S. State Department to help him get his friend and his family to the United States.

Now living in Northern Virginia, Hue, his wife Cam, and three daughters were sworn as U.S. citizens in November 1996.

With help from many of his friends, Hue has been able to send all three of his daughters to college. He works two jobs and is heavily involved with the Vietnamese-American community around Washington, D.C. He also buys a lottery ticket each week, hoping that a bit of luck will enable him to bring his two sisters, who live in poverty in Hue, to the United States to share in his good fortune.

Someday Hue would like to return to the city of his birth.

"The time is not right yet," Hue said. "The communist system is failing in Vietnam. It is only a matter of time. I have a strong feeling that my mission on earth is not over yet. In the meantime I will do whatever I can to help my people."

The other ARVN hero, of course, is Gen. Ngo Quang Truong. Now almost 70 and retired in Northern Virginia a few miles from his old comrade, Tran Ngoc Hue, Truong leads a quiet life, far from the national spotlight he once occupied during a brilliant 21-year military career.

He lives in a modest brick home on a quiet street in a Washington, D.C., suburb. On a wall of his living room is a framed depiction of the raising of the South Vietnamese flag over the Citadel on 24 February 1968 and a glass-covered memento of the four unit patches he wore during his career—Airborne Division, 1st Division, IV Corps, and I Corps. The two gifts were presented to him by friends and former colleagues during a ceremony at Fort Leavenworth, Kansas, in 1975 shortly after he arrived in the United States.

He is fiercely proud of his time as the 1st Division commander, especially during the Tet offensive. One of the photos he cherishes is of former U.S. Secretary of Defense Melvin Laird adding a blue streamer to the ARVN 1st Division colors after the unit was awarded the U.S. Presidential Unit Citation. The 1st Division is the only Vietnamese division to have received that honor.

Truong received his second star in June 1968 and was promoted to lieutenant general two years later when he was given command of IV Corps in the Mekong Delta region south of Saigon. Two years later, President Thieu, at the urging of his U.S. advisors, sent Truong back to I Corps to relieve his old boss, General Lam. Truong, with the help of massive U.S. firepower, was able to turn back the enemy's 1972 Easter offensive that had nearly over-run I Corps in an attempt to split the country in two.

It was this success that vaulted him to the top of a short list of possible candidates to succeed Thieu as presi-dent should such a move prove necessary. In the view of most Americans, the quietly efficient Truong was the most appealing candidate on a small list, a fact that Thieu him-self had duly noted, much to the detriment of his own personal relations with Truong.

Three years later, when the Communists finally over-ran South Vietnam, it was Thieu's suspicion of Truong as a U.S.-backed rival that played a significant role in the enemy's quick victory. Thieu, fearing that Truong had too big a power base, ordered the withdrawal of the Air-borne Division from I Corps to Saigon, a move Truong described as nothing short of madness. The normally reticent Truong was so dismayed, according to one pub-lished report, that he considered resigning or possibly mounting a coup against Thieu. In the end, however, Truong harbored no such desires. He decided to remain what he had always been, a consummate professional soldier, not some political conspirator.

When Da Nang fell at the end of March 1975, Truong had literally to swim for his life. A poor swimmer, Truong entered the surf near a former marine air base and, with the help of an aide, he paddled to safety aboard a waiting South Vietnamese patrol boat. Earlier that day, an ex-hausted and disillusioned Truong had received a phone call from Thieu ordering him to try and establish a beach-head on an island off the coast as a prelude to a counter-offensive to retake I Corps. Truong did all he could not to laugh.

Arriving in Saigon a few days later, Truong checked into a field hospital. He was suffering from a nervous problem and conjunctivitis. After a few days of rest, he was given a job as deputy chief of the Joint General Staff in charge of Saigon's defense plans, such as they were. Truong, who had managed to have his wife and two children flown out of the country, was planning to stay to the end.

On 30 April Vice President Ky ran into a bitter and broken Truong at the Joint General Staff headquarters at Tan Son Nhut Air Base. Truong was wandering the hall-ways, seemingly in a daze. When asked what he was do-ing there, Truong told Ky he was waiting for orders. Ky gave him one. He ordered Truong to join him in his pri-vate helicopter, and the two men, along with 10 others, flew out to the USS *Midway* in the South China Sea.

In March 1997 I visited Truong at his home, bringing the former Hac Bao commander, Hue, with me. We had tea and engaged in some small talk. Truong and Hue each had a cigarette.

"You don't smoke anymore?" the general asked me, remembering the days back in Hue when we both smoked.

"No, I gave them up a long time ago," I said.

"Good for you," Truong said with a smile.

Hue, who still calls Truong his "boss," told me earlier in the car that the general does not give interviews be-cause he does not want to live in the past. But, he said, the general was looking forward to seeing me again.

Truong recognized me from the outset and was genuinely happy to talk about the Battle of Hue. I asked him whether there were any inaccuracies in the books and stories he had read about the battle. He said no, everything was pretty accurate.

I told him I still regarded it as amazing that his small force was able to stop the NVA forces from overrunning the Citadel.

"There is the man who saved the Citadel and the man who saved my life," Truong said, gesturing at Hue. The two men exchanged nervous smiles. Truong pointed with pride at the painting of the Citadel flag raising on his wall and then got up and took down the glass-covered memento of the four military patches he wore from its place on the wall by his desk.

"I only had four commands in my career, all very good ones," he said with obvious pride.

We talked about the flag raising at the Citadel. I told him that I had had a chance to go on that raid and did not, a decision I still regret. He then rose and went looking for some photographs to show me.

While he was gone, Hue told me that the general was very poor. He and his family had left Vietnam with not much more than the clothes on their backs. After being debriefed by the U.S. Army at Fort Leavenworth, where he wrote several thoughtful studies on the war, Truong began a career as a computer programmer and systems analyst for the American Railroad Association. He retired in 1995 with a small pension.

Truong returned in a few minutes with a handful of 3-by-5-inch photos, none of which were of him. Among the photos was a letter Gen. Norman Schwarzkopf had written him in February of 1991 just a few weeks after the Gulf War. I did not look at it right away, thinking that it was private. Truong spoke to Hue in Vietnamese.

"The general wants you to look at the letter," Hue said to me.

It was only three paragraphs, typed on stationery bearing the four stars of the commander in chief of Operation Desert Storm. In it, Schwarzkopf thanked Truong for a note that he had sent him on how proud he was of one of his former U.S. advisors. Schwarzkopf replied by saying that Truong was one of his greatest teachers and that many of the strategies he used in the Gulf War were things he had learned from Truong. Truong beamed while I read the letter.

"General, may I copy this letter and use it in my book?" I asked.

"No, I'd rather not. It is private and personal," he answered.

I changed the subject back to how his small force was able to hold off two battalions of NVA troops in the Citadel back in 1968.

He looked over at Hue, sitting next to me.

"Because of him," he said. "He was born in the city and he knew every street and every building."

Hue smiled and then he made everybody laugh.

"I tell my Vietnamese friends here that if the NVA comes to the United States we will let them use the beltway [around Washington, D.C.] in a rental car," Hue said.

Before leaving I asked the general whether there was anything he would like to say about his career that had been overlooked by others. He shook his head no and then used the occasion to poke fun at himself.

"It is kind of funny that I ended my military career swimming in the South China Sea," he said with a wide smile.

CHAPTER FOURTEEN

The Aftermath

The sun was shining brightly as a helicopter bearing South Vietnamese President Nguyen Van Thieu touched down at the ARVN 1st Division LZ in the Citadel late on the morning of 25 February.

Thieu, in freshly starched fatigues, exchanged a salute with General Truong and then warmly shook his hand. With the ARVN 1st Division band playing in the background, Thieu reviewed an honor guard composed of the Hac Bao Company and then presented medals to dozens of ARVN soldiers and U.S. advisors.

Thieu, who had commanded the 1st Division in the early 1960s, smiled often and he even got Truong to exhibit a rare smile. The sense of relief felt by both men swept the parade ground like a refreshing breeze.

After a brief lunch Thieu's helicopter took off and headed south. From the air, Thieu looked down on the devastation that had turned his country's most beautiful city into a smoking, crumbling ruin. The main bridge across the Perfume River was a twisted, ugly scar, its rusting girders sticking out of the waters like the bones of a sea serpent. The Citadel walls, which had been pounded by air, naval, and artillery fire for over 3 weeks, were pockmarked with shell holes and reduced to piles of rubble in many locations. Except for a few areas along Le Loi Street, the south side of the river appeared to be in much better shape.

The refugee situation was critical. It was estimated that 116,000 out of a total population of 140,000 had nowhere to live. There was an urgent need for food, clothing, and medical attention. The possibility of epidemics was a major concern. Water and electrical services were knocked out. Bodies littered the streets, buildings, and waterways: the dead had to be buried immediately.

Many of the refugees were ARVN soldiers who had been caught at home on Tet holiday leave. Rather than defect to the NVA as the enemy had hoped, they had hidden in cellars and attics, waiting to be rescued so they could rejoin their units. Three days after the fighting ceased I found my Vietnamese jeep driver among a throng of refugees who had been detained at the province prison. When he saw me across the room he broke into a smile and rushed over to me. He fell on his knees and began kissing my hand. He, like many of the other detainees, thought the NVA had killed all the Americans.

One of the first priorities was to repair the railroad bridge at the western end of the Perfume River to allow vehicular traffic to flow to both sides of the city. The main bridge was patched up rather quickly so that it could be used for foot traffic, but it would be another 6 months before it was ready to accept vehicles.

The view from the air was bad enough but was far worse from ground level, where the smells and sounds dramatically highlighted the scope of the devastation.

So many buildings had been destroyed that there was no place for the refugees to live, sleep, and eat. Temporary camps were constructed of corrugated tin brought into Hue by air and truck convoy. In a matter of days, 100-pound sacks of rice grown in Louisiana were flown into the city. Whole families huddled within their tiny cubicles around makeshift fires to boil water for the rice. There were few vegetables and no meat. Vegetable gardens had been either destroyed or turned into graveyards, while chickens and pigs had fallen victim to soldiers on both sides during the battle.

ARVN troops were given time off from their military duties to help in the reconstruction. Many of them worked on their own homes. ARVN doctors made the rounds of the camps to test water and immunize the refugees, mostly for cholera and plague. The vaccines were provided by the Americans.

The smell of death hung in the air for weeks as the grim job of recovering bodies that had popped up from the rice paddies, rivers, and moats around the Citadel continued day after day. But that was not the worst of it.

About a week after the battle had officially ended, I received a phone call from a colleague about the discovery of mass graves in the Strawberry Patch section of Gia Hoi east of the city. I drove to the area and stood in horror as hundreds of bodies were exhumed by friends and relatives of the victims. Many had had their arms bound behind their backs with wire. Others had been buried alive in what appeared to be deliberate acts of slaughter.

A year and a half later, Vietcong defectors led U.S. troops to a creek bed deep in the jungle 10 miles west of Hue. Spread out in a ravine for about 100 yards were the skeletons of some 400 bodies washed clean by the running brook. The skulls showed that many had been shot or clubbed to death. Hue authorities later released a list of 428 victims, including ARVN soldiers, students, civil servants, village and hamlet officials, government workers, and ordinary citizens. All told, the number of executions approached 3,000.

In 1970, President Richard Nixon used the Hue atrocities as evidence of what would happen to the South Vietnamese if the United States were suddenly to pull out of Vietnam. Nixon called the NVA's brief occupation of Hue a "bloody reign of terror in which some 3,000 civilians were clubbed and shot to death."

North Vietnam officials denied that the atrocities took place. One of North Vietnam's senior architects of the Tet offensive, Gen. Tran Do, claimed that all the film and photographs of the butchery supplied by the Allies were "fabricated." Several years later, however, North Vietnamese officials finally came around to admitting that the atrocities had in fact taken place but insisted that they were just a by-product of war and nothing else.

"Large numbers of people had been executed, most of them either associated with the government or opponents of the revolution," wrote Truong Nhu Tang, a founder of the National Liberation Front and a minister of justice for the Vietcong Provisional Revolutionary Government.

But others had been killed as well, including some captured American soldiers and several other foreigners who were not combatants. I had questioned [NLF leader] Huynh Tan Phat in private about these atrocities. He had expressed his sorrow and disappointment about what had happened and explained that discipline in Hue had been seriously inadequate. Fanatic young soldiers had indiscriminately shot people and angry local citizens who supported the revolution had on various occasions taken justice into their own hands. According to Phat there was absolutely no policy or directive from the NLF to carry out any massacre. It had simply been one of those terrible spontaneous tragedies that inevitably accompany war.

There was little doubt the killings were deliberate and done in a way to humiliate the families of the victims. One of the tenets of Vietnamese culture is a strong sense of family, which includes deceased ancestors. The rites of burial and the tending of graves are particularly sacred. Peasants often put aside money to buy coffins to ensure themselves respectable burials. The same sense of family values applied to the Vietcong, as well. The Americans assumed that the enemy had carried off their dead whenever they could to hide their casualties. This was not the principal reason. The living carried off their dead, often at great personal risk, because they knew how important it was to their fallen comrades to have a proper burial.

There is also evidence that the same sort of vigilante justice was meted out by South Vietnamese forces when the battle was over. So-called black teams were formed by the South Vietnamese government to investigate and then prosecute all those believed to have aided the enemy during the fighting.

The city may have been declared secure, but the fighting and dying were not yet quite over. Flush with their long-awaited and costly victory, the marines were reassigned to chase down and eliminate as many of the fleeing enemy as they could. There were not very many of the enemy left.

As soon as the Citadel flagpole and Imperial Palace

compound had fallen, Major Thompson's battalion (1/5) joined its sister units, 1/1 and 2/5, on the south side of the river, while the ARVN took care of any remaining pockets of resistance inside the Citadel. It took several more days, and a handful of casualties, before the 19th-century fortress was truly secure.

South of the Perfume River, the marines continued to hunt down any enemy stragglers. On the first day of mop-up operations, 28 February, the marines walked into a South Vietnamese minefield and suffered a dozen casualties, including three killed. Later that day, four more marines were killed when a jet undershot its target on a napalm run. The dying was not quite over.

The marines swept south toward the bridges spanning the Phu Cam Canal against rear-guard forces that, in some cases, were determined to make the marines pay for every bit of ground. The marines persevered, and, on 2 March, Task Force X-Ray officially declared Operation Hue City over. Two days later, the exhausted marines of 1/5 were finally pulled off the line and sent back to Phu Bai to refit. On the next day, 5 March, Colonel Hughes and his regimental staff left the MACV compound and returned to Phu Bai.

Most of the advisors moved back to the MACV compound in early March. Within a day or two, my laundry, which had been taken away by a cleaning woman over a month before, was returned to my room, all clean and neatly pressed. A week later, in solemn ceremonies presided over by Colonel Adkisson, the MACV compound was renamed in honor of Specialist Frank Doezema, the young army machine gunner who gave his life fighting off an enemy assault on the U.S. billet the first morning of the battle.

The first thing I noticed about the MACV compound when I returned was the number of pockmarks and bullet holes in the facing of the hotel annex. Of particular interest were some dark powder burns surrounding an upper floor window. I was told that an errant round from a marine tank or a 106mm rifle had flown across the Perfume River and detonated in the room while I was gone. It being unoccupied, nobody was injured. It was the same room I had stood guard duty in for the first 8 days.

Captain Chase, the senior advisor to the ARVN 3rd Troop, 7th Cavalry, had an even scarier homecoming when his unit returned to its base at PK 17. It seems that while he was gone, some replacements had arrived at PK 17 and occupied 3/7's billet. A young lieutenant, brand new to Vietnam, was sound asleep in Chase's bunk when an enemy rocket flew in an open window and killed him.

Some units stuck around Hue for awhile. A couple of marine units continued patrolling in the southern section of Hue for a few more weeks and then returned to their duties elsewhere. The four battalions of the ARVN 1st Division's 3rd Regiment, minus those detailed to help deal with the various crises within the city, resumed their normal patrolling in a heightened state of readiness. The advisory staff made the daily round trip from the MACV compound to the Citadel with armed guards, weapons locked and loaded for any surprise attacks.

The Tet offensive in Hue had gotten everybody's attention, there was no doubt of that. None of us would see the war or our jobs in quite the same way again.

In retrospect, it was clear the enemy had failed to

achieve its principal objective—the collapse of the South Vietnamese government. The North Vietnamese had grossly overestimated their own political strength among the South Vietnamese as well as the likelihood that the South Vietnamese would participate in a general uprising. But, even though the NVA and Vietcong had been thrown out of Hue, they had made a powerful statement. They had grabbed the world's attention and held it for nearly a month, demonstrating a strength and determination that completely surprised the Allies.

Shunning their usually effective hit-and-run tactics, the NVA and Vietcong came to Hue with intentions of remaining put and slugging it out with the Americans, no matter the price. The Allies claimed a body count of 5,113 during the battle of Hue, but whatever the real figures were, it was clear that the enemy had suffered a substantial blow. An NVA document captured later admitted that the invading forces had lost a regimental commander, eight battalion commanders, 24 company commanders, and 72 platoon leaders during the battle. The Communists paid dearly for their bold gamble, but though they had clearly lost the battle, they eventually won themselves a nation.

The price was high for the Allies, as well. The ARVN reported 384 killed and 1,830 wounded, the U.S. Army suffered 74 killed and 507 wounded, and the U.S. Marines lost 142 killed and 850 wounded. Civilian losses were even higher.

Four men won the Medal of Honor for heroism during the Battle of Hue—Army CWO Fred Ferguson, a chopper pilot with the 1st Cavalry, S. Sgts. Joe Hooper and Clifford Sims of the 101st Airborne Division, and Marine Sgt. Alfredo Gonzalez. The marines also awarded 10 Navy Crosses for extraordinary gallantry.

"As a marine I had to admire the courage and discipline of the North Vietnamese and the Vietcong but no more than I did my own men," said Capt. Myron C. Harrington, commanding officer of Delta Company of the 1st Battalion, 5th Marines, which had fought in the Citadel. "We were both in a face-to-face, eyeball-to-eyeball confrontation. Sometimes they were only 20 or 30 yards from us, and once we killed a sniper only 10 yards away. I don't think that the North Vietnamese and Vietcong were about to give it up even if we'd surrounded Hue and tried to starve them out. We had to go in and get them out. There was no other way, except to dig them out."

Accomplishing that mission was a deadly business that, in the end, all came to nothing. Seven years later, and 2 years after the United States had withdrawn its combat forces, Hue and the rest of South Vietnam was overrun by the Communists in humiliating fashion.

When I left Hue in the summer of 1968 it was a far different city from the one I had first seen back in January. The battle had sapped the vitality and spirit of a once proud and carefree city. Fresh graves could be seen everywhere, in front yards, parks, and school grounds. The citizens seemed to walk with a slouch, with no bounce in their step. Frowns had replaced smiles. It was so ironic and so sad that Vietnam's most beautiful city had had to endure such a painful and prolonged trial by fire.

Just before rotating home, I received a light-hearted certificate of appreciation from the senior MACV advisor for enduring 6 months of "fog, rain, sun, water buffalo, Hue girls, bicycles, jackasses, asses, rice, chicken heads, alert drills and higher headquarters crisis management . . . 82mm mortar fire, rocket bursts, machine gun attacks, plastic noisemakers, B-40 agitators and sometimes personal wounds."

Hah, I thought as I looked over the colorful document, I didn't realize that I had had all this much fun. Fun? Who am I kidding. The fact that I survived 4 weeks of total madness without a scratch, either physically or mentally, was a bloomin' miracle.

SELECTED BIBLIOGRAPHY

Hackworth, David H. *About Face*. New York: Touchstone, 1989.

Hammel, Eric. *Fire in the Streets, The Battle for Hue, Tet 1968*. New York: Dell Publishing, 1991.

Herr, Michael. *Dispatches*. New York: Avon Books, 1978.

Karnow, Stanley. *Vietnam: A History*. New York: Viking, 1983.

Krohn, Charles A. *The Lost Battalion*. Westport, Conn.: Praeger Publishing, 1993.

Lowry, Timothy S. *And Brave Men, Too*. New York: Crown Publishing, 1985.

Nolan, Keith. *Battle for Hue: Tet 1968*. Novato, Calif.: Presidio Press, 1978.

Oberdorfer, Don. *Tet!* New York: Doubleday, 1971.

Page, Tim. *Nam*. New York: Alfred A. Knopf, 1983.

Palmer, Dave. *Summons of the Trumpet*. Novato, Calif.: Presidio Press, 1978.

Schwarzkopf, Norman. *It Doesn't Take a Hero*. New York: Bantam Books, 1993.

Snepp, Frank. *Decent Interval, An Insider's Account of Saigon's Indecent End*. New York: Random House, 1977.

Warr, Nicholas. *Phase Line Green*. Annapolis, Md.: Naval
     Institute Press, 1998.
Westmoreland, William C. *A Soldier Reports*. Garden
     City, N.Y.: Doubleday, 1976.

INDEX

ABOUT THE BOOK

This well-documented narrative by former U.S. Army Capt. George W. Smith is the most complete account to date of the longest continuous battle of the Vietnam War.

Charged with monitoring the huge civilian press corps that descended on Hue during the Tet offensive, Captain Smith, an information advisor to South Vietnam's 1st Infantry Division, was an eyewitness to the 25-day struggle. He recounts the separate, poorly coordinated wars that were fought in the retaking of the city, documenting the little-known contributions of the brave South Vietnamese forces that prevented the Citadel portion of Hue from being overrun and then assisted the U.S. Marine Corps in evicting the North Vietnamese Army. He also tells of the social and political upheaval in the city, reporting the execution of nearly 3,000 civilians by the NVA and the Vietcong.

The tenacity of the NVA forces in Hue earned the respect of the Allied troops on the field and triggered a sequence of attitudinal changes in the United States. It was those changes, Smith suggests, that eventually led to the U.S. abandonment of the war.

George W. Smith was formerly a sportswriter at the *Hartford Courant*.